The Six Questions

Acting Technique for Dance Performance

Daniel Nagrin

University of Pittsburgh Press

Published by the University of Pittsburgh Press, Pittsburgh, Pa. 15261

Manufactured in the United States of America

Printed on acid-free paper

10 9 8 7 6 5 4 3 2 1

Library of Congress Cataloging–in–Publication Data and acknowledgments of permissions will be found at the end of this book.

A CIP catalog record for this book is available from the British Library.

These pages are dedicated to *Helen Tamiris*
1902–66

She gave me and many others the liberating insight
that the art of dance and the art of acting were rivers
waiting to be joined as one.

Contents

Acknowledgements

I am blessed with a widely disparate group of friends and colleagues. With no conscience at all, I exploited a favored few by sending them the manuscript for their review. Sooner or later all responded and all from wildly different points of view. Some seized upon every misplaced comma, others circled garbled expressions and best of all some wrote "Yes!" in the margin. Some hoped I would trim the text and others longed for more. There was one sour note, some doubts and enough praise for me to risk offering this to the dance public. I list their names alphabetically and absolve them from any responsibility for what appears in this book. I alone am accountable for all that follows and yet I am profoundly beholden for the perspective and help they offered me; for this I thank them all:

William Akins, Ph.D., David Barker, Dominika Borovansky, Christy Funsch, Claudia Gitelman, Ryan Gober, Jacques Levy, Ph.D., Kathie Longstreth, Meredith Monk, Mel Rosenthal, Ph.D., Meriam Rosen, Suzanne Shepard, Phyllis A. Steele-Nagrin, Paul Taylor, Arthur Waldhorn, Ph.D. Out of this alphabet of thanks, I will in all justice pluck the name of my wife, Phyllis Steele-Nagrin, who helped me immeasurably by being the first to read and comment upon every page as it emerged from the printer.

Introduction

How many dancers believe that work on the internal life of a dance performance is every bit as demanding as work on the physical? Most professionals labor unstintingly to achieve absolute command of all the motions, spacings and musical problems of the choreography and then, as the climactic time of performance approaches, seize upon a quick fix for the questions of why and for whom they are dancing.

There is a very good chance that many dancers who read the table of contents on the previous pages will back off with dismay. "What? Does this man imagine that in order to perform, I must think of avoiding all those pitfalls and choosing all of those 'right ways' just to dance? I learn my moves, rehearse them, try to get into them and then go out and give it all I have. What more can be asked of a dancer?" More is possible. There are some brilliant dancers out there gracing our stages, but the problem is that they are simply "on," like a 2,000-watt lamp that glows without variation until the switch is flipped to "off."

At the heart of why we dancers do all that we do is an experience to which we all hunger to return if we are to continue. These are the times in classes, rehearsals and best of all in performance when we are dancing with power, authority and the uninhibited outpouring of all that we are. This free flow of the body is the expression of our feelings, our intellect, our inner vision, our beliefs—our totality. Having a solid dance technique paves the road to this place but it is only a beginning. Few experiences are so harrowing as performing when this state of being is lacking and when we try to *appear* to be deeply involved. We are forced to put on a show of immersion in the dance when in reality we are outside watching ourselves: a cold place to be.

There is a technique available to release all our powers in the act of performance, even in roles that do not come easily to us. It is a technique borrowed from the actors. In the late twenties, the actors and directors of the Group Theatre, who were pioneering in the use of Constantin Stanislavski's teachings, saw value in the work of the emerging modern dance and added dance to their training as actors, and still today actors do this. It is a bit late, but we can still return the compliment and find the tools to dance better than ever by studying and applying what actors have to teach us.

The moment a dancer enters the stage arena, he.she has assumed a role and the performance of a specific act, whether the choreography is abstract or dramatic and whether its style is ballet, modern, jazz, Flamenco or whatever. To be able to dance with clarity, authority and the consistent ability to release the deep sources of one's person, requires a technique. No spoken dialogue or scenes from plays will be used. This book will explore *in terms of movement alone* the acting techniques that can enhance and liberate dance performance.

The term *specific image* was the keynote of my previous book *Dance and the Specific Image: Improvisation* (Pittsburgh: University of Pittsburgh Press, 1994) as it is of this book. A peach is a peach if it has a pit. One doesn't see the pit unless one digs into the peach. The specific image for the performing artist is rarely known or seen as such by the audience. It may be sensed or felt, and when a performance is truly successful, the audience supplies a pit—a specific image—out of its own life and imagination. It is then that what we all strive for is happening: the audience is involved and the dancer, for whom the specific image is as real as the pit in the peach, informs all that she.he does with strength and conviction. Thus the act of a dance performance becomes a mutual act of creation by artist and audience. As these pages unfold, the meaning and use of *specific image* will be explored in detail.

Many of the exercises, games and structures described in *Dance and the Specific Image: Improvisation* (Pittsburgh: University of Pittsburgh Press, 1994) are vital to an understanding of acting technique for dance performance. They were originally conceived and developed to serve the life of the Workgroup, a dance company which I directed from 1970 to 1974. Its risky goal was the performance of improvisation. In my biased opinion we did succeed, and when the company disbanded I continued to teach and develop the techniques and exercises as I toured and worked in the university circuit. About eighty of these are here in this book: selected, modified and directed toward our present concern. The theory is the same, but the problem at hand is different. The earlier book was about improvisation—dancing without knowing what will happen next. This one is about knowing what will come next but experiencing it as spontaneously as an improvisation. It is about taking dance material that has been rehearsed in every detail and giving it the semblance of life.

This book has two major sections. Part I, "The Theory" (chapters 1 through 5) presents the theoretical aspects of acting technique for dance performance, referring the reader to specifically relevant exercises that are described in detail in part II, the Workbook (chapters 6 through 13).

It should be noted that the linear structure of part I is not necessarily the best sequence of approaching the work of developing an acting technique for dance. In the Workbook, the sequence of exercises *is* structured as a step-by-step guide for study and work.

It is too easily assumed that proper study is done in a group situation, either that of a dance company or a class. In fact, some of the most intense research, study and practice of our dance art is performed by solitary figures. I myself took fewer and fewer classes, spending hours and hours alone probing, testing new ideas and ways. All the exercises will serve groups of two or more dancers. Some can be explored profitably by a dancer working alone; each of these will be clearly tagged by a superscript dagger (†).

Wherever I teach, I suggest or require that my students read *My Life in Art* by Constantin Stanislavski. It is long, 572 pages, but it is a fast read, written simply and directly. It is the epic struggle of a man intoxicated by the theatre and a passion to be part of it. He stumbles from error to error and from revelation to revelation to emerge finally as a great artist. As his journey proceeds, an insight into his inspired method evolves more clearly than in any other book I have read on the critical matter of integrity and artistry in performance, including his own writings on acting technique.

I find it difficult to listen to anyone expounding a point of view without having some idea of who they are and what are the roots of their experience. Here are my sources: my initial training in dance was with Ray Moses in the Graham technique and later with Martha Graham herself. My first ballet study was with Mme. Anderson-Ivantzova and subsequently with Nenette Charisse and Edward Caton. I never achieved a significant control of ballet technique. Over the years, at different intervals, I studied acting with Miriam Goldina, Sanford Meisner and Stella Adler, all fine teachers of the art. In dance, my most significant teacher and associate was Helen Tamiris, one of the founders of modern dance and the one who helped me integrate my facility as an actor with my newly acquired skill as a modern dancer. For fifteen years, I worked with Tamiris in musical comedy on Broadway, during which time I danced lead roles and had a few minor speaking parts.

Professionally, I have worked as an actor in stock and Off-Broadway. In 1978–79, I adapted a novel by Albert Camus, *The Fall,* as a one man play and performed it Off-Broadway without dancing a single step. Subsequent to my fifteen years on Broadway, the major portion of my career has been as a dance soloist. What distinguishes my work from that of most of my colleagues is that whatever I do—as a dancer—I do not try to look like something, I am someone *doing* something. I never do abstract dance. Having said that, I will claim that the approach to performance presented here is nonetheless valid and useful to those who do perform abstract dance, and I may speculate that the best artists in that genre gain their strength from involvement with a poetic use of specific images.

Since Helen Tamiris figures so prominently in what follows, it is well to give this brief portrait, which I first wrote for *How to Dance Forever* (New York: William Morrow, 1988):

> Young, she found interpretive dancing in a settlement house on the Lower East Side of New York. As World War I ended, she joined the ballet of the Metropolitan Opera House. A few years of that was followed by dancing in Broadway revues, tours on the movie-vaudeville circuit and night club appearances. Dissatisfied and unconnected to all the dance training and dance culture she had experienced, she went into the studio and a year-and-half later emerged with her first solo concert in 1927, one year after Martha Graham's debut and a year before that of Doris Humphrey and Charles Weidman. The language of her body, infused with the energy of her time; the music contemporary, Debussy, Gershwin, Negro spirituals; her themes, human and immediate—all were the hallmarks of what came to be known as the Modern Dance. In her lifetime, five names were always credited with the creation of Modern Dance in America; Graham, Humphrey, Weidman, Holm and Tamiris. As a dancer she was a breath-taking panther and as a choreographer she was always probing and searching for new forms to express her central concern for human dignity.
>
> In the early forties she turned to work, with great success, in the field of musical comedy; choreographing almost twenty Broadway shows and a few Hollywood musical films. Finally, in 1960 she returned to the concert field to form the Tamiris-Nagrin Dance Company.
>
> In addition to her astonishing beauty and power as a dancer and her innovative choreography, she had a brilliant mind capable of searching analysis, exquisitely clear exposition and some of the best teaching I've ever observed. We were married and together for over 20 years. (Pp. 267–68)

In many of these pages, I speak from personal experience. I do not do this out of vanity or to claim that I have the answers. I do it precisely because I do *not* have the answers. There is no attempt here to present a general theory of dance performance that will apply to all for all time. All I have to offer are my own experiences, studies, hunches and guesses. If, at times, the tone appears dogmatic, don't be deceived. I may believe fiercely but *I am sure of nothing*. It is my hope that the reader will always be aware that this is the position of one man and that nowhere does he lay claim to *the truth*. By that token, the reader should be all the more ready to think, choose and reformulate for him.herself. Putting any of this in writing represents a peril. In some obscure little journal on Buddhism, I read that the Tantrist master never puts anything in writing because the minute it is on paper it is becoming false or irrelevant. In his book *The Presence of the Actor* (New York: Atheneum, 1984), Joseph Chaikin, the seminal theatre director wrote, "Theories and systems on paper are seldom what they are when they are an active process. Once on paper they get frozen by their most serious adherents, become intractable, and are applied for all occasions" (p. 34). Read it, study it, think on it, practice it, bend it, twist it or reject it. It's all here for you to use by your own lights.

Part One THE THEORY

1 *Work on the Self*

In the complex task of becoming an artist, there are profound yet subtle differences among the arts, all hinging upon the question of how much of the self is involved. The gap between an organist and a dancer is immediately apparent when one considers the instruments involved. One engages a multiplicity of ranked keys and pedals with the fingers and the feet; the body of the organist supports every action, but the focus is in front of the body. The dancer, however, is *in* her.his instrument—as is the singer and the actor. The difference is great and imposes special problems. There is no question that the persona of the musician is in the music but it is the organ we hear, not the organist.

The dancer-singer-actor fraternity is naked as it were. No instrument separates them from their audience. They themselves are the matter of their art. Yet there are differences among them. For the singer, there are the objective elements of the score, the breath, the vocal quality, the pitch, the rhythm and the pronunciation. Because these exist in their own integrity apart from the person, it is not at all unusual for them to become the prime focus of a performance style. We have all heard such singers. They have glorious voices, exquisite musicianship and yet, they leave themselves out of it.

Dancers similarly work to master the objectives of their craft: strength, limberness, balance, musicality, linear elegance and the elements of virtuosity in balances, turns and elevation. The task of achieving these interlocked skills can be overwhelming, leaving little energy or even interest for further work. The self is there, but is it on a par with those other concerns? So many times it tags along to the performance, puts on a smile, a yearning expression or most simply, allows no expression at all.

I will speculate that the actor is the most naked of all. True, there are the objectives of vocal quality, vocal projection, clarity of pronunciation and a general physical facility, all of which need to be mastered. But actors can not escape the reality that the raw clay of their craft and their creative process is their own personality. No matter what new and unexpected character a Dustin Hoffman or a Meryl Streep creates; the raw material is their own humanity. Undoubtedly, some actors are so technically accomplished that they can manage to keep themselves at a distance in their work and their performances. In fact, until this century, most actors worked that way, using skillfully devised gestures and expressions that were a part of learned, traditional, theatrical conventions. The use of self was limited to a few actors.

Everything in this book seeks to mine the self as the companion of the awesome beauty and power of an accomplished dance technique. Is there any excitement to equal the roiling ecstasy of two rivers joining? That is the joining attempted here. This first chapter examines what it takes to grapple with the complexities of a dancer mastering the art of performing as a complete human being.

Pride in Your Physical Presence

When I became aware that at some point in the future I was going to write this book, I began to tape-record classes for two reasons. First, it is much more difficult to write about this stuff than to teach it in a class of living, bumbling human beings. Their errors and triumphs are experienced firsthand and analyzed on the spot. Writing demands a good deal of anecdotal material to melt down the generalizations to vivid specifics. Second, in the heat of class interactions occasionally one speaks with a graphic clarity less easily achieved while seated at the computer. Witness this bit of a recorded outburst:

If you want to be a dancer you must have pride in your physical presence. Even the wildly beautiful have a reservoir of self-hatred and confusion about their bodies. Some women with visibly beautiful breasts are terrified of them because of the frightening and unwelcome attention they draw. People with long legs have trouble moving quickly and that embitters them. Both are envied by others lacking these qualities. Everybody is into crucifying themselves. We are our own worst enemies. And yet, some of the most successful people have something funny in their bodies. Have you ever noticed the inordinate length of Mikhail Baryshnikov's rump—and on such a short man! It happens to be what gets him up in the air, and when he steps out upon the stage to do his work, wherever his foot falls, you can read, "Misha was here!"

Every art has a spine upon which the entire structure rests. A singer with the most luscious voice and a range of four octaves is nowhere with a poor sense of pitch. A pianist can have a weak pitch sensibility but with an iron rhythmic control he.she can be one of the best. A percussionist too, can be tone-deaf but still be convincing and compelling. An actor with a magnificent voice, perfect articulation and a glamorous presence is not an actor unless she.he can play the game of "pretend" with relish and conviction.

A pianist can not go onstage thinking, "I must have good rhythm tonight." That has to be learned long before he.she adjusts the bench to play the concerto. The singer weighted with anxiety about pitch is gone before the mouth opens. A dancer standing in the wings can suffer all the self-hatred in the world, but at the moment of stepping into the lights, swells up with the feeling that says, "*I'm here!* I didn't rehearse enough, but *I'm here!* My legs aren't long enough, but *I'm here,* and at this moment there is nothing else in the whole world!"

Your pride in your physical presence should not depend upon being beautiful. Beauty is too cheap and too perishable. Too much garbage gets by on the basis of dreamy looks. All that matters is that *you are here!* You're a person with a big bust or an invisible one, with powerful shoulders or skinny blades, with long legs or bowed legs—whatever. You're one of us and you know something that nobody else knows. When you begin to dance you are doing something for us; you are helping us live with ourselves. What could be more beautiful or powerful than that?

A dancer without pride in her.his physical presence onstage is a mere shadow. There are dancers who have a linear elegance that other dancers would kill for, or with a complete battery of technical skills who, in effect, can disappear before our eyes. Odds are there never was a dancer who did not hate some part of his.her appearance, including the very best performers in the profession. But, and this is a big but, whatever self-loathing they might feel while standing in the wings, the moment they shift into that other world, the stage, they are transformed, and no cocky Gypsy in the caves of Andalusia has one bit more conviction that "It is now time for the world to stop and pay attention to only one thing. Me!"

Until recently it was a given that the complete dancer spent some time studying Spanish/Flamenco dance, not so much to perform it but to absorb that poem of pride into the bone and muscle of the spine. With Flamenco dancers, the conscious theme of much of what they do is precisely this "song of myself," to steal a phrase from Walt Whitman. With wondrous dancers, this pride is not in the forefront of their minds; it is the electricity that flows up and down their spines and radiates out through the legs, the arms and particularly in the carriage of the head.

It is sad if this force is weak in "life." It is a condition that cries for attention, but not from this book. But, what to do when it is fragile onstage? There is work to be done. For starters, reading a sixty-page poem might open a few doors or tear a hole in the ceiling and let you fly. The name of the poem is "Walt Whitman," written, of course, by Walt Whitman, in *Leaves of Grass*. After that, there is "I Sing the Body Electric," also by Whitman. Both will provide repeated joy and enlightenment.

One graduate student, Christy Funsch, had this to say on the matter of pride:

Pride onstage to me is the simple willingness to be onstage (which is not simple). I take pride in the blatant vulnerability that performing demands of me. Not many can stand so naked and offer up their "shortcomings" (their human-ness). The ability to do this at all should make one prideful above any physical imperfections.

When You Dance, You Can Lose Your Mind

Anyone truly caught up in dance has had an experience which may never have been consciously examined. We are dancing in class, rehearsal or onstage and, without noticing it, there is a shift. The music is coming from everywhere, there are no walls, we are everywhere, our powers know no limits, our senses are revved up. We are the music, the floor, the lights and at one with our fellow dancers. In street talk, it's a "high." Our language is rich in expressions and words that attempt to pin down this elusive state of being: ecstasy, bliss, delight, delirium, euphoria, in heaven, rapture, transported, beatitude, felicity, inspiration, fury, frenzy, sent, unselfconscious, out of one's mind, involved, submerged, with it, in it, out of it, flying high, trance, dream, reverie, loss of self-awareness, intoxicated, involved, absorbed, engrossed, immersed, rapt, rapture, (and finally, more than anything) losing all sense of time.

Whatever we call it, it happens unexpectedly and cannot be willed except by some very stupid and self-destructive means. Among performing artists one can discern three differing attitudes toward this loss of self-awareness: mad for it, in fear of it and ready for it.

Those who are mad for it demand it as the condition of all performing, all the time. Liquor or drugs hold the promise of guaranteed highs. The hazards of performances that coast on inspirations fired by the bottle or the needle are all too apparent.

Dancers who fear and avoid it prefer to be in conscious control at all times. They distrust spontaneity and the fluidity that welcomes every performance as a new experience and fear the surprises that well up from their secret caves.

Some performers do everything to make it possible, letting it happen as it may, never forcing it and never shunning it. This third way brings everything to bear upon the task at hand. If the performing ecstasy envelops them, they embrace it; if it doesn't, they plow forward, carried by all the thought, rehearsing and integrity needed for the performance.

When we are dancing immersed in this state of "losing our mind," we are not quite accountable, but *we are responsible for how we get there.* The route lies along a road carved by hard work, our taste, our training and our philosophy of dance and of life. That road is a synonym for who we are. It is my hope that in the work ahead, readers will discover a tool or two to cut through the thickets of debilitating self-consciousness to find those moments of timeless freedom.

The problem in starting any creative session—a rehearsal, a class, a workshop or a performance—is in getting the heart/mind warm, free and ready for any adventure, whether intellectual or emotional. The heart/mind is an elusive beast, a secret garden, a private hell—depending on what you have hidden there behind your body/face mask. Getting to it is one of the central problems of being an artist, and for that matter, of being a human being. It was the question that haunted Stanislavski and spurred the development of his seminal technique of performing.

A premise of our time and one that I accept is that we humans operate with two distinct areas of awareness: one, the intellectual, the cerebral, the mind; and the other, the irrational, the heart, the dream world, the unconscious or the subconscious. I fantasize an ideal way of being: that these two areas coexist, merely separated by a beaded curtain through which one can pass at will and, while in one area, maintain a glimpse of the other. *Heart/mind* is the word I like to use, thinking of the slash as that beaded curtain. I am troubled by anyone who elevates or values one of these more than the other. I tend to define mental and emotional illness as the domination of one or the other. We have health when the heart and the mind exist as an interactive unity.

The first techniques I found for myself and others of making it possible to arrive at "losing the mind" focused on the use of rhythm. Rhythm sparked my earliest work with actors, with dancers and with the Workgroup. It can be the ritualistic way to start work sessions and performances. Like a meditation—a movement meditation—it is a way of entering the body, getting it going, cutting loose from the mess of the outside, relaxing the militant control of the mind, turning the wall between the two consciousnesses into a "beaded curtain" and best of all, connecting with where we are at the moment.

WORKBOOK Spinning†
EXERCISES The Mind-Wash†
True Repetition†
Evolving Repetition†
Lose Your Head†

Relish the Game of Pretending

What we do onstage, we did as children: we "make believe" that what is not so is so. If this embarrasses, the performer is in deep trouble. Whoever feels silly in this game of pretending has taken the wrong train. It must be pursued actively, or only a part of the job is being done. I believe that there is no way to enter the stage space, to appear before the "others," the audience, without assuming a role, regardless of what the post-modern theorists claim in their manifestos. How can you present your dance material without having a specific character to which you will adhere until that time when you leave the stage and become something/someone different than you were a moment ago? You change when you step on the stage and you change when you leave it. In that interval between entering and leaving is what Stanislavski called "the magic if."

It is *as if* you were bits of hard light leaping off polished metal. It is *as if* you were a woman trapped in the body of a swan. It is *as if* you just lost the one who was most precious to you. It is *as if* you want nothing more than to please and amuse the audience. It is *as if* you are the living re-creation of a fragile, elegant design. It is *as if* there is nothing more important in the world than your skillful and precise execution of a string of movements given to you by a great artist. It is *as if* you see before you an endless vista of a rich land which you will plow and plant. It is *as if* you are the son of the king and your body can do anything you dream of. It is *as if* you are certain that your wife is deceiving you. It is *as if* you are making love to the music.

There is no end to these "as ifs." With each new choreography, each new role, each return to an old role, a dancer finds a new "as if." The dance comes to life when the "as if" is poetically relevant to the dance work, when it is believed with the conviction that a child brings to the game of "let's pretend" and when it charges the dancer intellectually, emotionally and down to her.his very bones.

Among actors and directors, one may occasionally overhear the phrase, "Oh, he.she makes such daring and wonderful choices." Within the context of preparing a particular dance there are always many choices possible—many ways of doing the same role. It is here that the choreographer can help the dancer by giving him.her the freedom to create a personal "as if" or, if the dancer is floundering, giving an "as if" that will challenge and spark the energy and the imagination in the game of pretend which is what we call theatre.

WORKBOOK
EXERCISES

All of the work asks for pretending to one degree or another. The exercises on this list emphasize the poetic leap of imagination.

Visualization[†]
Who or What Is Alive in the Music?[†]
Gesture Permutations[†]
Seeing Through the Eyes of Another[†]
The Inner Rhythm of the Role[†]
The Obstacle[†]
Passing Through a Physical Object[†]
Slalom[†]
Faces
A Duet
Not Naming[†]
The Other
Each Alone[†]
The Duet as a Structure
Prison[†]

Recall Your Earliest Performing Instructions

One year, before I taught acting technique for dancers for the first time, I attended a performance of one of our major dance companies. Though I was always critical of the direction of the work, I much admired the choreography and the beauty of the dancing. The three dances on the program were all abstract in nature but differed radically from one another. Somewhere deep into the third work, I became aware of something I had not noticed before. Despite the differences in costumes, music and choreography, the dancers were doing the same thing *all evening*. Not that the dancers were similar to each other. Far from it. One man was a severely earnest acolyte who flashed his lithe legs about like lethal sabers—all evening long. One woman continually tossed a shiny head of hair, letting everyone know how wonderful it all was, her face lit with a subtle smile. Another woman was grimly devoted to every moment. A man danced the most complex intricacies with a distant and passionless objectivity. And so it went. Every dancer had his.her own inner agenda which never changed over the course of three completely different works nor at any time during a particular work. The leader was another matter: he was never the same from one minute to the next.

I knew from talking to former company members that the choreographer gave movements and that was all. It was unthinkable to ask or even assume that a dance was about something or that there were individual characters to be developed for each piece. The only responsibility was to the movement, and much of it was elegant, virtuosic and full of surprises. That night, I suddenly had a vision of these dancers as very young children in their cute little costumes, gathered backstage for their very first performance. Their dance teacher is giving them what will become the most important instructions of their lives on the stage and *they will never ever forget what they are being told*. More accurately, they forget what they have been told but will always *do* what they were told.

When I arrived at the American Dance Festival to teach Acting Technique for Dance Performance, the first assignment I gave was to answer the question, "What were the instructions you received for your first performance?" In the years since, every such class started with that question. Following is a collection. (There is a reason for that little line to the left of each of the urgent injunctions listed below. Mark up this book with a check next to the ones that apply to your own earliest forays into the theatre.)

Linny had the longest list:

____ Smile at the audience.

____ Stop trying to be the star.

____ Look straight at the audience.

____ Stay with the group.

____ Never allow your "butt" to face the audience.

____ When you're onstage, turn on.

___ Give everything you got.

___ Never look down onstage.

___ Always try to be in the front.

___ Be aggressive.

___ Watch the other dancers.

___ Be natural, not fake.

___ When you perform—give!

___ If you make a mistake, don't let anyone know.

___ Be more dramatic.

___ Be less dramatic.

___ Never wear panties under leotards and tights.

Sharon:

___ Look over the heads of the audience to avoid eye contact.

___ Keep your expression neutral, but likely.

___ Keep going at all costs.

___ Smile only when it's appropriate.

___ Get into "character" before you go onstage.

Cecily:

___ Always a sense of giving, giving, giving, more, more, more, and out, out, out to the audience was emphasized, but what and how were left unattended. I often did not know what I was smiling about or projecting.

Denna:

___ Enjoy yourself and don't frown.

___ If you look like you're having fun, the audience will too.

___ Pale people need to wear lots of eye makeup.

___ Try to make all movements as sharp and clear as possible.

___ Never let the audience know when you are uncomfortable, whether you forgot something, you're hurt or whatever.

___ Don't cry onstage, because then you are no longer in control.

___ You can fake a cry, but don't really do it.

___ Don't upstage your fellow performers.

___ Try not to offend your audience.

___ Try to be as involved as possible with what is going on onstage.

___ Don't use a fake smile—but do try to let the joy of performing show through your eyes and let the audience know how much you love what you are doing.

_____ The show must go on—no matter what.

_____ The material that is being performed and the performance of it is far more important than makeup, costume, lights, etc.

_____ You must perform your material as honestly and fully as you can.

_____ Do your very best and hope the audience likes it.

Gail:

_____ I was told to rub a generous amount of Vaseline petroleum jelly on my teeth, before going onstage.

_____ Stare out to the audience with a pearly white smile.

_____ The one rule I follow and will never forget was given to me by my father, "Give 'em Hell, Gaily."

Matt:

_____ Broaden each emotion and gesture, because everyday, natural movement was not big enough and wouldn't reach beyond the first few rows of seats.

_____ Be vulnerable, be open, be willing to exchange energies with fellow dancers.

Heidi:

_____ The fruits of success could be ours if we had a great smile and really sold it. The smile was practiced by placing the index finger between the upper and lower set of teeth so there was a nice big space and pulling the lips back so all the teeth were showing.

Carol:

_____ Smile, project, focus on exit signs above the audience. Do not glaze the eyes.

_____ Put vaseline on teeth to prevent smile stickage.

_____ Use extra strength deodorant.

_____ Do not count with lips moving.

_____ The teacher walked around whacking dancers in the stomach and screaming, "Look like you enjoy yourself. No one wants to watch a dancer in pain."

_____ Work intelligently.

_____ No jewelry.

_____ Avoid tension. It develops violin strings in neck.

Donna

_____ Absolutely NO talking.

_____ Absolutely NO crying.

_____ Absolutely NO gum chewing.

_____ Absolutely NO eating backstage.

____ Absolutely NO jewelry with costumes.

____ Absolutely NO panties with costumes.

____ Absolutely NO dancers are to talk to the teacher the night of the performance, she has too many other responsibilities.

____ Never look at your feet.

____ Don't be nervous: Your mother will be backstage with you until the show starts.

____ You must do good because your mommies, daddies and grandmas will all be in the audience watching to see how much has been learned.

____ Dance to the fourth balcony.

Connie:

____ Never go onstage without false eyelashes.

Dorina:

____ The performer before going onstage has to concentrate everything of himself into the fact. He has not to think about himself or about the audience, he has just to consider himself and the audience into the same fact. If he makes the fact vivid, from this vitality there will come a growing life between the audience and the performer, between the audience and the audience and between the performer and the performer. To *exist* as much as possible onstage with himself and all the opposition factors he includes lightness and heaviness, wideness and narrowness, highness and shortness and play with freedom and control and all the colors in between them. Every performance should be like a birth till death and a death till birth. A circle in perpetual movement. Be generous in movement. Believe in what you are and what you're doing.

No name:

____ Breathe!

Among the psychologists who study learning, there is a phenomenon called *imprinting*. As described in the *Encyclopedia Britannica* (1973): "The phenomenon of imprinting is an example of behavior primarily learned . . . by which an early experience of a young animal determines its consequent social behavior. In one of the first experiments investigating this process, Lorenz [Konrad Lorenz, an Austrian psychologist who studied animal behavior in reference to human behavior] divided a clutch of eggs laid by a graylag goose into two groups. One group was hatched by the goose, the other was incubator hatched. The goslings hatched by the goose followed it as soon as they could walk; the incubator-hatched offspring, however, were exposed not to the goose but to Lorenz, whom they followed about as the others followed the goose."

Humans do this too. Invariably, when I introduce an exercise or game in an improvisation class or workshop, the pattern chanced upon by the person who begins the movement is picked up by almost everyone. The instructions given to children prior to the traumatic experience of that first time onstage are potentially an imprinted pattern that, unbeknownst to us, may be controlling us today in our adulthood.

Not good. Though many of them are ridiculous, pathetic and vulgar, a few are genuinely valuable and some are even poetic. It is worth more than a moment to relive those times when you were initiated into the theatre and to cull what may be guiding you to this day. Enrich it if it still serves to release your powers and shun it if you recognize it as pathetic.

WORKBOOK   **Your First Performance Instruction**[†]
EXERCISES   *Perform according to your first performance instructions.*

Observation, Imitation and Imagination

These three—observation, imitation and imagination—can be seen as the pillars supporting the bridge that arcs from "life" into art. Weaken one and the bridge will wobble or fall. Let the force of each bolster the other and there is a chance of arriving.

Observation

If you believe that there is more to dance than elegant athleticism, if you believe that beyond all those pliés is the possibility of becoming an artist, you will want to spend most of your life observing, observing, observing—not because you should but because of your insatiable greed to blot up all you can experience. You will be committed to the work of continuous observation whenever and wherever you are, without discrimination and without fastidiousness. You will be curious about the design of coat hooks, the texture of adobe walls, the movement of people's rumps, their intonation as they tell you how wonderful you look, and you will not be able to take your eyes from your sleeping cat.

Our work is to pay attention, to become a storehouse of information, all the time accepting an enormous responsibility: each of us is seeing things no one else sees. Each of us is experiencing things in a way no one else does. In this infinite universe, each of us knows very little, but some part of it *no one else knows but you*. We become artists when we know what it is we know that no one else knows and are possessed by the compulsion to tell the others of it. We peer into the dark and catch a glimpse of what we feel compelled to share with the others. What we observe is the raw material of our art.

The following is a transcript from a class at the American Dance Festival:

Daniel: Being truthful to an object other than you is the beginning of learning your craft. The inner life of a person who hardly moves could be a tornado. I suspect that most quiet people whom I know contain a tumultuous turbulence. It takes place deep in their salt mine, and all there is to observe is a barely perceptible tremor. If you penetrate into the salt mine you may find out what is there. How are you going to get into the cave, the salt mine, from the outside? You don't know what's inside, you're on the outside. The armor may be steel-plated but somewhere the wall is thin. Somewhere what's inside is entwined with the outside. You're looking at someone and, "Ha! What's that going on with the hands?" Sometimes the only time you can tell what's going on inside is by the angle of the neck. Everything else is concealed or controlled. You need sharp eyes. More, you have to *want to know* because some things in the salt mine may be upsetting.

Student: Yea, okay, and so you can identify what is going on in the salt mine. Then what?

Daniel: Then you either get scared and run away or you say just as quickly, "Now I am beginning to see. Now I think I know something of what's going on." What will you do with that hunch or insight? You will never know until and if it suddenly appears in the context of a creative act.

WORKBOOK EXERCISES

What Quickened You?[†]
Seeing Through the Eyes of Another
Walk Behind Another[†]
Slalom[†]
Rhythm Portrait[†]
Take a Walk in Your Own World
Faces
The Minnesota Duet
Tandem Solo
Relay Solo

Imitation

Imitation is the method by which we learned to say "Mama," learned to spot turns, learned to do something like the artists who made us breath faster, and finally learned the moves thrown at us by choreographers. A professional dancer is a professional imitator. A dancer who finds imitation difficult may be a rigid person, fearful of changes, deliberately creating and protecting a particular manner. There are dancers who amass a formidable technique encased in a cast-iron personal style. They audition well and drive crazy the choreographers who hire them.

As I was preparing the final revision of this text, I was reminded by the above paragraph of the profound influence of one woman and three men on how I grew in dance. I saw Louise Kloepper perform a solo in Hanya Holm's *Trend*. Her elevation was magical. It looked as if she were descending from the stage flies. She did a turning jeté I must have practiced a hundred times. I saw Leonid Massine in two of his own creations, *Three Cornered Hat* and *Gaieté Parisienne*. I was awed by his speed, double air turns finishing with absolutely perfect stops, intricate, articulate footwork and above all, the ever-present glittering intelligence and zest that carried him about the stage. Avon Long was Sportin' Life in *Porgy and Bess*. His jazz was unlike anyone's. He barely touched the ground. He too had speed—like a hummingbird's wings. His intricate footwork and fluent legs dazzled me. Most miraculous of all was a breath-taking split leap that came from nowhere. Hans Zullig was quite a short man, exquisitely shaped and in command of the most immaculate technique. Every position was an ideal, every move was like sweet cream and his turns like dreaming. Recalling him, I would spend hours launching into arabesque turns that started in deep demi-plié and in the course of the turning rose slowly to stop in full relevé. I think I succeeded once.

How many hours did I pursue the glories of this woman and these gentlemen? Not to be counted, and it has to be said that unbeknownst to them, they were among my best teachers. I studied for a couple of months with Edward Caton. His feet were like butter, and powerful. It was a delight to see him move, but my real teacher in that class was another student, the brilliant Leon Danielian. I came to dance with strong elevation but from the moment I entered that class, I became aware that Leon, who was a phenomenal jumper, was doing something different—something I was not doing. From then on, I saw to it that I was positioned behind him on the floor or in the diagonals, particularly when there was any jumping to be done. Being a good imitator, I could feel something better and after a few weeks, I realized that he used a blindingly fast and *shallow* plié. It was radically different from the deep, powerful plié of André Eglevsky, and it worked for me.

In the history of art, there are countless stories of artists making deliberate "copies" of those who fill them with awe; it is one way to learn important elements of the craft. This does not contradict my previous discussion of style and imprinting. Individuality is not lost through imitation but rather it is asserted, first because the choice is personal, and second because the artist uses what has been learned in shaping his.her distinctive statement. The process enriches the young artist and can be practiced in class, as I did with Danielian, or in the privacy of the studio. To quote Miles Davis, "You have to play a long time before you can play like yourself."

WORKBOOK
EXERCISES

Gifts
Medicine Ball
Outrageous Travel
Seeing Through the Eyes of Another[†]
Walk Behind Another[†]
Take a Walk in Your Own World

Imagination

Imagination is the third pillar supporting that bridge into art. Without it, it's all dry craft. Imagination is really a form of recombinant memory. You can't imagine anything beyond your experience, but you can take pieces of your experience and put them together in ways that no one has ever imagined.

Observation and imitation feed the skill of imagination. These three will shape your art. Your audience will probably never know your specific image, your X, but unless your artistic feet are grounded in experiences that have touched you, you are in great danger of telling lies, dancing generalizations, offering us fabricated information you barely experienced, interpretations you don't care about or a heat wave of physicality covering up an inner void.

If there's any world that has ever needed attention, it's the one we live in. If we don't pay attention to it, it may rot in our lifetime. I hope the artists take the lead. The scientists pay attention, but all too often they give us only better pesticides and missiles.

WORKBOOK EXERCISES *Any and all will serve. How can you begin to dance without the springboard of imagination? Still, in a quiet moment, resting, going to sleep, try either or both of these as journeys of the mind:*

Backdoor[†]
The Hub Meditation[†]

Keep a Journal

Daily, you are bombarded by impressions, experiences and golden bits you are resolved to remember and perhaps even use one day in your work. You will certainly remember some of these precious nuggets, and it is equally probable that too much may be lost. A remark by a teacher in the middle of the class illuminates your mind like lightning at midnight. A theatre reviewer's comment on Ophelia gives you a shocking insight on love. Looking at a maple tree blazing red in the fall, a wild line of words sings through your head. A crazy idea for a dance is there in front of you as you are late and dressing for class. *What is going to happen to all that stuff?*

If you do not write it down as soon as possible, half the time you will remember that you had a great idea but can't recall what it was. Do not write it down on a piece of paper which is fated to be lost the next time you clean out your practice bag. Write it in a bound blank book that goes with you, everywhere. Find a style that you like and buy a dozen—lined or unlined, locked or unlocked, scented or unscented—date them, and one day when you haven't an idea in your head, you will open the book and your motor will be running in high again.

Read a Book

"Read a Book" is short for being cultured, knowing where you come from and what your contemporaries are doing and what your ancestors did, not only in dance, but in painting, literature, music, architecture, film, history, anthropology, politics and whatever else is out there. "Read a Book" is not simple or easy, so plan to spend your life doing it.

It behooves every dancer to know what's happening in the field. And yet, seeing too much dance can crowd your mind and your creative machinery particularly when deeply involved with creating new material. There is a remarkable book by a British biologist, W. I. B. Beveridge, *The Art of Scientific Investigation* (New York: Norton, 1950). I have used it as the text for advanced choreography classes because I think it is the best book on the creative method for artists as much as it is for scientists:

> The research worker remains a student all his life. . . . It is usual to study closely the literature dealing with the particular problem on which one is going to work . . . however, . . . some scientists consider this is unwise. They contend that reading what others have written on the subject conditions the mind to see the problem in the same way and make it more difficult to find a new and fruitful approach. There are even some grounds for discouraging an excessive amount of reading in the general field of science in which one is going to work. . . . When a mind loaded with a wealth of information contemplates a problem, the relevant information comes to the focal point of thinking, and if that information is sufficient for the particular problem, a solution may be obtained. But if that information is not sufficient— and this is usually so in research—then the mass of information makes it more difficult for the mind to conjure up original ideas. (Pp. 3–5)

> Successful scientists have often been people with wide interests. Their originality may have derived from their diverse knowledge. . . . originality often consists in linking up ideas whose connection was not previously suspected. Therefore reading ought not to be confined to the problem under investigation nor even to one's own field of science, nor indeed to science alone. . . . [The scientist] rarely has enough time to do all that he would like to . . . and so he has to decide what he can afford to neglect. . . . However, I do not wish to imply that subjects should be judged on a purely utilitarian basis. It is regrettable that we scientists can find so little time for general literature. . . . One of the research worker's duties is to follow the scientific literature, but reading needs to be done with a critical, reflective attitude of mind if originality and freshness of outlook are not to be lost. Merely to accumulate information as a sort of capital investment is not sufficient. (Pp. 7–17)

Probably the biggest problem of all is keeping one's balance in a world of paradoxes. "Read a book" *and* don't read too much!

WORKBOOK EXERCISE   The Reading List†

Too Much and Not Enough

Every time I read about the serious problem of "hyperactive" children, a suspicion lurks in my mind that some of these "problem" children are actually high energy, spirited, creative individuals who terrify limited and unimaginative teachers and yes, parents. How many high energy, spirited and creative dancers have been squelched by limited and untalented teachers?

Speaking for myself, I will always welcome "too much" in a student and be distressed by those students who make virtues of control, "good taste," restraint and any number of rationalizations for doing less rather than more. My logic is simple. It is easier to trim, hone and polish raw, explosive energy than to light a fire under damp, unadventurous dullness. There are teachers who are literally threatened by the volatile and the unpredictable; their weapons are words like "too personal," "self-indulgent," and "You are emoting!" The tone of voice is clearly an indictment of bad taste.

Sadly, there are some students who have settled for mediocrity. At some time in their search for the ecstasy of dance, they decide that their talent is a limited one and resign themselves to work within safe and easily reached parameters. They acquire the basic skills, learn to look as if they are really dancing and after a while work their way to the status of a teacher of dancers and even a choreographer for others. These are probably the ones I am describing, the repressors of the irrepressibles.

Perhaps the saddest of all are the gifted ones who trash themselves as inadequate. They are the hardest to help and even harder to notice.

If dance is what you really need, know your limitations *and* your strengths. Reach past the weaknesses and around them. Hone your powers. Learn to see the full range of your talent in a clear light. This is not an easy task, but it is a required one. With the courage of a secret self-perspective, your limitations can become a part of your charm. Here's how I phrased it once in class:

> Raise your r.p.m.'s throughout, not just in the gestures that "connect" for you or in the technically hard places but also in the transitions and places where there's nothing "hard" to do. Find the movement motivation and its opposite. Find material that "lights your fire." Don't be afraid of taking up too much room or making too much noise. Assert your spine. Dance all the way. Don't be afraid of the big motion. All dancers are too short. What would happen if you allowed it all to come out? You would be rich, for you would have much from which to choose!

This argument is not for everything to be on a massive scale; one should not be afraid of the small motion either. What I advocate is the fearless response to what is needed at each moment—a shout or a whisper, a furiously percussive motion or a floating stillness.

This brings up the matter of taste. Taste is what you acquire if and when you become what we call "cultivated" or "cultured." It does not mean that your values agree with the majority or the cognoscenti (who are usually some fashionable clique). It means that you have an awareness of how you have evolved as an artist and a person, what is happening in life and particularly in art, and in the light of all that knowing, you have made choices. These may be choices which no one else may accept. If that is the case, all you will need is the courage to stay with what you found is true for you.

Poor taste or no taste are the marks of one who *weisst von gurnicht* (one who knows from nothing). Taste means choosing from an internal sense of rightness, by one who has the awareness and the capacity to make a wide range of choices. W. I. B. Beveridge uses the word in a more specialized way, identifying taste with the intuitive ability to pursue productive lines of research (*The Art of Scientific Investigation,* pp. 1005–08). In dance, there are talented people who make the fatal error of choosing and staying with a teacher or a choreographer who is wrong for them. It is called "failed taste." By the time the mistake is recognized too much time may have gone by.

To return to the matter of the fear of "too much," women frequently exhibit this syndrome. Someplace along the way of growing up, most probably very early, they learned that to be a girl, you mustn't make too much noise or take up too much room. Delicate, elegant, fragile and modest are the ladylike tickets to success as a female. Whatever move the teacher or choreographer gives out, these dancers trim it back to good taste and a "reasonable" proportion. Nothing could be more self-defeating. It is sad when a woman tries to appear female when that is what she is, and so it is when a man tries to appear manly—whatever that might be. There is no ideal template for female or for male, there are only the infinite variations and blends that go to make the complexity of humans. As the Beatles sang long ago, "Let it be," and do what needs to be done. Pay attention to the moment. If the door is stuck, push hard; and if it isn't stuck, open it with your finger. Don't perform. Forget style. Do each thing as fully as it needs doing.

> Student: The energy in me feels genuine. I don't feel hysterical but people say to me, "Gee, what a hysterical woman."
>
> Daniel: You have the loveliest error of all. I'd rather deal your problem of too much than not enough.
>
> Student: Yes, but though you're not afraid of too much, most people are.
>
> Daniel: Well, we have a serious question: What are you afraid of? Most people?

Every exercise in the Workbook is a challenge to deliver all that is necessary and nothing superfluous. What is the key to this delicate balance? There is the constant call to give up a focus on self and pour all of the attention upon the task at hand. If that becomes the way you work, the question of too much or not enough should not appear. If the door is stuck, push hard.

2 Eroding Elements of the Performing State

By the time most dancers are ready to become professionals, they have already ingrained in them qualities and ways of working that profoundly affect whatever it is they have to offer as artists. Some of these are taken for granted. Take the matter of style. It is a given that one must have style. For many, this means that one must be "stylish" (up to the minute). It is generally assumed that one must cultivate an attractive style. The belief presented here is that each of these three thrusts—having a style, being "stylish," and working to be attractive—is precisely what destroys the most precious gift an artist can offer: his.her individuality.

The Crutches of Style

The Crutch of a Personal Style

If a dancer cultivates a particular style, there is a whole world of otherness that is closed off to that artist. By proudly asserting, "This is what I do and I do it very well," there is the admission that, "There is very little else I can do." No. If you're a human being, your range of possibilities is awesome. You open them up by your unrelenting need to observe others, your skill in imitation and your faith in the boundless range of your imagination. You free yourself to dance in many ways by not protecting and defending one way.

The Crutch of Peer Style

Young people tend to be the victims of peer pressure. The terror of being "different" is the terror of being isolated from the group. Why is this fear so intense? For most, being young is a hard passage. At the core of this unease is the question of identity. The time

21

of commitment and the entrance into responsibility is approaching. "Who am I and what am I going to be and do?" The closest hook to an identity are your companions. Step out of their circle and you're nothing. It is at this stage that the mentoring of a compassionate teacher means so much. Think of Edward Villela caught up in dance but surrounded by a community that considered dance for a man as inconceivable. It was only by a delayed and convoluted path that he was finally able to plunge into the work of becoming a dancer. Truth to tell, there are not too many adults who have the nerve to walk alone, and many fall into imitative patterns unconsciously.

The Crutch of Charm

An article in the *New York Times* quoted the eminent actor, Frank Langella, discussing his work as the lead actor in Arthur Miller's *After the Fall*: "It could be the single worst trap for an actor: to want to be liked. . . . It's a stultifying insecurity. It's in me, it's in all of us, and we must fight it. To want to be liked is to ultimately compromise. You begin to live for other people. It shouldn't rule your life and it shouldn't rule the roles you play" (November 5, 1984).

If this charm gambit is a trap for actors, it certainly is pervasive in dance. For centuries, the chief focus of dance was entertainment, seduction and yes, charm. In our field, there is the ever-present self-conscious decorativeness of dancers with which every director and choreographer must deal.

During the second evening of an improvisation workshop, I slid a folding chair out into the center of the room and deliberately pointed to an attractive, skillful and elegantly decorative dancer and said, "I have a challenge for you. Can you pass under that chair without moving it?" It looked to be an impossible task and yet, with careful maneuvering and much concentration she emerged on the other side of the chair, disheveled, panting a bit and somewhat confused. I asked, "While you were trying to achieve what you thought was a ridiculous and somewhat impossible task, were you aware of how you looked?" Wide-eyed, she shook her head. "Were you trying to look good while you were doing it?" "No," she said, still somewhat confused by this weird assignment in a dance workshop.

Having given this task many times since, what am I getting at? Almost every minute and detail of every dance class we have ever taken is an arrow pointed clearly at the ideal of looking good, looking beautiful. That's what the whole thing is about, isn't it? What's wrong with trying to get an audience to think you look beautiful? For some, this exercise is perhaps the first time they just do something without trying to look good doing it. The object, to pass under the chair without moving it, is not muddied with a focus on appearance or style.

Stanislavski has an even better story: An acting student is given a situation by the director: her mother has lost her job and there will no longer be any money for her tuition at the theatre training school. A friend, who has no cash to lend her, offers a valuable brooch. The gift is refused. The friend, unnoticed, pins the brooch in the folds of a curtain and as she leaves says, "I have left it for you somewhere in the room." The student rushes back into the room and flees from one spot to another with bold and tragic gestures of anguish. There is a great show of searching everywhere and finally the student returns to her seat flushed and triumphant. The director asks to see the brooch. She, "Oh, I forgot that," and rushes back to the stage to look for it. The director calls out to tell her that if she does not really find the brooch, she will be dismissed from the school and no longer be able to attend the classes. This time there was no demonstration; the search was a search—intense, slow, careful and quietly desperate. When questioned afterward, the student much preferred the first way, "I was excited, I suffered." The director told her that she was believable the second time. "Your first search was bad. The second was good." "Oh," she said, "I nearly killed myself the first time" (*An Actor Prepares* [New York: Theatre Arts, 1972], pp. 35–37).

Can one lose focus on one's own person and throw all one's attention to the object? Is it possible that one can achieve a beauty, a self-realization, yes, even a virtuosity, by this discipline of losing the self? What is being projected here is indeed an aesthetic and an implied ethic, not unlike that of the ancient Chinese Taoists. The search is for the revelation of what is, not with what is made. Beauty is identified with light, with vision, with insight, not with ordering. Highly significant thinkers in art have said that art is the bringing of order to the chaos of life. The Taoists of ancient China believed that life is ordered, not chaotic, and that understanding, insight, science and art are engaged in *finding* that order. How to do this? For the Taoists, it lies in being open to The Way, The Tao, to what is there. This means paying attention and being receptive on all levels without preconception. It means that focus on the self neglects vision of the object. It attempts to dispense with history—to see as a child sees. For adults this is difficult and well nigh impossible on a pure and absolute level. How to even approach this way, this mind-set? The first step is to forgo the deadly demand for the "pure and the absolute." The second is to look past the self and seek the object, the task, the other. Observe the surfer who succeeds only when totally absorbed in the vagaries of the wave he.she is riding at that moment. You can't surf the last wave or the next wave, only this wave.

If at the center of your reason for being on the stage is to be liked, to be admired, to be loved for any reason—for your skill, for your looks, for your sexuality and yes, even for your great talent—there is a very good chance that you will be. How will you achieve this "success"? You will flaunt your technique, your fabulous musculature, your stunning figure or your refined profile. You will aggressively call attention to yourself whether or not you are the central figure. What happens to the choreography, to the intentions and design of the choreographer, to the character and quality of the role you have been given? It is bent, distorted or lost in the blaze of your brilliance, your sexiness, your gorgeous tresses or whatever treasure you so generously share with the audience. More important, what happens to you? In this flirting with the audience, you learn to give them what you think they want, not what you have to offer as an artist.

And Yet What Is Style?

From my second year in college, I not only studied dance, but I worked in a few dance companies. My first truly professional company was directed by Anna Sokolow. With a barely adequate technique, I was taken into the company in the 1939–40 season that culminated in my first Broadway performance in the Alvin Theatre. Late one afternoon, I was returning from rehearsal in the company of one of the other dancers, a man called Maurice Silver. He wasn't very good either, but what was Anna to do? There were so few male dancers, choreographers took what they could find.

As we were waiting for the train, Maurice, who was usually a kind man, said to me, "It's true, you are really working very hard, but you don't have any style. That is going to take a lot of time. You'll just have to be patient." Of course, I was jolted and hurt and may have angrily asked, "What are you talking about? What the hell is style?" No reply from Maurice sits in my memory, only my offended pride.

A few weeks later, also in a late afternoon, I had a few minutes to rest after a rehearsal and before taking the subway home. I was alone, sitting on a park bench in Madison Square Park, just looking at the bare branches and enjoying the crisp early spring air, when from nowhere a sentence appeared in my mind: "Style is personal authority." Just the thought of it released a band of tension through my whole body. At the time, I did not analyze why I felt so much better about myself, but recently, as I told this story to my wife, it became clear to me. How could I, just a beginner, have personal authority when my dance control and knowledge were so pitifully limited? Maurice was right. I did not have style, but with work and patience I would acquire style and I would then be responsible for what I did as an artist.

Good professional dancers do have style, defined as personal authority. They have the craft and the knowledge and the taste to make the vital choices that go into the creation of a dance role and a style that is inherent in that role. This is quite different from having a particular style that curtails the dancer's performance options.

WORKBOOK EXERCISES

Medicine Ball
Outrageous Travel
The Obstacle†
Passing Through a Physical Object†
Walk Behind Another†
The Inner Rhythm of the Role†
Your Familiar†
Each Alone†
Before, After and On†
Take a Walk in Your Own World
The Spine of Style†
Possessed by a Mannerism†
I Dare You†
The Minnesota Duet

Performing for the Audience: Seen and Unseen

More times than once I have had my eyes opened to a new way of seeing what I have been looking at for years. Many such illuminations have been provided by Joseph Chaikin, the director of the Open Theatre.

On the Audience

One of the baffling questions for the actor is "Who is the audience?" . . . Every performer makes some decision about the audience in his own mind: personalizing, making specific the anonymous. He makes a secret choice, in the course of events, as to "who" the audience is. In attributing a particular quality to the audience, one invites the participation of that quality. Who is he secretly addressing? The casting agent present in the audience? The critic who could advance his career? His parents? The ghost of Gandhi? His greatest love? Himself? The same action addressing each of these has in it a very different message. To whom does the actor personally dedicate his performance? (*The Presence of the Actor* [New York: Atheneum, 1972], pp. 140–41)

Chaikin suggests here that this choice tends to be made without thinking, a choice that becomes an integral part of our theatrical baggage without our being aware of it. He is saying that we cannot allow these patterns to act upon us unquestioned. They need to be raised up to the level of our conscious thought and consideration. Nothing in what he says applies exclusively to actors. It is addressed to everyone who ventures upon the stage and actually to all who present the self to the public in any art form.

You can dedicate your motion at any time: in class, in rehearsal, in performance, in creating a dance. Rather than to "someone," it can be to "an animal of which you are in awe," or to "a place of great beauty." Many variations are possible. In an improvisation session, when I call out, "Dedicate your motion to someone who is not here," I always witness a subtle change in the dancers, usually in the direction of greater intensity, a sharpening of the movement and sometimes an elaboration of the original phrase. Most striking is to listen to the dancers after they have done this for the first time. There is often a preoccupation and a wonderment in their faces. It may have been the first time they danced for, with and to someone or something that really mattered to them. Not rarely, that "who" or "what," that "someone" or "something," was a surprise, unexpected and strangely affecting. It becomes one of the first lessons in what it means to fill a motion with action—an action from within. By action, I mean to *do* something, to recognize that an arabesque is a metaphor for an action.

The reader and I are quite aware that there is a whole school of dance that totally rejects what I have just written. To them, the paramount significance of an arabesque is itself. To them, loading it with meanings and metaphors drags it down into sentimentality or sets it up as a mysterious sign which the bedeviled audience is required to decipher instead of simply exhilarating at the movements they are witnessing. To me and to Tamiris, who schooled me in my beginning, the sheer elegance and physicality of an arabesque is one of many ways of seeing and experiencing it, not the only way. It can be a metaphor for flight, for offering oneself to another, to baring one's vulnerability to others, or it can be an exquisite and awesome configuration. The list will go on and on as long as there is choreography—in spite of the purists.

One could also give the challenge, "I dare you to dance for the audience," and who does that better than the dancers and artists of Las Vegas and Broadway? Their task is clear and unequivocal: to entertain, manipulate and seduce the audience; an audience that comes to be entertained, manipulated and seduced. What could be more honest? But what of the concert stage? A work may begin with a profound interactive life, a life that has no awareness of an audience; but in the finale, the dancers turn their faces, attention and smiles, forward to signal the imminence of the end and the cue for vociferous applause. Many performers involved with an inner scenario that does not include an audience nevertheless dance face front, attention front. The only "audience" for the Prodigal Son is his father, who is onstage. Romeo and Juliet are alone together. The theatrical convention of "dancing for the audience" tells many dancers, and unfortunately choreographers, that the proper focus is front regardless of the material.

Although I am wary of all rules, I will state one now: Looking directly front tends to recognize the audience *as an integral part of the choreography*. There are exceptions, as when the metaphor is to address "society," to be struck by some powerful vision, or when front is clearly one of many places to focus upon, as in a ritual. Otherwise, to establish a life onstage that does not include viewers, a dancer can look in any direction *except straight front.*

Technical matters aside, the relationship with the audience boils down to an ethical matter. The stage can have the climate of a creative, risk-taking world or an arena for seduction, competition and judgements. It is possible to regard the audience as collaborators in the same world and in the same struggle which you had in the far country from which you have come to them, to bring them into the full weight of the experience that you have had and that you are trying to illuminate. Conversely, you can treat the audience as dummies who need every subtle point explained, or as a gold mine that has to be captured from the other performers. You can pander to the audience, or you can challenge it. Whichever way you go, there are portions of the audience that will cooperate with you and support you. Either you pass out rose-colored glasses or you take all the risks involved by treating the audience like adults and letting them share in the shit and the roses that make up the life you have discovered for them. It's your choice.

WORKBOOK	Dedicate Your Motion[†]
EXERCISES	I Dare You[†]

The Intolerance of Uncertainty

At a certain period in my life, I was preparing to reroute my energies to becoming an actor. I had become negative about dancing, not realizing at the time that it was the life of Broadway that was wrong for me. To further that direction, I convinced the director of The Mt. Kisco Playhouse in Westchester, New York, to take me on as his only regular actor. Everyone else was jobbed in for each play.

It was opening night for *Anastasia*. I had a minor role as one of the conspirators assisting the Baron who was involved in the attempt to establish the legitimacy of the supposed daughter of Czar Nicholas II. As the curtain went up on opening night, I was lighting a cigarette, picking out a candied sweet and feeling very good about how smoothly my stage business was going when, on cue, the Baron entered. I hopped off the trunk I had perched on and stood there. There was a lengthy pause and then the Baron roared, "Sergei, do you not greet me when I enter?" I mumbled, stumbled out a lame, "Good evening, Baron," three times without stopping. At intermission, I rushed back to the actor's dressing room to apologize for missing my cue. "Nonsense," he said, "Bobby Lewis said, 'Always look for the obstacle.'" (Bobby Lewis was one of the great teachers of acting in New York City and original member of the Group Theatre.) What he meant was, "Always look for trouble. That's where the life lurks. If you are full of your intention and you know who you are, the unexpected and the unplanned are juice for your battery."

No honest performer, dancer, singer or actor will enter the stage without hours of intensive, careful thought, preparation, research and rehearsal. The hazard wrapped up in all that planning is rigidity. There are artists who resist the slightest change. They cannot face the reality that no two performances are alike. The flexible ones delight in surprises and literally gain energy when "things go wrong."

Creatively, the rigid ones love systems that provide all the answers. The teachings of Francois Delsarte (1811–1871) had a strong effect on acting in America, on American dance, and particularly on Ted Shawn, whose book, *Every Little Movement*, gave his understanding of this approach. Basically, Shawn said that "every little movement" did have meaning. On page 56 of his book is a drawing of a man in profile extending his arm in eleven different angles, each one of which has been assigned a precise meaning, from the lowest, "It is evil," to the highest, "It is enchanting." To extend the arm straight forward would mean, "It is." Delsarte assigned a particular meaning to almost every imaginable position of the body. Actors and dancers trained by mastering this dictionary of attitudes and motions. (See fig. 1.)

The massive change in thinking introduced by Stanislavski directly opposed this type of system and the set lexicon of broad operatic gestures that dominated the stages of Europe in the nineteenth century, both in the theatre and in ballet. These conventions are alive today in most opera, in much of ballet, in TV sitcoms—but have disappeared from contemporary theatre. With Stanislavski, there were no stencils, no molds,

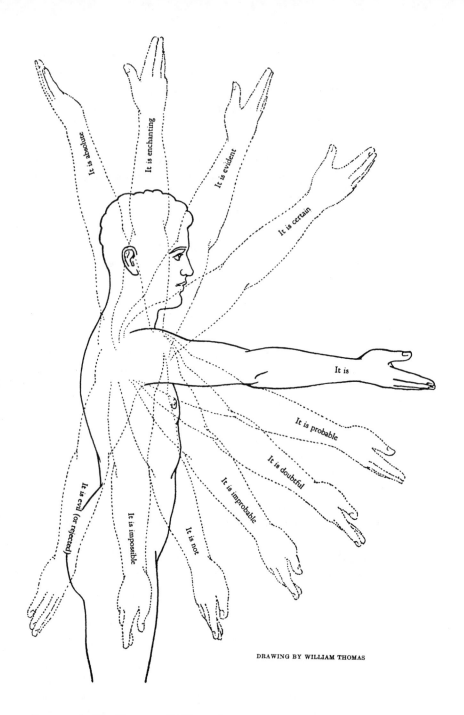

DRAWING BY WILLIAM THOMAS

FIGURE 1. The Degrees of Affirmation.
From Ted Shawn, *Every Little Movement* (New York: Dance Horizons, 1954), p. 56.

no clearly defined models to emulate. Each role and each performance created its own rules and its own surprises. One of the marks of Helen Tamiris's work was that it could not be easily identified or characterized. Each new work was an unexplored country that had to be recognized for what it was rather than portrayed in terms of what had gone before. Her choreography did not just accept uncertainty as a necessity but exulted in the thrill and adventure of the creative process.

You think those newscasters are speaking to you. You think they are looking at you. No. In front of the lens of the camera is a tilted sheet of glass. Below the camera is a continuous role of paper on which the script is printed, mirror image. As newscasters speak to the teleprompter, the mirror image words unroll and are reflected correctly for them to read aloud. The camera lens doesn't see reflections, only the speaker.

It is possible for a person to appear to be looking, listening and responding to what is going on when in fact he.she perceives everything in terms of preconceptions, anticipations and prejudices. As noted above, Stanislavski used the term "stencils" to describe the error that entraps many performers. They know ahead of time the "right" way to do a role. They come to work with an ideal persona in mind. Many dancers suffer from this way of working. Instead of coming into the rehearsal or the class with a wide-open receptivity that asks, "What is new here? What is special and different in this choreography and its demands?" they come armed with a certainty of a correct style, spirit and manner of how they will dance. Such rigidity will erode whatever richness of expressiveness the artist has. The dancer might even "look good," but the work will undoubtedly suffer.

No. Enter the work space like a blank sheet of paper. Wait to be inscribed by the unexpected—and accept the premise that the ideal cannot be fully achieved. If, after working it to the hilt, it feels wrong for any reason, do whatever needs to be done: talk about it, express your unease, or leave. How to achieve this state of mind? The artists of Asia have profound resources to offer us. Some use meditation, finding various ways of emptying the mind as a prologue to their creative work.

WORKBOOK EXERCISES   *Any and every improvisation exercise is an exercise in uncertainty.*[†]

Vanity Versus Self-hatred

Would it be false to say that at times most of us bounce back and forth like a pinball between vanity and self-hatred? Bad enough, but what of those who get locked into one or the other?

One of my cousins had a passion to become an actress. She went to New York University, majored in theatre, fell in love with her instructor, enlisted her father's money to back a production starring her and directed by the loved instructor. But whenever it was her turn to speak, she either had the greatest difficulty resisting the impulse to turn to face upstage or, to her horror, she would give into that evasion and speak to the rear wall. I admire the fact that when she realized what was going on, she gave up acting.

Deep in the middle of a jazz class I noticed a student who had just come into the class crossing in an energetic diagonal. I stopped the class, telling her it was hazardous to enter a class in the middle. Near tears, she said, "But I was here from the beginning!" I was embarrassed and apologized. The next week, I looked for her and after a while found her in the farthest corner of the room with three people between her and me. After the class, I beckoned to her and said, "I am now taking back my apology. I didn't see you because you didn't want me to. You have been hiding in this class. You probably can barely see me, which would indicate you are making sure that I do not see you. Do you not want me to teach you?" The next week, she was in the front row and remained there for the rest of the semester, trying every moment to let me know that she did want to be seen and to be taught.

Sadly, not everyone would be as courageous as this young woman. Some would fade even further away when challenged to be seen. I have observed students who had genuine talent choked by a demeaning concept of themselves. It is no simple matter for a teacher to draw them out. In my teaching, there is a small collection of these self-loathers whom I managed to coax from behind their screens. It distresses me to think that with the kind of impatience and abruptness that I occasionally bring to bear in classes, I may have lost sight of a frightened talent.

In 1947, Helen Tamiris and I went to London to stage *Annie Get Your Gun,* she to direct and I to re-create her choreography with the British dancers. One of the very best of the performers was the man who played the role of Charlie Davenport, the business manager of Buffalo Bill's Wild West Show. He quickly caught the American accent, and his vitality filled the stage in every rehearsal. Came the first dress rehearsal, we could barely find him. He seemed to disappear, or rather seemed to be playing a different role. It took a good ten minutes to figure out what was going on. Not only was this slightly overweight man of over fifty still putting on a pink juvenile makeup, but the whole vibrant characterization went into another gear. Not the abrasive, aggressive wisecracker we loved but a charmer who was still wearing the first makeup he ever learned.

In the audition, we were convinced we had made a great find that had been ignored by the British theatre. It was a mystery why he wasn't a star. In the rehearsals, he was a stunning performer but here in the dress rehearsal he had slipped into—what? Tamiris said: "He's got to get rid of that makeup. Go backstage and see what you can do with Milligan." (I can't recall his name so I'm inventing one.) I found him in his dressing room: "The scene is wonderful, but there is something very unreal about your makeup. You have a fabulous face but you're covering it up. Could you do a more natural make-up? You have wonderful brows and you covered them up to make thin elegant brows. Why?" Well, he was so charged up about being in that show, wanting to please and thinking Helen and I had been dropped from heaven, anything we said had to be true. "Oh, of course, you are so very right." He grabbed a towel and began to work on his eyebrows, rubbing away the thick grease with such intensity that he tore off a piece of skin above his eye and blood trickled down his cheek.

Obviously, much was involved in that face he was rubbing out. This was the makeup he learned when he was eighteen, and he probably had a bit of success with that face. Now, he had a plethora of lines, jowls and fierce wonderful brows over piercing eyes, all of which he had tried to conceal with the face of a juvenile. This was the pathetic piece of vanity to which he had been clinging all his adult life.

Sensing I had done all that was possible for the moment, I said, "Helen needs me out front. Let's talk about it later." Before the next dress rehearsal, he and I sat down and worked on a strong makeup that revealed his own crafty, cynical face. We never again lost sight of his vibrant presence.

Vanity or self-hatred are exactly the kinds of self-focus that destroy the very meaning and purpose of performance; concern for self supersedes the actual stage task. The great artists of the theatre have one quality in common: They are ruthless in their perception of themselves, their strengths and their weaknesses. One knows she has no waist and will badger every costumer to cover up that fact. Another knows he has a miserable arabesque line and finds every way to avoid it in profile to the audience. Still another knows he isn't tall enough to cope with a costume that cuts him in two. A cool self-appraisal is required as admission to the profession. Once on the stage, those successful ones find a fierce focus on the role—not on the self.

WORKBOOK EXERCISES
Any of the following may *expose some tender area that affects your work as an artist and is asking for your attention.*

Your Familiar†
A Duet
Why Do You Dance?
Possessed by a Mannerism†
I Dare You†
Inside the Outside†
Rituals of Power
The Minnesota Duet

Reaching for the Result

In many ways, this innocuous phrase, "reaching for the result," encapsulates everything I've said in this chapter. How many choreographers have called out in desperation to their dancers: "Come on! Give it some life!" "Move it!" "Feel love!" "Be more lyrical!" "Some energy, please!" "Be strong!" "Express wonder!" "Be abstract!" "Reverence!"

"Stop emoting and just dance it!" "Joy, I want some joy on that stage!" Every one of these all too common pleas reaches for a desired result, for the emotion, for a generalization or an abstract dynamic.

The peril of these goals in performance is banality. Asking a group of dancers to feel pride or to be lyrical or "to make it beautiful," is to guarantee a studio awash in clichés. And yet, this is exactly the kind of direction dancers so often receive. Perhaps the dreadful and unconvincing performances that flow from this mind-set are the reason so many dancers and choreographers have opted for the classic stone face of modern dance. To them, facial expression of any kind is in bad taste and dismissed contemptuously as "emoting." By avoiding the bad taste of synthetic emotion depictions, these apostles of "good taste" have lost much of the humanity that could enrich their work—if they could find an honest path to that goal.

The central aim of this book is to open the door to genuine, deeply felt emotion in performance by learning how to get there. Most simply stated, the "result" should be the product of a specific action in a specific context, and what that result is will inevitably contain surprises not only to the audience but to the artist. Working this way, the dancer never knows quite what the result will be and is patient enough to wait for it to appear.

The next chapters present an acting technique for dance performance. As noted earlier, it may appear far too complex. It is and it isn't. The fundamental concepts that bind all the parts together can be encompassed by six simple questions, but the parts are many and all deserve awareness and thought. However, they are at no time to be regarded as a checklist when "real" life takes over and performances are being prepared for the stage. Every dancer finds at one time or another a part that fits so well that the less thought and analysis the better; all that is needed is the plunge into the material. Then there are the roles that don't work—at first. They demand a long reach and resist coming to life. It is at these moments that the professional is armed with a battery of techniques to penetrate the complexity. In fact, the ability to bring a vivid beauty to difficult roles is what qualifies a dancer for the term, *professional*.

WORKBOOK
EXERCISES
A well worked understanding of the following chapter will make it possible to reach profound emotional states in the act of performing without reaching for them or worse, without the curse of making them up.[†]

3 *The Six Questions*

The Syntax of the Performing State

Alice: Marjorie, when you did the crooked walk this last time, it looked different than when you first showed it.

Marjorie: No, it was the same. Well, I was thinking something completely different this time.

—*from a class at the American Dance Festival, 1987*

Syntax is a lovely word defined as "the way in which words are put together to form phrases and sentences." The performing state, similarly, is at its best an elegantly linked structure. When it's right, all the parts feed each other to make a single expressive entity. The analytic work on the role described here need not be done in every situation. There are artistic expressions that burst forth like a spring flood. A wise person accepts them gratefully, rides the crest, asks no questions and doesn't analyze. But a dancer dedicating her.his life to the profession cannot expect that every role will emerge effortlessly, right and inspired. Some will be downright difficult. The style of the choreographer may be alien, the music unattractive and the character, a far cry from what comes naturally. The professional dancer can have the craft to understand what is needed and have the tools of analysis that will make an awkward and difficult role every bit as beautiful and as successfully realized as the one that came spontaneously.

We analyze only when we have to, and when we have to, it is well to have the tools. One of the most important contributions of Helen Tamiris was her recognition that Stanislavski's method of breaking down a role for actors was there waiting to be used by dancers. At the heart of Stanislavski's teachings and Tamiris's development of them lies a creative act which amazingly enough tends to be ignored most of the time by much of the dance profession. It asks the imagination, the heart and the mind of the dancer to build the entire performance around a specific set of images which are linked as if they were a model sentence having a subject, a predicate and an object with subordinate clauses. The entire process can actually be encapsulated in one sentence: *Who (or what) is doing what to whom (or what) and where, in what context and under what difficulties and why?*

It may appear ridiculous but this one sentence is what most of this book is about. Diagrammatically, it looks like this:

1. *Who or what?* (the subject)

2. *Is doing what?* (the verb)

3. *To whom or what?* (the object)

4. *Where and when?* (the context)

5. *To what end?* (the reason for the action)

6. *The obstacle?* (justifies theatrical viability)

These questions are disconcerting to some, inartistic to others and libérating to many. Considering how most dancers are trained, the heart of this technique is nothing less than revolutionary. The tradition has been to focus on abstractions: on energy levels, on an emotion, on movement per se, on technical virtuosity, on generalized vivacity, on charm, on being attractive, on being brilliant, on dancing beautifully and finally on anything except what the dance is about and the particularity of each dance role. The specifics, when they are needed, are provided by costume and set designers. A funny hat can make a dance comic. A romantic dance needs but a slight expression of yearning or perhaps a beret will do. An abstract movement piece has the de rigueur expressionless face. How many dancers carry on the identical inner life in every dance regardless of the role? All they do is change hats and dance "beautifully," whatever that may mean.

Before we go further, it is well to recognize that some very great artists would regard what is being pursued here as pernicious nonsense. "I can teach and explain to pupils what to do better, but not because there's a reason. . . . You have to be very careful when you use your mind . . . or you will get into trouble. . . . Don't ask why it must be like this. Don't analyze. Just do it."

These words are attributed to George Balanchine by Gelsey Kirkland in *Dancing on My Grave* (New York: Doubleday, 1986), pp. 48, 78. She claimed she was continually mocked or ignored by him whenever she tried to discover the meaning of what she was dancing. Of course, Balanchine continually contradicted himself. Suzanne Farrell, who worked quite closely with him for over twenty years, tells of one of the first times she danced for him in a ballet called *Meditation*:

> I was to enter from the back corner behind him [Jacques d'Amboise] with three simple steps—full step on my right foot, up to pointe on my left and then pointe on my right, stopping in fourth position. . . .

Mr B, of course, didn't mention any story line; he described only what he wanted physically. It was as if I were parting an invisible curtain, parting clouds. . . . "You just hold on to the air when you're up there [on pointe]," he said. "You're riding on air." (*Holding on to the Air* [New York: Summit Books, 1990], pp. 12–13)

It's a perfect illustration of that contradiction. He disdains to give a "story line," but because she was having a balance problem he gives her a truly exquisite *specific image*, "holding on to the air." She herself creates her own lovely image of parting clouds with her arms. Why did Gelsey Kirkland get a blank door and Suzanne Farrell the gift of a bit of poetry? Perhaps because, although we try hard to be consistent, we invariably slip into contradiction. Undoubtedly, if anyone took the trouble to seriously examine what I have stood for as a choreographer, teacher and writer, they would encounter contradictions. Here, in this book, I state my conviction that sheer movement is one of ten thousand exquisite reasons for dancing.

Who or What?

Who or what is dancing? This question is the key to the entire process. All dancers, be they principals or one of the ensemble, need to shape their internal life around the core of a specific identity within the context of a specific image. Who gives the answer? In the theatre, the play script defines the specific character for the actor. In dance, ideally the choreographer should do this, but some bridle when asked, "Who am I supposed to be?" or "What am I doing here?" They give Balanchine's answer, "Stop thinking and just dance." Then the dancers are thrown upon their own resources and must resort to a private session of imagination.

There are an infinite number of images possible for each dance part. How do you know when you have found the right one? A hard question with no easy answer. First off, did the image come of its own accord rather than by a logical and rational choice? Second, does it (to adapt the immortal words of Jim Morrison), "light your fire"? Does the image and its action excite, energize and free your motions? Third, is the specific image one that illuminates the poem of the dance work? Fourth and critically, is the choreographer happy with your interpretation of his.her choreography? If yes, dig in and keep developing what you have found. You don't have to tell anybody what imaginative inner life is driving your dance; that is your own private artistic property. If it's working, discussion and analysis would probably water down the intensity of your work.

If the choreographer rejects your danced interpretation of her.his work, you must listen very carefully to what is not being accepted and grasp at every indication of what she.he does want, no matter how vague or generalized the words are. Pay attention not only to the words but to the tone of voice, and note the facial and bodily expression. Use all of that for a new meditation on the role (Hub Meditation—see chapter 10).

With these directions, the spoken and the unspoken, let the image find you rather than the other way round.

At no time let yourself be seduced by a blurred or generalized image, no matter how interesting, intelligent or inspiring. Pursuing a generalized image will result in clichéd interpretation of your role. You will discover what has been discovered and look like what has been seen in generations of dancers who have gone before you. The awesome power of the *specific* image, and the *specific* identity, is that it is a poetic metaphor that is yours alone—yours as the singular person that you are. It will help you discover details and textures that will not only surprise the audience but you as well.

The two columns below illustrate the generalized versus the specific image. One is a huge, ill-defined area; the other is always characterized by an action and not by a feeling. The point is that the action will generate the feeling.

Generalized	*Specific*
A balmy wind	A cooling, moist wind racing across a dry, hot plain.
A brooding prince	A young man who has everything and nothing he wants and senses that what he is searching for is not of this world. (Consider Nureyev in *Romeo and Juliet*. He seemed to be fully alive in the last century and absorbed the details and the specifics of romantic ballet as if it were the first time they had ever been done. Hence, he was not banal.)
A lyric force	Any strong force balanced by an equally strong force: a pair of lovers, each with his.her own face and name; a dancer pitted against a soaring piece of music; a votary seeing in his.her mind's eye an elusive god and reaching for it.
A virile peasant dancing	A man dancing under the duress of a gun pointed at him; a man dancing to arouse the woman he desires.
A bravura dancer	Legs and arms are flashing swords, flexible foils, the eyes shine as brilliant jewels and every finger displays a precious ring.
A dancer in a work choreographed by chance methods	The dancer as a dancer luxuriating in the movement, aiming for precise control of every motion.

Generalized	Specific
A sexy jazz dancer	Auditioning to be a Dallas Cowgirl, knowing you have it all.
One in love	One who cannot tear his.her eyes from the beloved; one who cannot bear to be far from the beloved; one who shields the beloved from harm; one who feeds the vanity of the beloved; one who would keep the beloved warm in the cold. (Trying to *feel* love, banality will reign, but *doing* any one or a combination of these will create a feeling of love in the doer.)

WORKBOOK EXERCISES The Two Dances

In every viewing and analysis of these performances this matter of identity calls for attention.

Who or What Is Alive in the Music?[†]
The Inner Rhythm of the Role[†]
Circles[†]

Gives the muscular and physiological texture that forms the basis for becoming X and achieving the quality of movement that belongs to the role.

A Duet
The Hub Meditation[†]

This is the central tool for finding the specific image.

Before, After and On[†]
The Spine of Style[†]
Ham and Clove
Rituals of Power

Is Doing What?

Whether it is the stage, film, opera or dance, we go to the theatre expecting to see something happen. To say that action is the driving force of dance is obvious but, as in the matter of identity, its expressive force is too often blurred and oversimplified.

In modern dance, there is an early tradition of a dance of happiness, a dance of celebration, a dance of work and play, a dance of mourning. This tradition of generalization is kept alive in choreography classes all over the country where studies focus on high energy or low energy, in curved space and angular space, in joyousness or in grief.

The rationale is that these supposedly less complex problems are appropriate for beginners in choreography. (The argument may be valid—I have rarely taught beginners and have never used this approach.) The imprint of this early teaching makes generalized feeling and emoting the accepted practice throughout their careers. As choreographers create they create works that carry the same mood or action from beginning to end. If it's the same at the end as it was in the beginning, has anything happened?

In traditional ballet, literal pantomime conveys all the fluctuations of the story line, and when everything is made clear, the dancers are free to dance. What goes on in the minds of the dancers when they float above their brisé volés? In the rarest of cases, this devilishly difficult step becomes a part of a constantly evolving poem. In an Anthony Tudor ballet, like *Jardin aux Lilas,* every step, turn and pause is weighted with shifting meanings and actions without unnecessary time-outs for pantomimic explication of the plot. Tudor's work is a rare exception in the world of ballet where most of the time the dancers are just dancing full out on the crest of a feeling without any shift from beginning to end. There is no question that the great artists of the ballet like Galina Ulanova, Alicia Alonso, Jean Babilée, Nora Kaye, Rudolf Nureyev did not get buried in technical preoccupations nor in simplistic moods to carry them through a performance. They came onstage with a mission—to do something quite specific—and acted on it either to fail or triumph.

Action analysis is a process in which the action, the "who is doing what," can become clearer if three aspects are considered: the spine, the beats, the subtext.

The Spine

At an American Dance Festival class in acting technique, a truly lovely dancer from Hawaii, Karen Miyake, performed a substantial chunk of José Limon's magnificent solo, *Chaconne,* which she had the good fortune to learn from Betty Jones. The line and the placement were impeccable, as was her musicality; and yet what she did had little impact. It was stiff, self-conscious and mannered. The phrasing was disjointed. Always asking the students to give their opinions first, I heard consensus that it wasn't working. One student talked about disconnected phrasing, another about the uncertain focus, another that it lacked a lyric force, another that the arms should be more expressive, and so on.

At times, I will draw a student aside and give a direction out of hearing by the rest of the class. My reasoning is that if the other students hear what I am suggesting they may see it happen even though it doesn't; or, they may expect a certain result that fits their personal imagination and fail to see the value of what the dancer actually does. Less frequently, I speak my suggestion for all to hear because I sense that the public statement will charge the dancer. This time, I addressed Karen from my seat and for all to hear:

Daniel: Do you think this is a good dance?

Karen: Oh yes!

D: Did you ever know José?

K: No.

D: Do you admire his work?

K: Oh, I do!

D: Do you owe José anything?

K: Oh yes! (And her eyes fill quickly.)

D: So why not thank him for what he gave you?

There was an uncertain pause and then she indicated to the student who was running the cassette player to cue it up and play the Bach score again. She danced almost weeping and we almost wept too. She had a sweep and a fullness that would have drawn thanks from José.

The questioning with its final, "Then why don't you thank him?" ignited an action that filled the whole dance. An action that does that is called "the spine." One cannot always hit upon a spine of a dance so simply and so energizingly. Usually there is considerable fumbling before the right spine, the right over-arcing action is clarified. This time, I did hit it and she caught it entirely.

There is no rule or law that a spine cannot be radically altered at some point as the dance develops. There is no rule or law that a spine has to be crystal clear. How many in our culture thrash about without knowing what they want? How many fight without knowing the face of their enemy? How many carry the burden of guilt for crimes they have forgotten? Any one of these can be a dynamic spine to drive a performance. It has been the self-appointed task of artists to probe deeply into vague and uncertain areas of our lives seeking something more specific than a hunger or a fear without a name. Art is a seeking, but to seek does not ensure finding. An uncertain feeling or a nebulous vision can be a specific image that will significantly infuse a strong performance.

WORKBOOK EXERCISES

The Two Dances

Your Familiar[†]

Possessed by a Mannerism[†]

Each Alone[†]

The Hub Meditation[†]

The Duet as a Structure

Why Do You Dance?[†]

The Spine of Style[†]

Inside the Outside[†]

Rituals of Power

Adam and Eve

The Beats, Bits or Units

The spine alone is not enough. American teachers of Stanislavski technique say that the action has two aspects: the spine and the beats. Actually the term *beats* is a misnomer. Stanislavski called them *units*. Elizabeth Reynolds Hapgood, who edited and translated *An Actor's Handbook* (New York: Theatre Arts, 1963), speculates that the first great teachers of Stanislavski's methods in America were Russians who would thunder at their awed students, "Where are your *bits*?" But what the American actors heard was, "Vere arre your beets?" Certain that the acting gurus were not asking for a vegetable, they heard it as "beats." Stanislavski wrote:

> In order to work out the score of the play . . . we had to break it up into small units. . . . Remember, the division is temporary. . . . It is only in preparation . . . that we use small units. During its actual creation, they fuse into large units. . . . As you put on your makeup, you will think of the first unit. . . . You play the first unit and are carried along to the next and the next. (P. 154)

On occasion, he used the word "bits." The spine is the main action that pervades the role; it is the highway. The bits are the shifts and changes that occur along the way. Many dancers do go past generalizations and find an action or a spine that carries them through the time of the dance, but all too few have the slightest idea or awareness of bits. They are on a superhighway, constructed as straight as it can be. If there is a curve, it's long and soft—no sharp curves, no hairpin turns and rarely a right angle. The path of a good actor is the country road that constantly yields to the contours of the earth, buildings, trees, fields and so forth, though never losing sight of the main objective.

When a superhighway is built, homes are demolished, farms shaved thin, forests split open and the sides and summits of mountains sliced away. Sounds brutal doesn't it? Well, too many dancers tend to do the same. They ignore the convolutions and changes going on about them and hew to one overriding action or mood. If it is good choreography, there are bound to be subtle or abrupt shifts and changes from moment to moment, the music is constantly evolving and the actions and configuration of the other dancers may flicker like a fire. How many dancers pay attention to all that? Dancers can learn from good actors. Every change in the inner and outer life demands a response if the performance is to be alive. These small changes within the major action, the spine, are the beats, bits or units. In the creation and performance of a role, a rigidity that hews to the spine remorselessly risks being unbelievable, one-dimensional and, worse, boring.

In the summer of 1992 at the American Dance Festival, a class in Acting Technique for Dance Performance was honored and blessed by the presence of a major talent, a dancer-choreographer from Indonesia, Martinus Morito. In several of the first improvisation exercises, he danced with magnificent daring and imagination. He was electrifying in his imaginative use of personal movements and chunks of traditional Indonesian gestures. All the more disappointing was what he did when he presented his first of The Two Dances. (It would be helpful at this point to read this exercise in the Workbook, chapter 7.)

Mr. Morito's first presentation was a traditional Indonesian dance in honor of a king. It was like witnessing an exquisitely detailed teak carving come to life. All the more reason to be confused by the fact that I was watching it from afar—untouched and uninvolved, though in awe of his craft. Whatever the reason— the lack of a proper costume and makeup, the setting of a classroom rather than a ceremonial area and occasion—it was a flat, uninvolved performance with limited inner life, in spite of its technical excellence and polish. It may have been a dance he had performed with success but which had never felt right to him. That I never learned.

I threw a mess of questions at Morito: Who is doing this dance? A loyal noble pledging allegiance? Another king who has been vanquished? A professional dancer? A conspirator distracting the king preparatory to an assassination attempt? Are there any changes in the course of the dance? Is the dancer saying one thing all through the dance, "I revere my king," and that is all? Or, does he, in the beginning offer his reverence, then show how brave he would be defending his king, then how heroic the king himself is and finally how all must bow to the gods, the king and the soldier? I told Morito that I gave him this scenario as an example and that his task was to forget the details of what I said, only to remember the questions and to answer them for himself.

A few weeks later, he came back to repeat the dance, but to our eyes it was very different; the dance for the king came to life. Did he answer in his own terms all the questions I had put to him? Did he create an inner life composed of changing bits that carried him through the dance? When something really works, I am reluctant to ask questions. I fear that analysis and exposure will cool the heat of the dancer's conception and inner life. I never learned what Morito did to make the dance for the king so moving this time. The class and I were merely grateful. We applauded, murmured our appreciation and we went on.

In the appendix I present a close unit analysis of one of my own solos, *Dance in the Sun*. This goes against all my resistance to ever explaining any of my dances. I betray this one dance, which is not being performed by me or anyone else, in part because it can be seen on videotape and be used for study by those interested in this technique. Another good reason is that this is a lyric dance without the strong dramatic overtones which characterize so many of my solos.

Does every dance need a close analysis noting when each and every beat impacts upon the dance? I believe that any dancer who is taking this book seriously should subject at least a couple of dances in her.his repertoire to exactly such a process. After a time, she.he will know in what way to make use of bit analysis. My guess is that if there is clarity on the six questions, a moment-to-moment analysis would usually not be necessary. The specifics of the role will give birth to the bits one by one without a deliberate and conscious checklist. When and if a section of the dance is muddy and unfocused, a bit analysis would probably save the situation. Of course there is the paradox present in every complexity: extensive and prolonged analysis can be deadly, not unlike an operation—the longer the patient is lying on the table opened up, the dimmer are the chances of surviving. (You want simple answers? Read another book.)

WORKBOOK	The Two Dances
EXERCISES	Justification[†]
	How Does Your Tree Dance?[†]

In the course of a dance, or even in the course of a dance phrase, the source of the movement impulse can change.

Before, After and On[†]

The Subtext

How many times have your dance teachers exhorted you to do the opposite of what you are apparently doing? You are going into a grand plié and they hiss at you, "Pull up! Pull up!" Or they sing out, "Press the air down with your arms!" Or when you are spinning they shout, "Aim for stillness!" To be in balance is to be constantly recovering from losing balance. My first real teacher, Ray Moses, who had been an early member of Martha Graham's company under the name Lillian Ray, said to us, "You must learn to move your legs as if they were your arms—with the same lightness and articulation of your arms, and learn to move your arms as if they have the architectural power and weight of the legs." When I see a dancer always moving in a thin atmosphere, I question whether he.she is really dancing. A dancer has the capacity to make the air through which he.she moves thick. A port de bras can be a victory. If the very texture of dance movement is infused with counteraction, what of the mind?

The theatre is an arena of conflict. Music, from the polyphony of Bach, to the theme and countertheme of harmonic music, to the tensions of modernism, gains its vitality from conflict. If there were no trouble there would be no need for art. Conflict in art is a metaphor for the strife found in life.

The first place to locate conflict is within the person. We appear to be such and such, but what is going inside? Think of any of the arts and this principle is visible. Consider the dynamic figures of film: Marilyn Monroe—the manner of a slut with the persona of an innocent; her flaunted, fleshy sexiness versus her awe, childishness and air of constantly being surprised. Marlon Brando—a demonic force contained by a soft-spoken man who barely moves. Brando speaks softly because it's obvious that if the wrong buttons were pushed, he would explode; he doesn't need to make that obvious by yelling. Heard the other night while scanning the TV channels for something to watch: Charles Bronson looks into the darkness, speaking from under the deep shadow of a Western hat to a man beside him:

"You know what I hate more than anything else?"

"No. What?"

". . . being afraid."

That says it best. Find the opposites: a gunman whose angry pride conceals a feeling of inferiority, a clown whose physicality and daring stem from impotence and childishness, a tightrope walker whose calm, debonair persona conceals her terror of falling, the gentle charmer who is a con man.

Every dance role is incomplete without its contradictory elements. A student brought in an extraordinarily well-danced solo of the most unabashed declaration of love to an indifferent person. The moves were rich, personal and virtuosic, but neither I nor the students of the class could experience more than watch him go through his agony from a distance. His fault lay in a simplistic focus on the pure pain of an unrequited passion. That made it his problem—not ours. I gave him this challenge: Do everything with a shell of calculated, controlled moves so that the declarations of love take on the air of mockery. All the while be determined not to let your deep devotion show, but without realizing it, the inside tears loose, intermittently and unexpectedly. He understood the direction, performed it fully and we were caught up in his longing.

A dancer brings in a very well executed tango which she has worked up with a modestly competent partner. They want to enter a ballroom contest. The work is clean, occasionally exciting and flat. To them I say, "Forget this is a tango in a competition. Who are the two of you? What do you want of each other? The man is the leader in the tango. Perhaps the woman should take over? How does the man cope with that?" They look at each other doubtfully. Suddenly, the woman says, "OK, let's try it." Their tango becomes a duel and she appears to be winning until the last vicious lift and he has her, but does he? She whips spinning out of his grasp to smile triumphantly and bow before he does, opening up a whole new set of possibilities. He bows uncertainly and they look at each other from a distance. We bang on the floor and clap our hands in excitement.

It is not enough to know there is a subtext, an inner contradiction to what appears on the surface. One must enter the stage with it alive and present even though it is not visible. I recently witnessed a powerful duet choreographed by a colleague. Two women progressed at a painful slowness diagonally from upstage left toward downstage right, one woman supporting the other. Several times, they paused as if unable to continue and then suddenly flung their arms up in the air with a violent gasp only to resume their deadly progression. The unexpected arm fling should have been startling and drawn us deeper into their struggle. Instead, I was distanced a bit from a dance in which I had been strongly involved. I am assuming that the error lay not in the choreography but in the minds of the dancers who came to that moment and thought, "Now is the time we do that gasp." They should instead have had the impulse to do the gasp from the beginning, even before the lights came up. The impulse is there but is held in check, for whatever reason that is appropriate to the inner life of the dance. When the gasp finally occurs, it does so in spite of the repression.

The subtext—the contradiction—needs to be alive within the dancer from the start and, better still, part of the preparation for the performance.

WORKBOOK Inside the Outside[†]
EXERCISES

To Whom or What?

There are dancers in group works who do not relate to the others except in the most formal, abstract fashion, even when the choreography calls for interaction. Not to relate is the equivalent of not doing the choreography. For the soloist, the imagination populates the stage with people and objects no less real than if they were actually there. In a group work, the imagination plays just as rich a role because the other dancers are all pretending to be what they are not. There is and must be a focus for one's actions at all times, whether internal or external. Actually, the mind always has a focus of one kind or another, even in sleep during dream intervals. Thus, in performance, not to direct one's attention within the context of the choreography and the nature of the role is really a breach of performer's discipline and responsibility. The body may be doing the work, but the mind is not.

My theatre training was on the job. With comparatively little performing experience and less dance technique, I got my first professional job in 1940 (Depression time), dancing at a summer theatre in the Pennsylvania Pocono Mountains. It was Unity House, the summer resort of the International Ladies Garment Workers Union. The company included actors, dancers, comedians, singers, writers, composers, a full orchestra, and almost all first-rate professionals. We did original revues, plays and gave concert nights. Getting ready for a performance, I learned makeup by watching my neighbor or by being scolded by him for not recognizing that I had no upper lip worth talking about. "Build it up. Build it up." (Build it up I did—and do so even today.)

But the voice of Jack Berry, an awesome young actor, threw something into the air that helped me more than anything to cope with the outrageous challenges of that first season of work. He had been studying with Benno Schneider, one of the leading actors of the Habimah Theatre, a part of Stanislavki's Moscow Art Theatre. On the first night, or soon after, I heard Jack shout from the other end of the long dressing table at which we all sat, ". . . and Benno Schneider says that the shortest distance to the audience is through the other actor!" (Everything Jack said had an exclamation mark after it, but this comment deserved it.) "The shortest distance to the audience is through the other actor!" became my slogan. I had so many justified fears at that time: my technique was at its bare beginning, my experience in professional theatre nil and my self-esteem was continually deflated by my failures. This slogan always brought my focus back from the audience to the work at hand: absorption with the life onstage. Best of all, by relating to the other—an actor, singer or dancer—I was able occasionally to forget my panicked self.

<table>
<tr><td>WORKBOOK
EXERCISES</td><td>*Every exercise or dance role calls for a focus of one's attention and energies upon an object, be it a person or a thing, beyond oneself or within oneself.*[†]</td></tr>
</table>

Where or When?

The awareness of context enriches a performance. The time and the place of any event or of any dance movement are factors which must affect and color what is done, but only if the reality of the time and place live vividly in the mind of the dancer. I have always had difficulty with neat schemes and systems because I think all that we live and do is messy, complex, layered and anything but pure. To me, Rudolf von Laban's categories of movement qualities were a noble attempt to simplify the complexity of human motion. I think it went too far, and so I offer here my own mess of qualities. They are all about the where and when that must be present in our awareness as we dance. Ideally, every one of these abstractions needs to come alive in a specific image. If movement is either controlling or being controlled, active or passive, finding a specific image enriches the work of the dancer: it is not simply a passive motion, it is a warm, moist wind that moves the limbs so gently.

**The Dichotomies Which Mark Out the Limits of Movement
and Imply the Possible Points Between**
Weak/Strong
Light/Heavy
Linear/Rotational
Random/Organized
Flowing/Spasmodic
Slow/Fast
Accelerating/Decelerating
Still/Moving
Vibrating/Sustained
Accepting the given parameters/Resisting the given parameters Small/Big
Released/Controlled
Focuses on positioning/Focuses on the motion

Moving in relation to an object ("it")
Controlling it/Being controlled by it
Carrying it/Being carried by it
Pushing it/Pulling it

Moving in relation to a surface, where the surface or "it" is the other part of the dichotomy. "It" could be a hard slick ramp or a trampoline. Each "it" changes the movement quality.

Resting on it

Sliding on it

Rubbing it

Pressing it

Hitting it

Piercing it

Pushing off it

"It" can also be:

Air/Solid

Slippery/Sticky

Soft/Hard

Dry/Wet

Flat/Inclined

Rough/Smooth

Weighted/Weightless

Cold/Hot

Resilient/Rigid

Movement can be initiated by:

A part of the body/The whole body simultaneously

Movement can be initiated from:

Within the body/The peripherals of the body

Movement by a part of the body or the whole body can be:

As a unit/As a flowing, wavelike succession

To deliberately and specifically choose among all these possibilities is not necessary. All that is needed is for the performer to visualize vividly and specifically where and when the dance is taking place and the answers will fall into place without even being named. It's called imagination and is the best set designer in the world. A dancer in command of the six questions will have no need to think or plan or select the appropriate dynamic for any motion. It will happen as unconsciously as the energy exerted by a student late for a class on the top floor of a building without an elevator.

The Two Dances

Or any dance in the repertoire of the dancer.

The Schizoid Little Fishes of the Bering Sea
Justification[†]
Dedicate Your Motion[†]
An Event, a Recurrence, a Ritual[†]
Each Alone[†]
The Hub Meditation[†]
Visualization[†]
The Duet as a Structure
Emotion Memory[†]
Inside the Outside[†]
Processional[†]
Adam and Eve
Prison[†]

To What End?

"To what end?" is inextricably bound up with the spine of the dance, but it is essential to keep in mind that the action that initiates and drives the dance, "the spine," can be diverted anywhere along the way. Think of all the changes that race through the Moor in the course of José Limon's *The Moor's Pavane*. As in life so it is onstage. It is possible on any journey or endeavor to get lost in the moment and lose sight of the intended goal only to pick it up again or lose it forever.

One of the most moving duets of recent years is by Lar Lubovitch. In *Mozart, K. 622,* two men enter from opposite sides of the stage and greet each other with a gentle warmth. The duet itself is an extended series of intertwining moves and exhilarating lifts that speak of dependence, mutual admiration, ambivalent love, and then they take leave of each other, exiting on opposite sides of the stage. What brought them together? What did each of them want? What happened between them in the course of their time together? Why did they choose to leave separately?

You could say, "because the choreographer told them to." No. I worked as a movement director with a brilliant theatre director named Gene Frankel on several plays. One of these was *The Umbrella*. It should have been a smash: Geraldine Page, Franchot Tone and Anthony Franciosa. A mangled script and contradictory conceptions were wearing down all of us. At an afternoon rehearsal, while on the road in Philadelphia (where the show died), Gene was giving notes to the cast on the previous night's performance. "Tony, don't say that line to her *after* you're in the taxi. Do it just before you enter." "Gene, you told me to speak *after* I was in the cab." Gene, one of the fastest men with a reply, said, "Tony, by now you must know that that is the worst reason in the world for an actor to do anything." Yes!

Going further, it is the worst reason in the world for a dancer to do anything. Regardless of what the choreographer says, at some point, *before* the time of performance, the dancer must reinvent her.his own inner scenario and reasons for performing the stage actions. Does it have to appear to the choreographer that the dancer is following the directives? Yes. Is the objective that empowers the actions of the dancer a secret known only to the dancer? Yes!

I once attended a Town Hall concert by Cecil Taylor, the avant-garde jazz pianist, and a group he had assembled for the occasion. Cecil opened with his dazzling speed and thunder. He was followed by a trumpeter, who though remarkably facile, barely commanded my attention. After him, a saxophonist stepped up to the microphone. He was much older than the others and in no way as theatrical as either Cecil or the trumpeter but I found myself hanging on every note. It took several minutes to realize why. *He was trying, really trying, to get someplace.* Where? How would I know? As proof that I was involved, I had found my own answer—vague, but an answer. And the trumpeter? Why was he boring? He was caught up in his own fleet, convoluted phrasing that displayed his superior technique and went nowhere.

From that concert on, I was so much more aware of this difference among performing artists—in any field—music, dance, theatre. Some are caught up in technique and virtuosity, while others are reaching beyond the moment to become what they are not or to arrive at where they are not. Unloading all the words, it is called *the objective.*

Every exercise given will come to life if it is energized by the object that is inherent in it.[†] Certainly The Two Dances could be analyzed in respect to the object that drives them.

The Obstacle?

There are two kinds of obstacles to the action: internal and external. An internal obstacle creates a conflict *within* the character. A simplistic performer, one who lacks ambivalence, is boring. What is alive pulls two ways.

An external obstacle: If you are healthy, you are a constant battlefield in which your immune system almost always wins out. Sometimes you get a cold and there is a slight setback. The most beautiful tree is swarming with bugs bent on destroying it. The essence of organic life is layered with positive and negative elements. From this, I draw the belief that there is no role onstage that is not in fact layered with a complex agenda. It may be played or danced as if it were a pure essence—a simple oneness—but that is moving away from what it is to a fantasy that to me is neither credible nor interesting. Purity does blossom in performance in those wonderful, unplanned moments when the performer "loses his.her mind"; when all the work and all the complexities come to a swift flowering. Generally, consciousness onstage is anything but single faceted.

Passionate Romeo under the balcony is never for long unaware that he is being very bad and in great danger. This woman is a Capulet, a hated enemy. Juliet knows she is bad, talking to a boy without her chaperon. The cool of Carolyn Brown delivering those immaculate, perfect and near impossible balances blankets the terror of one who has no choice other than being perfect. Merce Cunningham may disagree. He may be right. John Cage's program notes denying meaning to Cunningham's movements may be the truth, but I've never seen Merce Cunningham move without shadows, signals and signs of hidden hungers and passions flickering behind a densely wired fire screen. Granted, I create some of them, but I also believe Merce's stage is crowded—in his mind.

Resistance to the actions, internal and external, creates a vibrant life. The obstacles energize every motion that fills the stage. The ax is defined by the tree trunk. In the section above on the subtext, I made the point that movement life depends on opposition, a point that cannot be stressed enough. Historically, it was the awareness of this principle of opposition in motion that was one of the distinguishing marks of the emerging modern dance.

WORKBOOK EXERCISES

Again, every exercise would be enriched by the awareness of an obstacle. For the few that are listed here, that awareness would be more obvious than most.

The Obstacle[†]
Justification[†]
A Duet
Slalom[†]

Emotion Memory

Among American directors and teachers of Stanislavski's technique there is a sharp schism on one point. Lee Strasberg, originally of the Group Theatre and later the director and guiding spirit of the Actor's Studio, laid great stress on the use of personal experiences emotionally similar to those in the script. Sanford Meisner, also an original member of the Group Theatre and a seminal teacher, taught that truth in the role could be found from an imaginative life within the text. He believed that concentrated attention on an inner life based on a personal experience would of necessity be away from the context of the script and thus produce distortion. Both teachers sent out into the world staggeringly brilliant actors and yet they were diametrically opposed! Strasberg used a strongly psychological approach, suggesting to an actor playing Hamlet, for example, that he ponder his relation with his own father. Meisner, on the other hand, thought that if you focused compassionately on the character's time and context, your own life experience would reverberate within the role.

I studied with Meisner and found his approach exactly what I needed. It is quite apparent that for actors, the difference between the two teachers is great and makes a significant difference in how they work. When I have worked as an actor, using Meisner's approach, I would study the character and find all my images and metaphors within the script. It is not so simple to analyze what I have done as a dancer. Dance by its very nature is more fluid than the spoken theatre. There, words have a precise progression of meanings, while dance has a fluidity that brings it closer to poetry. By and large, my images and metaphors flow out of the context of each dance, but I suspect that more than once I have found them from some part of my personal history, even though they were far removed from the framework of the particular dance. Regardless of which approach you adopt, the greatest gift of an artist is to dig deeply within the welter of your life experience, within the self and beyond the self, and to shape what is found for the rest of us.

WORKBOOK EXERCISES *Every one of these contains the possibility of using emotion memory, memories out of your own experience, as material for your imagination.*

The Two Dances
Emotion Memory[†]
The Duet as a Structure
Ham and Clove
Inside the Outside[†]
Rituals of Power
Prison[†]

Direction

Giving Direction

Giving direction is a rare talent, difficult to analyze, to teach and to do. Some of the best directors are tyrannical horrors and some are supportive angels. The ideal director regards each dancer as a singular entity requiring a particular kind of incentive. Some dancers need only a hint in order to work out the inner life of a role. Others do best when they are given a good deal of information. Treat them like muscular automatons and expect either the performances of automatons or a stage full of performers each infused with a radically different point of view distantly or not at all related to the thematic material of the dance. I have often heard from dancers that the choreographer never told them what the dance was about or who or what they were in the dance. Movement was given, plus various exhortations about quality, energy, or loyalty and that was it. This is true not only of my student choreographers but of any number of professional choreographers, some of whom have produced major dance works. Style and method are a matter of philosophy and taste. You take your choice and you go your way. If the desire is to direct dancers in the ways outlined here, something more must be given to direct, lead and inspire the mind-hearts of the dancers.

WORKBOOK
EXERCISES The Two Dances

Have a student redirect the performance of one of the dances.

Taking Direction

Some directors can be quite evil; they enjoy exercising their power, manipulating and denigrating their dancers. Some are not only insensitive to dancers' fatigue but push them into hazardous work. Do you accept this? If you need the job, perhaps you do. Perhaps it is not worth it. No one can decide for you whether you stay or not.

Some dancers are quite evil and competitive. Finding a choreographer who lacks self-confidence, they will challenge the leadership, break discipline and be openly critical in a way that deflects the authority that should hold the group together. Hope that your professional work is never cursed by either of these.

WORKBOOK
EXERCISES The Two Dances

Work with a fellow dancer or student who is directing one of your dances.

"Bad" Direction; "Bad" Choreography

The responsibility of the director or choreographer is obvious. The responsibility of the dancers should be just as obvious. It matters not whether the choreographer is world famous or a fellow student struggling with her.his first dance assignment. The dancer has only one function: *To realize the choreographer's vision and to make whatever movement is given look beautiful and sublimely inspired.* Anything less is unprofessional. Are you being given good or even great choreography? Congratulations are in order. Most dancers, most of the time, perform choreography that is mediocre or occasionally even bad (the same is true of direction). You are really good when you try to see the world created by the choreographer through his.her eyes. One of the reasons that people go to the theatre is to see the world through your eyes. Can you do less for your director/choreographer?

Question. Can a dancer ever give an opinion—a criticism—of the direction or the choreography? First, assume that every director/choreographer is a singular entity. Some would actually welcome feedback from the dancers, some would feel threatened and some would be aghast at the temerity of such behavior. Best to know to whom you are talking. Assuming that it is appropriate to speak up, the next question is when? Unless the director or the choreographer pauses to ask for an opinion, wait until the rehearsal is over. A discussion during rehearsal, particularly one initiated by a company member, breaks the rhythm of the work, and that rhythm is the most precious tool of the director/choreographer.

There is the choreographer's metaphor and there is the dancer's. They are not necessarily the same. Learn, sense, absorb, imagine the choreographer's metaphor. If it works for you, if it ignites you, fine. But supposing it doesn't? You must find your own, searching until the image that drives you from the inside results in what the choreographer wants to see on the outside.

WORKBOOK The Two Dances
EXERCISES

Summary of the Six Questions:
Questions, Doubts, Paradoxes and Contradictions

One of the hazards of the six questions is that they seem to demand a rational logic as the inner life of a dance. No. Our business is mystery. As artists, our attention is drawn to what baffles us. Our creative process seeks to probe the enigma of some part of our experience that ensnares all our senses. If we pursue it, some coherence may appear while more of the unknown is hinted at.

I had the good fortune—and the misery—to have a scholarship with Martha Graham for the 1938–39 season while I was still a student at the City College of New York. I was raw and barely tutored in dance. Who was in the class? Erick Hawkins, Merce Cunningham, Jane Dudley, Sophie Maslow, Frieda Flyer; in other words, these were the glory days. I said "misery" because I was so painfully aware of my shortcomings. Who knows? I may have been better than I thought, but what difference did that make? I was living with my self-condemnations.

There was one exercise that I always welcomed. I had good control of the first part of it. (Toward the end, I fell apart.) It was Martha's defiant reply to the grand plié of ballet. Standing in first position, there was a relevé and the arms were lifted above the head and the upper torso with a straight spine slowly tipped forward until the back was parallel to the floor, at which time we began to move into a full, deep plié with the back still horizontal. At the depth of the plié, to become erect, we contracted and began to rise with the arms curved over the head to a full extension of the legs and feet at which time we went to our heels, released the arms out to the side, let the head fall back as we lifted the sternum looking like one of William Blake's angels swimming upward beside a page of his poetry. The phrase climaxed with a contraction that lifted us to relevé and sent our arms and our energy piercing through the ceiling. The next move was a quarter turn to the right, the right foot in front of the left, to repeat the entire sequence facing right.

Was it the first time I did the exercise or was it when I had a slight grip on the moves that I saw the leaf? Whatever, as I faced right and tipped forward, I clearly saw a pebbled sidewalk, wet with a recent rain, and there before my eyes was an autumn maple leaf: red with a faint blush of yellow. I saw it all the way down in that perverse Graham grand plié and lost it in the contraction that brought us back up. In the course of those eight counts tipping forward and into the grand plié, I was alive with a powerful excitement in an island of my own. There was no Martha, no Erik and not even Frieda, on whom I had a futile crush. There was only a wet autumn leaf on the sidewalk, and while I saw it I was very strong and sure of myself.

I did not see the leaf when I did the phrase to the other side. Why? There are certain questions that should not be asked. All I recall, as vividly as if it were an hour ago, is the strange quiver of excitement as I looked down and saw that autumn leaf draped over the tiny, stony bumps of the wet sidewalk. Where did the image come from? Don't ask. What did it signify? Don't ask. Was it a sign? *Don't ask!* It appeared but it was not sought. I was very young at the time and quite foolish about many things, but I was wise when I took that quarter turn to the right and saw the leaf and never tried to analyze what was happening. The image of a wet autumn leaf appearing unbidden was a souvenir out of the dark. I used it to give me strength and the frail beginning of my personal authority as a dancer. If I were an artist, which I was not at the time, it could have led me to a new place. Who knows? It may still do that.

How specific does the image have to be? Should you be specific all the time? We live in a sea of powerful forces that move and excite us while they elude precise description: things without names, shapes with foggy outlines, feelings concealed behind clouded intentions and irrational actions pulling us in all directions. They are what our art is about. It is exactly these that we are trying to confront, see clearly and release or bury. A powerful specific image is the metaphor that hooks into the mystery and opens us and our audience to the forces within. If our art is meant to bring a little light into this dark turbulence of our lives, then how lovely it is to find a metaphor that gives a clue to the nameless and draws a face out of the shadows.

Can a specific image be nameless or foggy or barely visible or shadowy? My predilection is for the concrete. If you are close to a creative idea, having a feeling that rocks you but is no more than vague, you're on a hot track, but don't stop there. Resort to the Hub Meditation (see the Workbook, chapter 10), placing the feeling at the center of your awareness. Allow that feeling to generate a multitude of images until one refuses to budge, regardless of how many new ones float by. (That strongest image may even be the first to emerge, but continue on, testing its staying power.) Then, regard the image and sense the feeling. Do they resonate? Does one call up the other? Yes? You have your specific image. No? Return to your Hub Meditation and continue the hunt.

In spite of the above, I suspect I have danced extended passages with images that were not concrete. Experiment. If it ignites your dance, hang on to it.

In traditional theatre and dance, the central focus has been on the "how" of a performance: "How to look?" "How to walk?" Considerations of style take precedence over matters of substance. Picasso, in his most abstract period, only wanted to find different ways of looking at things. The things he chose were a café table, a wine bottle, a newspaper, a pack of cigarettes—all objects with little intellectual or emotional weight. The buzzword that kept the presently exhausted avant garde inspired for twenty-five years was *process*. *What* was said was not as important as *how* one said it; *what* was danced was not as important as *how* one danced. It is the premise of this way of working that the *how* is determined by answering the six questions, "Who or what is doing what to whom or what and where, in what context and under what difficulties and why?" It must be noted in passing that for some choreographers the "how" is what their dance is about.

A man slaps his hand on the table. *How* does he do it? No, *what* is he doing? Quieting a meeting? Making a point in an argument? Killing a fly? If he wants to kill a fly, he will not pause to ask himself how he is going to do it.

It was while I was in my third year at City College that I decided I had to try to be a dancer. The cautious solution for this incautious ambition was to change from a psychology/sociology major to health and physical education, with the prospect of teaching dance in a college. Aside from the rules of badminton, we had to experience a full range of gymnastic work including what was called a "swan." One stood at one end of a not very soft mat, jumped from our two feet into a swan as do the divers, landing on the mat on both hands and keeping the arch, rolling down the chest, to the thighs, to an arched lift resting on extended arms and the insteps. It looked so pretty. I can still see a slender blond fellow student spring up in the air and down into the most mellifluous roll-up. The swan terrified me and I managed to get a Bachelor of Science in Health Education without ever doing one.

More than twenty years later, I was working alone in the Tamiris-Nagrin Studio on lower Fifth Avenue, choreographing a solo for a larger work called *American Journey*. On tour, the year before, I had traveled up the West Coast from Los Angeles to San Francisco and had been dumfounded by the rolling hills and dips of green coming right down to the waters of the Pacific. In the solo I was making, I wanted to draw the contours of that coast with my body. It was late and after an hour or more, I felt that I had carved out a good chunk of the solo and thought, "Enough for the night." I gathered up my stuff and headed for the dressing room. As I got to the door, I was stopped by the realization that in the course of the choreography, I had just done two swans! "Oh no! How did I manage that?" I dropped my shoes, sweater and practice bag and headed back into the space to try it again. Two steps into the studio and the old terror closed in. I thought, "No. Wait until tomorrow," and with great speed I dressed and left.

That night and the next day, I constantly shoved the thought of the impending swan out of my head. By late evening, the studio was emptied of all but me and my rehearsal time. As I began to dance what I had done, I forced myself to concentrate on one action: drawing with my body the undulating coast of California. Woosh! I effortlessly did one swan and the next one and continued working on the solo—and all of this on a hardwood floor! I never dared practice the swan in isolation, only within the context of what I was doing in the dance. It was every bit as smooth as the swan of that blond man I envied so.

Since the time Helen Tamiris helped me take down the wall between acting and dancing, I have continually found virtuosic moves through inner actions, even when my technique was still quite raw. (One of her greatest solos was *Joshua Fit the Battle of Jericho* in which she convinced all who saw it that Joshua did not use a trumpet to level the walls of Jericho—he had to have danced them down.)

One of the most upsetting experiences for a dancer is returning to a role that always worked and finding it empty and cold. That irrational, unnamed but perfect flow of energy and passion can all too easily go dry, and we face the worst embarrassment of all: appearing as if we are filled with a torrent of energy when in truth we are empty. It is precisely in this kind of situation that a technique of performance must come into play. The worst solution is to put on the face of the proper emotion. Better to seize upon the spine and the actions as they develop, staying with them with patience and without trying to pump up the performance beyond what is felt at the moment. The technique of action keeps the performer on the road to inner truth and gives the best chance of finding the heat again. *The heat* is an unpoetic and simplistic term for what Stanislavski called these hidden forces which we need to give us the magical lift. He used the then fashionable term, *the subconscious*. The words matter little; we all know what we are talking about and how utterly essential it is to perform and sooner or later experience that "high," that "inspiration," that "lift," that release of our hidden creative forces.

I had always suspected that the tragic deaths of Janis Joplin, Jimi Hendrix and Jim Morrison were hooked into the need for "getting high" at each performance. They were the apostles of ecstasy; what were they if they had a show and didn't feel it? Could they put it on—like a hat? The suicide note left by Kurt Cobain, leader of the rock band, Nirvana, hammers home the point: "I haven't felt the excitement for so many years. I felt guilty for so many years. The fact is, I can't fool you, any of you. I don't have the passion any more. The worst crime is faking it" (*The Arizona Republic,* April 11, 1994).

Yes, faking it is a crime. What the six questions offer is a way to find your way back to feeling the passion. How? By finding the specific metaphor and the specific action that will create a valid performance; one that is different than every other. Some will be hotter than others and some more resonant of subtler meanings. Did Cobain have a rigid idea of what constituted a valid performance? If he did, he was automatically in trouble. If he did, he was locked into the error of reaching for the result instead of finding out what was different there on the stage—every night.

The act of performance contains a tension that cuts through every other human endeavor: paradox. It is a lie which is trying to reveal a truth. To perform is to pretend to be what you are not.

The Judson Church gang, who generated postmodern dance, set out to dissolve this paradox and I think for awhile they fooled us, certainly the dance critics and themselves. I recall seeing Robert Morris wearing work gloves and overalls playing with a four-by-eight sheet of masonite and *pretending* to be a workman, while a naked woman reclined on a couch covered from head to foot with talcum powder and wearing only a black velvet neckband, *pretending* to be Manet's Olympia. What was in her mind as she lay quite exposed and stretched out on the couch in the dark waiting for the lights, and was there a change when the lights came on? Was it the same? Why was she motionless? And Morris, standing in the wings slipping on his work gloves, balancing the sheet of masonite and then striding in with it. Was there a change in him when he entered?

I see Yvonne Rainer going through a long technical movement sequence while a tape of her voice droned on about her intention of writing an essay on sleep. She was doing a workout, but it was a pretended, organized and choreographed workout that looked like a workout, and I'll wager she did a workout in order to perform that workout properly. By performing it with that impressive deadpan expression, she was reenforcing the ideal of *not performing*. The odds are that for the first performance, if not at every subsequent one, while she appeared so "cool," her heart was beating violently in response to the excitement, challenge and hazards of performing that long technical sequence.

Observing someone at work, it is easy to assume that that is what they are doing. Can you be sure that the carpenter driving in the nail is simply driving in that nail or is it a metaphor for something entirely different? Could he be "giving it" to his boss? Ironically, I *did* carpentry onstage in an evening long 1977 work, *Ruminations*. I built a small bench during the intermission and at the performance's end either gave it away or auctioned it off to the audience, the money to go to a "good cause," all to be determined by audience vote. These were sturdy little stools and I'm certain many still exist and find use all over the country. As I was making the bench was I pretending or was I performing? Or, was I proving to my long-gone father who had magical hands with tools that I was not as inept as he considered me?

Before anyone catches me in the contradiction of this entire book: I constantly rail against neat systems and schema, and yet what could be simpler or more schematic than the six questions? Does it not appear that I am holding this method forward as the best way to work?

There is no doubt in my mind that there are any number of good and great artists in dance who work in ways radically different than I describe. We are all guessing, and this book is my guess. Do I think it better than other approaches? Yes. I wouldn't use it or teach it if I didn't.

The strongest reason for my belief in the six questions is how open-ended they are. Using them as a guide, the performer is let loose to follow her.his own imagination and values. In the hunt for the who or what, the amazingly complex universe of each individual's life experience is there for the artist to choose from—with no one to guide or lead. No style is glorified, and the inner life is the creation of the artist, not the director or the choreographer. The dancer can take a suggestion or a direction, but from that point on, it can be transposed and transmuted to a personal metaphor which need not be known by anyone, ever. In fact, it is best for an artist not to share an inner vision. It too easily loses its vigor when exposed to the social air. Some of the most potent images may sound silly or even childish to others. What they do for the artist is what counts. This is the reasoning behind calling the character X, i.e., the unknown, because it is the private property of the artist performer.

This is a good moment to explain my use of the term *X*. It represents a someone or a something that takes shape in the mind of the dancer while learning and rehearsing a dance role. This identity can initially be established by the choreographer, but it must be developed and enriched by the dancer. Or, it is an identity that the dancer creates in his.her mind if the choreographer chooses not to communicate this information. In either case, as this conception of X develops it becomes part of the creative storehouse known only by the dancer. What is created by the dancer arises from observation, imitation and imagination. Ideally, the matured image of X is shared with no one. It becomes the private creation and seed of the dancer. In mathematics, X is the unknown factor in an algebraic equation. Study the problem and perform all the operations that point to X and you will find an answer. Can we say that the dancer begins with his.her X and if the performance is well-conceived, deep and rich, every person in the audience will arrive at their own answer as to who X is?

WORKBOOK	The Two Dances
EXERCISES	The Duet as a Structure

This chapter is the heart of the book. Everything else is essential but peripheral. Understand and put into practice the six questions and you will have at your command a way of dancing that is alive, textured, full of surprises and, best of all, that will use what you are from the depths of your being. Working on The Two Dances and the six questions can be the foundation for your understanding acting technique for dance performance.

4 *More Work on the Role*

In chapter 3 we examined the fundamentals of analyzing and creating a role. This chapter will cover a miscellany of techniques and considerations that help polish the initial work. Inevitably, there will be a few overlaps, but discussing the same thing from a different angle can bring new insights into view.

Impulse Analysis

Sometimes, even the magnificent English language fails us. In teaching the business of movement impulse in modern dance technique, there have been the obvious terms: centripetal and centrifugal, internal or peripheral. Without exception, the terms are cold and unpoetic, exactly what one does not need for a dance class. "Move from the center!" "Do a succession!" "Lead with the right arm!" Such language gives the chills.

A few years ago, I saw a Peking Opera troupe at Lincoln Center in New York. I caught a pervasive quality in their dance movements of which I had never been conscious. I realized that I quite often used just such a way of initiating movement, as do Flamenco dancers and many of Martha Graham's phrasings. Watching those Chinese dancers helped me see that there were not just two ways of initiating dance moves, from the inside or from the outside. There was a third way: *all at once.* Searching for a language to call up vivid images of each of these three ways of moving, I consulted my scholarly colleagues at Arizona State University, hoping to find just what I needed in the Greek or Latin or Chinese languages. Nothing. Finally, someone said, "Take a leaf from the Chinese who have such wonderful names for moves in T'ai Chi Chuan, such as, "embrace tiger" or "return to mountain." I liked that suggestion and came up with:

How many ways does the tree dance?
from the flowers, the leaves and the branches　；
from the trunk
the whole tree dances.

The first two are obvious and well taught. Some will say that ballet initiates movement from the flowers, the leaves and the branches and modern dance initiates movement from the trunk, but in fact both dance forms use both ways, sometimes within the same phrase of movement. But in none of the dance classes or rehearsals that I have attended, have I ever heard the following thought articulated (though I have seen it demonstrated): the whole tree dances. There are dance moves wherein the impulse comes from the entire body *all at once* and the move is completed by the entire body *all at once*. If you are a dancer, spend a bit of time in the studio playing with this. It is bound to be familiar, but it is rarely described and thus is just as easily lost as done. If you are not a dancer, watch for these three ways at the next dance concert.

I have omitted one important movement impulse, perhaps because it does not easily fit the metaphor of the tree dancing. A succession is a movement impulse that can start at any part of the body and flows or ripples through the rest of the body. Wood does not take easily to flowing or rippling. This impulse came from the German modern dance and though it is present in some American teaching, it is not in the forefront of our consciousness. It can be quite lovely, yet it is rarely seen in dance today.

In approaching work on any dance role it is well to ask, What is its dominant impulse source? Discerning this should not lead to the oversimplification of making that dominant impulse source the only one. Allowing for the shifts and turns of the choreography, the other two impulses will surface, making for a richly textured dancing.

There are obvious metaphors for the three ways. "Leading with the flowers, the leaves and the branches" tends to gives the sense of the mind being in control. "Leading with the trunk" gives the feeling of responding to deep inner forces. "The whole tree dances" gives the sense of a passionate involvement where the mind and the body are synchronized. (Metaphors for succession movements are not so obvious: waves, evocations of sensuality, passive response to an external impulse.) For each of these, there will be as many metaphors as there are dancers, and some of them will certainly contradict what I have just said. The goal is not agreement or consensus but awareness that the impulse source of each role, phrase and movement should be known by the dancer and be a part of his.her expressive warehouse.

WORKBOOK
EXERCISES

The Two Dances
How Does Your Tree Dance?[†]
I Dare You[†]

Relationship to the Music

Student concerts can be fairly interesting, despite the limited experience of the young dancers, but the opening of one of them yanked me upright in my seat. A dancer I had never seen was alone, downstage right, slashing virtuoso arcs with the strongest, most eloquent pair of legs I had seen in some time. Her whole body was engaged in a bold, bravura statement. Who was she? As the dance progressed, two other dancers joined her, and the group moved downstage left where they engaged in allegro unison activity that was of mild interest. I suddenly became aware that I had lost track of the dazzling dancer; but there she was, in full view at the peak of the triangle of dancers. What had happened? Squinting, as if to back off analytically, I caught it. She was behind the beat! The other two were, if anything, a little ahead of the beat.

The lesson is obvious. The dancer who is behind the beat is bringing the news *after* the others who are on or ahead of the beat. This suggests uncertainty or a tendency to follow. A dancer who is always ahead of the beat may be unduly aggressive; one who is always square on the beat may be cautious, safe, uninteresting. (See *How to Dance Forever,* p. 189.) On Broadway the style is predominantly ahead of the beat. That accounts for the frenetic, unrelenting, show-business energy that is designed to overwhelm the audience. On the concert stage, an indiscriminate use of this musical phrasing is bad taste.

It is only a naive musician who regards the written score as the exact way to perform the music. Some things cannot be written—they are inherent in the style, the intent and content of the music. Similarly, a dancer is truly musical if she.he regards the beat as a fluid possibility. Riding with the style, the moment, the phrasing and the intent, the dancer can and should have the freedom and musical skill to slip in an imperceptible hair ahead of the beat, slide in with a lingering breath behind the beat or step full square on the beat. Most unmusical of all is the dancer who never alters his.her relationship to the beat.

Then of course, one can counterpoint the rhythm of the music. Who does this and why is a complexity. Technically, going against the beat requires a high degree of musicality and, in terms of character, suggests an independence or a rebelliousness or an indifference to what the music calls for.

WORKBOOK   Who or What Is Alive in the Music?[†]
EXERCISES   The Inner Rhythm of the Role[†]
           Before, After and On[†]
           The Spine of Style[†]

Sense-memory Work

Though sense-memory exercises are a staple of the actor's training, no dancer can afford to neglect them. It means what it says: having a vivid, sensual memory of actions with a real object and the ability to re-create those actions without the object. In performance the real object is imagined or remembered or sensed, and the motion of the performer is determined by the truth of the remembering. It is the essence of the theatre—pretending that what is not, *is*.

Sense memory is the foundation of imagination. Any game of sense memory is an exercise in imagination, and imagination is a muscle. Use it and it will get stronger and more vivid. Ignore or forget its value and it will atrophy. Sense-memory exercises are the pliés of your imagination.

The moment I knew that I had to be a dancer, I also knew I had to begin the study of ballet. My initial training and loyalty focused on modern dance, but I was quite aware that if I was ever to gain employment as a dancer, I would need more virtuosity than was then being taught in modern dance classes. In ballet classes, I felt like an awkward visitor in a foreign country. One day, early in my induction into the ballet form, in a class given by Mme. Anderson-Ivantzova, we were doing a particularly florid battement phrase at the barre with baroque arms flowing everywhere. I was embarrassed and inhibited. "What is a nice boy from the Bronx doing making these fancy gestures like some eighteenth-century fop?"

The moment that question streaked through my skull, I saw myself as a *sixteenth*-century fop. I knew exactly what I was wearing: very expensive, black silk tights; a black velvet doublet belted with twisted silver; great puffed sleeves slashed to show green, red and white satin; all surmounted by a great white starched ruff that lengthened my neck. Best of all, I had precious rings, one for each finger! All my technical problems remained, although the extra lift and the bland assumption of an authority to which I had no right did give me my first few double pirouettes and did wonders for my carriage and port de bras. Ah, but my style! Madame Anderson-Ivantzova: "What iss, Danyell? You make such magnificent preparation for grand pirouette and then poof, you are on floor! What iss?"

The following was recorded in one of my classes at the American Dance Festival:

Fifth position is an imaginative act. Posture is an act of imagination. When it is done in a way that achieves poetry for you and for those watching it, you have made a leap from now to there—a new construct. A ramrod was used to load rifles with gun powder—stiff and straight. Now, sit up with spines like ramrods! That's an act of imagination. Let your head float far above your chest. And, that too is an act of imagination.

Sense memory is used many times unconsciously in performance. A really poetic person may be dealing with the wind without being conscious of it. In the welter of living, we have all been caught in a wind strong enough to make progress difficult and exciting. . . . There are people who run across the floor and they become the wind or they breast the wind.

One literal sensory experience can bring back a world. Proust called up a memorable scene from the smell of a cookie. The possibilities for sense-memory exercises are all about you. Wet your face, pluck a towel from the rack and dry your face. Put it back and do it all over again without the water or the towel. Pick up anything and put it down. Do it a few times. Remember it, then do it without the object. It's a fundamental leap of imagination: to pick up something that's not there. Keep this exercise simple for a while and take all the time you need.

In the theatre, all we have is 700 to 2000 square feet, a hole on one side, a canvas at our backs and flats or drapes on either side—and that's it. We do need a strong imagination muscle.

WORKBOOK EXERCISES *In addition to those listed below, see the chart of movement dichotomies in chapter 3. Dozens of sense-memory exercises can be spun out of these many categories, if a specific image is found for each of the qualities.*

What Quickened You?[†]
Passing Through a Physical Object[†]
Visualization[†]
Slalom[†]
Faces[†]

Passive or Active?

Is the force creating the movement coming from the mover or from outside the mover? It is hard to imagine anything other than these two alternatives, and yet any number of dancers actually achieve what appears to be a neutrality. They lack vitality and presence. It is as if they have not thought through who and what they were and what they have been doing.

Most dancers can give a convincing and exhilarating performance of an active impulse wherein the body is the triumphant expression of an inner will. Even the best dancers have a difficult challenge dancing a passive role. The danger is slipping into a limp mode. Actually, passive movement gains excitement and drama when the body that is being moved maintains its integrity and heft. A giant tree in a high wind may bend but it will still keep its configuration. A keen sense memory will add to the texture of the movement. Passive movement presents a subtle and difficult problem to any dancer.

The Two Dances

Analyze each from this perspective.

Goldfish bowl
Blind Journey[†]

These will require an oscillating blend of active and passive actions.

Before, After and On[†]

Controlled or Released?

I never thought about control versus release until I began to teach. I had fiercely sought to gain control of a body that came late to dance, all the while contending with an innate inclination for going wild and letting go. Then, when I left Broadway for the concert world, teaching became a necessary economic lifeline. In too many classes, I would be frustrated as I observed obviously talented dancers moving within the compass of a tight rein. "Let it go!" I would implore—and too often fruitlessly. The few wild ones with their lack of discipline were the kind of challenge I much preferred.

Control and release color every act, choice and motion that we perform. The balance, the *proportion* between them is the profile and the very texture of how each of us dances—and lives. One can even use these terms to characterize epochs, cultures and nations. In the court of Louis XIV, even the removal of a handkerchief from the pocket was performed as if it were a prescribed and controlled ritual. Seventy-five years later, during the French Revolution, France, and particularly Paris, exhibited a storm of released passion, jubilation, triumph, individual freedom and rage. In the next century, also in Paris, a new "war" raged between two beautiful dancers, Marie Taglioni and Fanny Elssler. To quote the erudite Lincoln Kirstein, writing of Taglioni: "Under the vague outline of skirt and bodice, there is pure strength; geometry the base of every arabesque" (*Dance: A Short History of Classic Theatrical Dancing* [Dance Horizons, 1977], p. 244). Theophile Gautier on Elssler: "Fanny is quite a pagan dancer. . . . exposing her thigh. . . she bends freely from her hips, throwing back her voluptuous arms" (p. 247).

Many promising careers in dance are either cut short or are never quite realized because, in spite of talent and technique, there is a destructive imbalance between control and release. To insure clarity, I'll define the terms. *Control* is the ideal of knowing clearly and specifically what it is you wish to do and doing exactly that, no more and no less. *Release* is "going with it," "letting go," and permitting an impulse to flow without needing to know or control what will happen next.

Control, if exercised at all times by a performer or a choreographer, creates dispassionate and alienated work; the only emotion visible is the passion to be "correct." Yet lacking control and always "going with it" are literally definitions of self-indulgence, sloppiness and the loss of craft. In spite of having a secure technique and all the skill needed, such dancers disregard their power of control in favor of needing to "feel deeply" what they are doing at every moment.

If the balance between these two essentials is so vital and delicate a matter, how much conscious choice needs to be exercised? I think none, unless you sense something is not right with a phrase of movement or a particular role or, most serious of all, what is happening to your career.

This interplay between control and release may operate within a single measure of music. The waltz can present a stumbling block for young dancers if they try too hard to be correct by precisely and deliberately spelling out each beat. It becomes a waltz when they learn that the downbeat must be *done* and the "2, 3" just *happen*. A musical and dynamically right downbeat or "1," creates, gives birth to, the "2, 3." To dance the waltz, you don't do the "2, 3," you let them happen.

Every movement, every performance and our entire lives are sculpted by where we choose to direct our actions and when we allow ourselves to flow with the moment. (See *How to Dance Forever*, pp. 205–06.)

It is well not to confuse control-release with the oppositional pair of active-passive. One can be controlled and still be in either an active or a passive mode. Similarly, release can be performed actively or passively.

The climate of the creative process is turbulent and constantly subject to change. Those who feel they cannot function as artists unless they are always in full heat and flowing are in serious trouble. Similarly, those who constantly seek the cool, objective detachment that gives them complete control over all that pours out of them are unwilling to risk the surprises and full life of an artist. For most artists capable of expression, there are periods of work where an intoxication possesses them and the work flows like a mighty river. These same artists are quite capable of slaving away for long periods of time in the cold tunnel of creation, remembering, re-creating and laboriously editing. They willingly bear tedium and hours of detailed concentration that to an outsider would appear dealing with minor minutiae.

How many dancers have at the crest of an improvisation felt that they had flown beyond the limits of gravity, and in the cold moments that followed knew that they might never recapture that ecstasy and those elegant phrases? The great artists patiently and stubbornly pursue that ineffable moment, and in time they hammer out a shape that may not be precisely what they have lost but is, in effect, a lovely poem about it. The journey of artists is a gamble through the fire and ice of the creative process.

The Two Dances

The balance of controlled/released movements should be examined for each of the two dances.

Spinning[†]

This sets the stage for released dance.

Why Do You Dance?[†]

Doing this fully may reveal your predilection in regard to control/release.

Lose Your Head[†]

Focus: Internal or External?

Is there ever a time when we are not looking at something, whether in dreams or awake? I don't think so. Even in the most disordered state, something—perhaps a chaotic mess— is there. Certainly, everyone who steps out onstage does so with the passionate hope that the entire audience is focused upon him.her. What is the audience looking at? Someone who is looking at something. The important thing here is not to confuse or limit seeing with what we do with our eyes. There is, as Shakespeare put it, "the mind's eye." If the attention of the dancer is continually alive to the intent and action of the choreography at every moment, there would never be a need to even raise the issue of focus.

Undoubtedly, there is a noticeable difference when a dancer is focused externally as opposed to internally. To make the point, I have faced a student and asked, "Am I looking at you or something else?" As the student watched, I would shift my focus from the specifics of that person's face to an image in my own mind. Invariably, the student can perceive the difference; an audience, even in a big house, can do so as well *if the dancer is clearly focused.*

When the focus is external, it should not matter whether the object of attention is a palpable object visible to the audience or exists only in the imagination of the dancer. For the dancer, they should have an equal reality. This is particularly the problem of the solo artist. Having worked extensively as a soloist, I have been asked, on occasion, what special skills are required. I have never had a good answer but as I write this paragraph, I finally do: a good soloist has the facility to create an all but palpable world onstage.

Looking directly front presents a special problem that needs addressing and awareness (see also the discussion in chapter 2). Many dancers and even some choreographers accept it as a given that they are communicating with the audience when they look front, even though within the choreographic context there is no audience. To look at something is to create its existence. Choreography that asks the performers to be aware of the audience permits direct visual contact out front. If within the imaginative realm of a particular dance there is no audience, looking directly front can be misleading and a betrayal of the work's premises.

In *Afternoon of a Faun* as choreographed by Jerome Robbins, the two dancers use front as the mirror in a dance studio. Done well, they create a wall between themselves and the audience, because gazing at oneself in a mirror is not at all the way one looks at an audience. Much depends on the context. Looking front can be seeing a vista a great distance away. In my memory of one of Martha Graham's early solos, *Frontier,* she spent the greater part of the dance looking forward. I'm certain that not one of us in that audience thought for a moment that she was addressing us. It all depends upon what's in your head—or rather the head of your X. Whether the mind is scattered or crystal clear will determine the quality of the focus. You should be able to create a place that is turbulent or serene. Your imagination and its instrument, your focus, can create whatever is demanded by the choreography.

With an external focus, there is a technical detail that needs attention. In most cases, and particularly in large performing spaces, one should not look with the eyes but with the cheekbones. Merely sliding the eyes left or right without moving the head is to perform an act that in the broad context of dance movement in a large theatre space is either not seen or has little impact. For the focus to be visible to an audience, the full face must turn toward the object being looked at. The exception that comes to mind are the extraordinary eye movements of East Indian dancers. They, however, are performing an art that was originally designed to be seen in intimate spaces, and further, their makeup has a wildly stylized highlighting of the eyes. I have the impression that when an East Indian dancer is doing something that relies heavily on the use of the eyes, head motions are amplified, the body's motions are reduced to a minimum and there is less movement in space. In western dance and in western theatre spaces, eye movements independent of head movements tend to be ineffective.

I am not suggesting that Western dancers emulate East Indian dancers in regard to their makeup but it should be noted that modern dancers, especially the men, tend to make up the eyes ineffectively. If the material of the dance is abstract, with little or no human interaction, a strong eye makeup is not a critical necessity. If expression plays a part in the choreography, effective eye makeup in required. The face has two outlines: the outer one that follows the shape of the skull, the ears and the jaw; and the inner outline, a triangle from the corners of the eyes to the mouth. *This latter is the only part of the face that is expressive.* Thus it follows that it must be seen. Depending on the size of the theatre, the mouth and eyes need a makeup strong enough to be clearly visible to everyone in the audience.

Since focusing is not merely a matter of the eyes but also of the mind, it is not unreasonable at this time to ask the question, should one think ahead while dancing or is it better to live in the moment, letting it give birth to the next moment? Are there different answers to this question depending upon whether we are talking about rehearsal or performance? This chapter is basically devoted to preparation, that is, to rehearsals. My premise is that rehearsals reach their objective when it is possible to dance at "concert pitch." Does "concert pitch" mean being finally free to be immersed in the present?

When the work is new, in classes and rehearsals, when it is unfamiliar, not memorized, not mastered, thinking ahead is a necessary tool. A cool, observant mind thinking ahead makes for swift learning. One of the chief reasons for "repetition," which is the more accurate French word for rehearsal, is to link the sequence of events so firmly in the neural patterns of the performer that the moment comes when there is no need to think ahead. For a well-rehearsed performer, the completion of one motion reveals the need and inevitability of the next motion. The time to let loose is when the moves are all etched deeply into the nervous system and the muscles.

"Living in the moment" and "focusing on the immediate action" need some clarification. "The moment" at the center of the attention may not be the actual move being done; the thought, energy, drive are directed to the end of a phrase, which may be quite long. In talking about pirouettes, Tamiris would say, "Don't focus on the turn. Go for the finish." Try it. It works. Even if the turn is shaky, an authoritative finish will make it appear to be solid.

At times, it may be appropriate to think ahead. If X is a liar, his.her answer will be carefully constructed before being uttered. If X must be in absolute control at all times X will tend to think ahead. Otherwise, most actions are responses to the present, not the consequence of previous planning. It is called spontaneity, and when it is present, it gives dance a sparkle that makes every performer with that quality endearing.

WORKBOOK
EXERCISES

Any exercise that calls for intense observation is automatically an exercise in focusing. All the Workbook exercises for observation demand clear and intense focus. See also chapter 1.

Gifts
Medicine Ball
Outrageous Travel
The Hub Meditation[†]
Visualization[†]

These two involve internal focus though the body is at rest.

The Duet as a Structure
Rituals of Power

Both of these begin with an unwavering focus on the other(s). Where they go as they progress will be a variable depending on developments.

Focusing

An Event, a Recurrence or a Ritual?

This is a critical question that needs a conscious answer from the choreographer; if that is not forthcoming, the dancer must make her.his own choice. "Is what I am dancing an event that is taking place for the first time, or is it a recurrence, or is it a ritual?" A recurrence is merely something that has happened before, while a ritual is a prescribed act or ceremony that must be enacted exactly as tradition demands without variation or improvisation. Quite obviously, the style and quality of the identical dance phrase would be radically different performed as an event in its first occurrence, as a recurrence, or as a ritual honed by time and tradition. Always be ready to recognize that within a ritual, an unexpected event may intrude. Any one of these may be mixed with one of the other.

When I lived in New York, I never failed to get a charge riding the subways, particularly in those cars where all the seats line the sides and face each other. The range of people always stimulated me. I would get a special kick out of trying to guess whether the couple across the aisle were out on their first date or whether they had been out together many times—or even married.

WORKBOOK
EXERCISES
The Two Dances

Each dance not only needs to be seen but danced from this perspective.

An Event, a Recurrence, a Ritual†

The Inner Rhythm of the Role

There is a remarkable book by Chieh Tzu Hua Chuan called *The Mustard Seed Garden Manual of Painting* (trans. Mai-Mai Sze [Princeton, N.J.: Princeton University Press, 1956]), written in China in the seventeenth century:

> In estimating people, their quality of spirit (ch'i) is as basic as the way they are formed; and so it is with rocks, which are the framework of the heaven and of earth and also have ch'i. . . . Rocks without ch'i are dead rocks, just as bones without the same vivifying spirit are dry bare bones. How could a cultivated person paint a lifeless rock?
>
> One should certainly never paint rocks without ch'i. To depict rocks with ch'i it must be sought beyond the material and in the intangible. Nothing is more difficult. . . . If I may sum it up in a phrase: rocks must be alive. (P. 127)

All the practice, all the control and all the thinking that go into work on the role go just so far, and yet there is an existence impervious to the conscious mind that needs to be reached and unleashed if the role is to attain that level where it is not merely good, but where it glistens. No matter how thoroughly one researches the facts and imagines the life and details of the character, there is just so much we can know about anyone—*including ourselves*. Each of us is different and each contains a unique physical-emotional motor that drives us through our lives in ways we hardly suspect and rarely notice. Performing the inner rhythm of the character stirs up the animality that lurks in the shadows of everyone. The inner rhythm stirs up elements that cannot easily be reached by reason or analysis. Everything is shaped by rhythm and I think of rhythm as central to the creative act. Rhythm is the pulse of the irrational center. If one finds the rhythm of the person or the thing one is supposed to be onstage, one is closer to penetrating the truth of what is being danced.

How does one go about finding an inner rhythm? It can be as elusive as a barely remembered dream or as palpable as your left hand. Elusive or palpable, it is there to be seen, sensed, felt because everything has a rhythm: the clouds before a storm, the kitten studying its image in a mirror, the breath of a lover, the scuff marks on your dance floor, the stride of Othello, the virtuoso in a demi-plié before a double air turn. It is there waiting for you to take it into your body. You fill yourself with the object of your attention by looking, touching, remembering, visualizing and imaginatively entering into it.

Does the inner rhythm have anything to do with the rhythm of the dance—with the rhythm of the music? Of course it does, but it is not the same. It has a life of its own that is alive within the other rhythms. It should be an integral part of every performance, a part known only to the dancer.

WORKBOOK
EXERCISES

Rhythm Portrait[†]
The Rhythm Series[†]
Inner Rhythm

Contradiction

We are—all of us—a mess of contradictions, and thus it follows that the theatre and the dance are arenas for conflict. This point has been made earlier, but I mention it again because (1) I think it is a critically vital aspect of the dancer's art. (2) It is easy to work hard and fully on a role and not realize that this dimension has not been explored. (3) Not many teachers of dance and acting speak of it at all. Every vital performer and work of art is animated by inner contradictions. Or as *The Mustard Seed Garden Manual of Painting* says, "attains ch'i."

WORKBOOK
EXERCISES

The Two Dances
The Obstacle[†]
Dedicate Your Motion[†]
Hot to Cold to Hot[†]
The Duet as a Structure
I Dare You[†]
Inside the Outside[†]

Living with the Magic "If"

Constantin Stanislavski, an eloquent and passionate man of the theatre, had a profound influence on the theatres of the world, on Helen Tamiris, on myself and all that I write and teach. The following passage was precipitated by his dismay upon returning to roles he had played with some degree of success in the past. To read it properly and gain value from it, it would be well to keep a few things in mind: first, take into account that this was written in 1924 and it is couched in the romantic mode of expression of that time, not our "cool" time. Second, the thinking is not dated and is as valuable now as when it was first uttered. Third, try to act like a computer and do a "Search and Replace." Every time you see the word "actor," replace it with "dancer," and it will make sense for those to whom this book is addressed.

Why was it then that the more I repeated my roles the more I sunk backward into a stage of fossilization? . . . God, how my soul and my roles were disfigured by bad theatrical habits and tricks, by the desire to please the public, by incorrect methods of approach to creativeness, day after day, at every repeated performance! . . . What was I to do? How was I to save my roles from bad rebirths, from spiritual petrification, from the autocracy of evil habit and lack of truth?

. . . At one of the performances given by a visiting star in Moscow, I watched his acting very closely. In my capacity of actor, I felt the presence of the creative mood in his playing, the freedom of his muscles in conjunction with a great general concentration. I felt clearly that his entire attention was on the stage and the stage alone, and this abstracted attention forced me to be interested in his life on the stage, and draw closer to him in spirit *in order to find out what it was that held his attention.*

In that moment, I understood that the more the actor wishes to amuse his audience the more the audience will sit in comfort waiting to be amused, and not even trying to play its part in the play on the stage before it. But as soon as the actor stops being concerned with his audience, the latter begins to watch the actor. It is especially so when the actor is occupied in something serious and interesting. If nobody amuses the spectator there is nothing left for him to do in the theatre but to seek himself for an object of attention. Where can that object be found? On the stage, of course, in the actor himself. The concentration of the creating actor calls out the concentration of the spectator and in this manner forces him to enter into what is passing on the stage, exciting his attention, his imagination, his thinking processes and his emotion. That evening I discovered the greater value of concentration for the actor. . . . The entire physical and spiritual nature of the actor must be concentrated on what is going on in the soul of the person he plays. . . .

The actor must first of all believe in everything that takes place on the stage, and most of all he must believe in what he himself is doing. And one can believe only in the truth. Therefore it is necessary to feel this truth at all times, to know how to find it, and for this it is unescapable to develop one's artistic sensitivity to truth. It will be said, "But what kind of truth can this be, when all on the stage is a lie, an imitation, scenery, cardboard, paint, make-up, properties, wooden goblets, swords and spears? Is all this truth?" But it is not of this truth that I speak. . . .

The actor says to himself: "All these properties, make-ups, costumes, the scenery, the public nature of the performance, are lies. I know they are lies, I know I do not need any of them. *But if they were true, then I would do this and this, and I would behave in this manner and this way towards this and this event.*"

I came to understand that creativeness begins from that moment when in the soul and imagination of the actor there appears *the magical, creative "if."* While only actual reality exists, only practical truth which a man naturally cannot but believe, *creativeness has not yet begun.* Then the creative "if" appears, that is, the imagined truth which the actor can believe as sincerely and with greater enthusiasms than he believes practical truth, just as the child believes in the existence of its doll and all around it. From the moment of the appearance of "if," the actor passes from the plane of actual reality into the plane of another life, created and imagined by himself. Believing in this life, the actor can begin to create.

Scenic truth is not like truth in life; it is peculiar to itself. I understood that on the stage, truth is that in which the actor sincerely believes. I understood that even a palpable lie must become a truth in the theatre so that it may become art. For this it is necessary for the actor to develop to the highest degree his imagination, a childlike naiveté and trustfulness, an artistic sensitivity to truth and to the truthful in his soul and body. All these qualities help him to transform a coarse scenic lie into the most delicate truth of his relation to the life imagined. All these qualities, taken together, I shall call the feeling of truth. In it, there is the play of imagination and the creation of creative faith; in it, there is a barrier against scenic lies; in it is the feeling of true measure; in it is the tree of childlike naiveté and the sincerity of artistic emotion. The feeling of truth, as one of the important elements of the creative mood, can be both developed and practiced. (*My Life in Art* [New York: Theatre Arts, 1952], pp. 458–67; italics added)

In these few paragraphs, Stanislavski enters the heart of the entire approach. If you can spare the time, reread them.

WORKBOOK
EXERCISES
There is no single exercise which leans upon the magic "if" more than any other. The whole business from beginning to end is a game of pretend. A grand plié will attain magnificence if we pretend it is the architectural motif of the Doges' Palace in Venice, or it can be a squat with a straight back.†

Justification

"Justification" in the theatre means finding an inner reason for doing anything and everything you are asked to do. For "inner reason" read your own reason and one that quickens your pulse, not a mechanically correct intellectual reason. If the dancer is lucky, the choreographer or teacher provides the impulse. If nothing is forthcoming, the dancer is beholden to his.her craft to find a powerful reason for being onstage and doing the moves that have been given.

There is an ideal place and time to develop the skill and the poetry to do this: the technique class, whether ballet, modern, or jazz. The moment you have mastered a given dance sequence is the moment for your inner poet to go to work. What is this like? What does it feel like? Who is doing this? What was the spirit or the devil that inhabited the teacher when she.he demonstrated the sequence? What is it in the voice of the choreographer/teacher as he.she is counting that is telling me what this is really all about? "Oh! She is on to something so beautiful. I will walk right into her body, become her and find out what is there."

Never fear this ploy of "becoming" the teacher or someone in the class that inspires you. You will not lose your identity. You will be you dancing *your* understanding of that person. This is unquestionably one of the fastest ways to learn anything, and if you pick the best, you have everything to gain.

To sum it up: in performing technique or choreography, every moment needs justification, either clearly understood or deeply felt on a less than rational level. The performer's task is to justify whatever is given, good or bad. Penetrating even deeper into the matter, the performer who is an artist finds the contradiction *within* the justification—a reason or reasons for not doing what is to be done. Everything holds its opposite.

WORKBOOK
EXERCISES

Again, one could make a case for every exercise as an exercise in justification. Those listed below, at least on their surface, call on dancers to more consciously find the justification that brings their dance movement to life.

The Two Dances

Each should be examined in terms of justification.

Dedicate Your Motion[†]

This is a teacher/director's device to lead the dancers into the practice of justification.

The Hub Meditation[†]
Who or What Is Alive in the Music?[†]
Each Alone[†]
The Duet as a Structure

This is the classic structure in which the justification evolves into the complexity of improvised interaction.

Living with the Game of Oscillation

I was in a small college in the South and spent an extra day there after the performance before moving on to my next engagement. I borrowed one of those old workhorse tape recorders from the piano teacher for a rehearsal. Finished, I returned to her studio with it and stayed for a bit to have some tea at her invitation. She was a Chinese woman, quiet, reserved and probably in her mid-thirties. In the course of our conversation, I asked her whether she toured or performed.

"Oh no. I could never be a performer. I learned that a long time ago."

"What do you mean? How did you learn that?"

"My teacher told me that I did not have a pure concentration. In fact, that is why I found your performance last night so awesome. You have that pure concentration."

Until that moment I had never even considered whether my concentration onstage was pure or impure. When I am onstage, I am a very busy man with many things on my mind, in my mind and under my mind. As for purity—"Oh no," I said, "My mind is a swirling vortex of more things than I can count or be aware of. I am deep in the heart of the dance and there is no audience and no Daniel—only the life of the dance and suddenly I realize I am too near that splintered area upstage right and carefully maneuver away from it. That throws the rhythm and I work to dig back into the music. Without knowing it, I slip back into the colors of the swirling vortex and Daniel and his problems with a splintered spot and a muddied musical phrase become one more bit in the turbulent mosaic of my mind. And that is the way it goes, in and out. A hyper self-awareness or audience-awareness brings a loss of self within the folds of the dance. No professional is ever purely in a piece for its entire length. There is a constant oscillation, in and out." She listened and said nothing. We talked of other things, I thanked her for the tea and I never learned whether my speech changed anything.

At this juncture, the reader probably will interject that Stanislavski does not seem to allow for such impurity. Just a few pages back, I quoted this sentence: "I perceived that creativeness is first of all the complete concentration of the entire nature of the actor." This the language of the nineteenth-century romantics for whom the words "complete," "entire," "pure," "unconditionally," "utterly" contained the gems of truth. Stanislavski may have thought and written that way, but I will wager that is not the way he acted onstage. He *had* to oscillate between total absorption in the life of the character and an awareness of self and the stage space. Failing that, he'd fall into the footlights.

After his autobiography, *My Life in Art* (1924), Stanislavski wrote three more books on the actor's art and technique. They are cast in the same dramatic form: a director, named Tortsov, is teaching a group of young would-be actors. Their interactions are the books. In *Building a Character* (New York: Theatre Arts, 1981) he deals directly with the oscillation of the performer's concentration. Two of the brightest and most aggressive of Tortsov's students, Kostya and Paul, are devastated when he speaks Othello's lines that begin, "Like to the Pontic sea . . ." and between the lines says out loud what would be in his mind to make the speech effective.

> *Ne'er ebb to humble love . . .*
> The moment has come to pull out all the stops!
> To mobilize all means of expressiveness!
> Everything to the rescue!
> Tempo and rhythm!
> And . . . I'm afraid to say it . . .
> Even loudness!
> Not a shout! . . .
> *'Till that a capable and wide revenge*
> "Swallow them up. . . . (Pp. 163–64)

Kostya and Paul are horrified and confused by this exposition and beg to talk with Tortsov. He invites them to his home that evening. Kostya explains to him how crushed he had been

> to find that inspiration had been replaced by theatrical calculation.
> "Yes . . . ," admitted Tortsov. "One half of an actor's soul is absorbed by his super-objective, by the through line of action [the spine], the subtext, his inner images, the elements which go to make up his inner creative state. But the other half of it continues to operate on a psycho-technique more or less in the way I demonstrated it to you.
> "An actor is split into two parts when he is acting. You recall how Tommaso Salvini put it: 'An actor lives, weeps, laughs on the stage, but as he weeps and laughs he observes his own tears and mirth. It is this double existence, this balance between life and acting that makes for art.'" (P. 167)

For my taste, this mathematical division of the consciousness of the performer—half of this and half of that—is an oversimplification. Out of my own experience, I prefer to think that what is going on in our minds onstage is better described as an organic, asymmetrical oscillation, rather than a twin track of equally active thought processes of conscious control on the one side and an unthinking, emotional involvement on the other.

WORKBOOK
EXERCISES
Every exercise will call for this balancing act in the course of rehearsing or performing.[†]

Taste

In *The Art of Scientific Investigation* (New York: Norton, 1950), W. I. B. Beveridge offers these insights on the matter of taste:

> Taste can perhaps best be described as a sense of beauty or aesthetic sensibility, and it may be reliable or not, depending on the individual. Anyone who has it simply feels in his mind that a particular line of work is of interest for its own sake and worth following, perhaps without knowing why. How reliable one's feelings are can be determined only by the results. The concept of scientific taste may be explained in another way by saying that the person who possesses the flair for choosing profitable lines of investigation is able to see further whither the work is leading than are other people, because he has the habit of using his imagination to look far ahead instead of restricting his thinking to established knowledge and the immediate problem. He may not be able to state explicitly his reasons or envisage any particular hypothesis, for he may see only vague hints that it leads towards one or another of several crucial questions. (P. 106)

Among the characteristic remarks by sophisticated actors discussing the work of other actors are "She makes wonderful choices," or "I really like the risks he takes in his choices." In this all-important game of imagination, the choices of images, the taste we use to create what no one else sees, all play critical roles in how we dance. What can one do to have a "wonderful" taste? Nothing will guarantee that, but some things might help: knowing history, poetry, the music of the Bushmen of the Kalahari desert, visiting museums constantly, an awareness of your dance culture, thinking about it all, writing poems and more of the same. Certainly having a hunger to absorb these things will open up the range of your choices. And then there is taking your time, doing nothing sometimes, learning to tap into your insides and having the nerve to stay with what "feels right," even if a part of you is aghast at what you find and particularly if others are horrified by your choices. Being a nice person has nothing to do with it. If you rein in your vision because you fear it will be disturbing to pervading tastes, you betray yourself and your talent. Almost every abrupt and inspired movement in art was greeted by charges of "bad taste." Good manners parading under the banner of "good taste" spawns dull art. The essay "The Duende" by Federico Garcia Lorca that concludes this book confronts all of this head on.

WORKBOOK EXERCISES

Live. Taste many things. Be alive to every moment. Read a book. Listen to your guts.[†]

Pursue the Mannerism/Probe the Cliché

Any dancer who is locked into mannerisms or invariably falls into clichés of performing has serious problems. Teachers, directors and choreographers have good reason to be distressed by such a dancer. Sadly, the usual and least productive solution is to tell the dancer *not* to do something: "Stop jutting your head forward!" If only it were that simple. One of the least productive lines of thought in rehearsal and/or performance is *not* to do something.

Joseph Chaikin dealt with the cliché in his direction and writing. "The temptation to play the cliché is always present. If the actor is spending a lot of energy keeping it censored, the actor may be staying inside the temptation. Sometimes if the actor plays the cliché out, he is more likely to go beyond it" (*The Presence of the Actor* [New York: Atheneum, 1984], p. 20).

In the Workgroup, we actually built works around our clichés. The premise was that whatever mannerism we had was a covert metaphor for something that was very important to us. The games we learned used them, exercised them, developed them, all to dig deeply into them. We found that we could make our mannerisms and clichés little gold mines.

WORKBOOK Your Familiar[†]
EXERCISES Possessed by a Mannerism[†]
 I Dare You[†]

Determining Style

If the dance artist works at answering the six questions in preparation for a role, the odds are that a basic style will emerge. However, when there is an uncertainty in this matter of style there are more questions that will reward the attention paid them.

Wearing What?

Even in the rehearsals, long before the costumes are available, fitted and worn, it is well to dance in a makeshift version of the costume-to-be. Sometimes, all that is needed is a hat to give the feeling of an entire costume.

WORKBOOK The Two Dances
EXERCISES *If possible perform the two dances in costume.*

 The Duet as a Structure

 In this one there must be a costume, either imagined or pulled together for the studio work. Either way has value.

 I Dare You[†]
 Props Fantasy[†]

Where Is the Action?

Again, long before the settings and the lights are experienced, the imagination should be called upon to do its work as a scene designer during the rehearsals. Movement is transformed by the space, the floor, the weather, the entire physical context that is implicit in the particular dance work. The work of the imagination is to re-create a context that is true to the dance.

WORKBOOK EXERCISES

The Two Dances
Who or What Is Alive in the Music?[†]
The Duet as a Structure
Inside the Outside[†]
Ham and Clove
Rituals of Power
Adam and Eve
Prison[†]
Signs of the Times[†]

What Are the Hands Doing?

The hands need attention. It matters not at what age a student enters a dance class for the first time, the hands are the most highly trained and skilled part of the body. By that very token, they are the most mannered part of the body. Each discipline of dance immediately seizes upon the posture and use of the hands, controlling the shape, motion and style to a fine degree. Before the dancer is aware, a manner is born, and for some it never alters from the beginning of a performance to its end—and for that matter from the beginning of a career to the farewell performance.

Play a game. Extend either arm in any direction. Seated where you are, and without looking at your hand, do the following actions:

Try to touch the wall to your side.

Use your hand as an instrument of benediction for someone.

Reach your hand out in the dark.

Make the salute gymnasts return to the judges before they start.

The hand is poised to caress the head of an infant.

The hand is poised to kill a gnat.

The hand is the simplest extension of an extended arm.

The hand is a decorative model of elegance.

The hand is a lethal weapon.

The hand is in the ideal configuration of a classical fifth position.

Obviously, there is no limit to the hand's range and expressiveness, yet rigid mannerisms freeze the hands of many dancers. There is not enough attention paid to what the hands are doing from moment to moment in relation to the specifics of each dancer's role and actions. Is there any multiplicity as dazzling as the many shapes of leaves the world over? Yes there is: the infinite number of shapes, actions and poems possible with the hands. What will determine the shape of the hands? If the six questions find their answers in the body in motion, the question of the shape, motion and style of the hands will never arise.

WORKBOOK
EXERCISES

Hot to Cold to Hot II†

Focusing on the hands.

The Arms?

What follows is addressed to modern dancers, teachers and choreographers, not to the ballet community. The best of the latter have a free and fluent use of the arms. Many modern dancers, on the other hand, have, in a misguided thrust at "good taste," perpetrated a limiting and stilted use of the arms. In order to avoid the flossy, sentimental use of the arms endemic to "bad taste" ballet, they have opted for arm movement which ignores the elbow and yes, the wrist. The consequence? Arms are used like oars. Arms are rarely released to find the easy moment before the strong thrust. Arms are always in the control mode and never in the released mode, thus making for a limited style of dance. This is so deeply ingrained in contemporary dancers that I find in every intermediate or advanced technique class at the most one or perhaps two dancers who can accept a fluent, easy arm motion as a counterpoint to a strong, controlled arm movement. The rest are surprised and confused by the challenge to add another dimension to the use of their arms. You are blessed with a most fluent instrument—your arms. Use its fluency when it is needed. Discover your elbows—and your wrists—and your fingers! They are yours.

WORKBOOK
EXERCISES

Any improvisation deliberately focusing on the arms, particularly one that posits specific images that call for fluidity.

Hot to Cold to Hot II†

The Face Versus the Body?

Observe the young dancer, ecstatic because she has been accepted into a major dance company. In rehearsal, she is flying across the studio with her powerful leap, legs stretched to a delirious 180° and happier than she has ever been. The choreographer lets out a shriek. "Stop! How dare you smile doing my choreography? My choreography smiles!"

In Chapter 2 there are a few words on this matter of facial expression—the face versus the body. A significant number of dancers, both in ballet and in modern dance, deliberately and carefully avoid any facial expression. They regard it as unacceptable stage behavior, believing that dance expression belongs solely to the body and that an animated face will detract from the purity of the body's eloquence. This becomes a deliberate style. Is it valid? Is it a better way of working?

Take note: this volume is not a brief for facial expression in dance. When I perform, I never know what my face is doing. It never occurs to me to "make a face" or to inhibit facial activity. I have but one goal, an inner and outer unity around the specific focus and action of the moment. With that as a way of working, it is inevitable that my face will reflect what I am thinking/feeling/doing. Undoubtedly there have been those who reject my "style." Does that mean that I, on my side, reject the style of those who restrain their faces? I have indicated a pejorative when I use the term "stone faces." Actually, I have experienced exquisite and moving performances by some who have what one might call "stone faces."

Only once have I, in a desperate moment, told a student or directed a dancer to "make a face." (It didn't work.) That is not the purpose of my teaching. What I seek is an aura that the performer brings onstage. It is what we all look for as human beings: the light that comes from a union of the insides and the outsides. It's what happens when you get up in the morning, brush your teeth and greet the day or whoever you're with, and *all of you is there*. That's not easy—onstage or in the bathroom. The excitement of a performance occurs when you sense the rivers of a person's existence being present. To do that as artists is the great gift we can offer each other. It requires more than good intentions. It wants a skill and a craft to be able to deliver this consistently. Any number of "stone faces" have this light, this aura, this inner-outer dynamic.

There are theatre forms, like opera, where vivid facial expression is a necessity. Musicals, revues, commercials, dancing in clubs all demand a lot of face and a lot of smiles. That is an integral part of those arenas and no one should go near them unless one joyously accepts that ground rule.

There is no question that it is possible to exert so much facial energy that it is literally difficult to take note of what the body is doing. That makes no sense. The ideal for which I strive is the unity of all that I am; the face is not an entity apart from the body with special problems, etiquette and techniques. Within this context, I may go from a "stone face" to a violent grimace. How does one decide how to work? It is one of the major choices every dancer has to make. Your own taste and predilections will lead you. Of course, if you are working with a choreographer who has an articulated point of view, then as a professional, you will take that point of view, justify it and bring it to a brilliant life.

WORKBOOK   Making Faces
EXERCISES

Speech and Dance?

If you're going to open your mouth, learn how to do it. Among my notes for a graduate class in choreography at Arizona State University I came across this critique of a particularly talented student:

> A very strong dance done to a monologue. The problem: the words are too often hard to hear and understand. The suggestion—for her and all dancers who choose to speak and dance: face the fact that if they find it necessary to speak while moving, particularly moving vigorously, they face a problem much more difficult than that which confronts most actors. It behooves dancers who wish to incorporate speech in their dances to work at pronunciation, vocal projection, vocal quality and strategic choices about the *direction* in which the voice is thrown. The best actors talking upstage or down into the floor suffer diminished vocal impact and the clarity to be understood, let alone dancers who lack vocal training.

Actors study body movement, usually taught by movement specialists or dancers. Dancers think nothing of deciding to speak in a dance without the training or the sophistication of an extraordinarily difficult craft. The problems are many: being heard, being understood, an appropriate pronunciation, having a vocal quality that befits the material. Few people who speak in the theatre ever achieve a solid craft at this skill without working seriously for a substantial amount of time with a vocal teacher, privately or in classes. (Even this skill may be declining with the advent of body mikes and sophisticated sound engineering.)

Some dancers think they have solved the problem by recording their voices and assuming that playing the resultant tapes through a public address system at full volume solves everything. *Au contraire:* it usually sounds terrible and unintelligible. It rarely occurs to them to really listen to what they have recorded and, more important, to test what they have done for intelligibility by playing the tape for several people who have never heard the text. The human voice is one of the most difficult of sounds to record with any degree of accuracy, clarity or truthful quality. Alas, there is the treacherous trap of speaking into the pathetic little microphones that are built into our rehearsal cassette recorders. Those mikes are ghastly and offer none of the remarkable adjustments that good sound engineering can do for the human voice.

I myself have suffered enough hearing loss so that when I go to theatre, films or conduct a class, I use a hearing aid. It works—up to a point. Many times I miss some things and am distressed by my problem, only to learn later that people in the audience with excellent hearing did not understand either. How do you ensure that you are heard and understood? *By having very good theatre speech.* In recent years, more and more dancers are adding speech to their dance. If that's the way it goes, fine. Whatever problems there are can be solved, but only if the dancers realize that there are problems.

More from the notes on the dancer who spoke:

She handled very well at what most speaking dancers fail: the timing of words and action. Her words slipped in and out of the dance with a music all its own that yet counterpointed the physical rhythms, and when they did coincide, it was startling. Almost all dancers who use words fall into the trap of synchronizing them with their motions: emphatic words fitting right in and on beat with emphatic gestures that mean the same thing. In ordinary human communication, this is the convention. In dance, it is gratuitous. Synchronicity of dance gesture and words becomes illustration. It is no different than the TV advertisements for a revolutionary set of knives that will never wear out. Emblazoned on the screen is "Only $19.95!" and the voice-over exults, "Only $19.95!" at the same time. Words and motion should have the same relation as the sophisticated handling of movement and music, complementing and counterpointing each other so that each enriches, highlights or even contradicts the other and only rarely and strategically concur. What is stated here is both a performance and a choreographic problem.

WORKBOOK EXERCISES *There are none here. If you are asked or choose to talk and dance, get some professional help on voice production and speech.*

Brechtian Consciousness or Stanislavski Involvement?

Bertolt Brecht (1898–1956) was a German playwright who by his theories, writing and direction had, like Stanislavski, a profound effect on world theatre. He rejected the theatre of illusion because he felt that it permitted an audience to experience compassion and tears *in the theatre;* afterward, they could return to their self-centered indifference. He wanted a performing style he called "the A-effect," A standing for alienation as opposed to the empathy aroused in the theatre of Stanislavski. "The premise at the center of Brecht's work is that *people can change. Things could be different.* The epic theater, as he came to define and redefine it, asks for a removal of pity by the performer and audience, since pity is a response to that which cannot be changed" (Chaikin, *Presence of the Actor,* p. 35). Brecht wrote: "It has been the aim of this technique of alienation *(Verfremdung),* to make the spectator assume an enquiring, critical attitude towards events" ("A New Technique of Acting," trans. Eric Bentley, *Theatre Arts* 33 [January 1949]: 38).

Not many dancers, either as performers or choreographers, deal with this attitude toward performing and this particular kind of confrontation with the audience. In my own work, *The Peloponnesian War,* I continually faced and challenged the audience, never letting them forget that this was a man dancing for them who was throwing out ideas and situations that involved them and even threatened them. I even fired a rifle in their faces. I used similar challenges to audiences in *Poems Off the Wall* (1981). Bill T. Jones's *The Last Supper at Uncle Tom's Cabin* is a powerful example of this kind of dance theatre. Most "performance art" involves this relationship to the audience: the performer is drawing the spectators into the action by deliberately relating to their anticipations, clichés, hopes, fears and prejudices. I have seen Bill T. Jones do this throughout his career, and to great effect. Pina Bausch, the artistic director and choreographer for Tanztheater Wuppertal, makes this the central style of her work.

In my mind, whenever I did work like this, the audience became a character and a force *within* the context of the work. I danced *The Peloponnesian War* in Guam for a substantially unsophisticated audience. Early in the piece, "The Star Spangled Banner" is played in a collage of at least six different keys. I rise to stand, hat across my chest. In New York, no one in the audience stood, though there was some restlessness. On the road, some would stand and some not. Whispers would fill the theatre, "Why are you standing?" "Why aren't you standing?" In Guam, everybody stood, including a little boy who marched up and down in front saluting and facing left, right and about face. At a reception after that performance, a young man blurted out: "I resented what you did to us. You put us on a stage and you were standing there looking at us." In his anger and emotional turmoil, he cut right to the core of what I was doing and what the entire evening was about.

This manner of working the audience has nothing to do with dances that ask the dancer to look at the audience, to dance for the audience and above all, to charm the audience. That way is close to traditional musical comedy wherein all the artifices of the theatre are admitted and the audience is continually called upon to participate in the action by laughing and applauding. We do get swept away by the romanticism of the songs, the glitter of the costumes and sets and dazzling dancers. For a while, the musicals of Broadway tried to emulate the unbroken flow of drama. *Pal Joey, Oklahoma, Fiddler on the Roof* all demanded a different kind of performer—and a different kind of dancer. Few musicals today make this effort.

In this Brechtian approach, it might appear that Benno Schneider's cry, "The shortest distance to the audience is the other actor," is being contradicted. Not at all. There are times when the *audience is the other actor,* or just one more factor at the heart of what is going on in the theatre. Thus, Brecht did not leave Stanislavski behind, he just dragged him off the stage into the house with the audience.

There are none. Question: Have you ever choreographed or been cast in a dance work where the dancer as the dancer unequivocally confronts the audience? What effect did that have on your performance experience?[†]

Dancing in Unison?

Dancing in unison raises several questions. Is the point of it virtuosity? Aside from looking leggy and sexy, the Rockettes do little that can be called virtuosic, but "Wow! Thirty-six women kicking their legs to the same height at exactly the same time!" That is something. As individual performers, their mind-set is to be cheerful and exactly in line with the dancer to their left and right. Anything more complex would be asking for trouble. If only two dancers are doing identical motions, the difficulty quotient is diminished.

Something more is needed to justify and quicken such a performance. When do two or more people do the same motions for an appreciable length of time? The military makes a very strong point of its soldiers' discipline, proving it with unison marching manoeuvres. Hitler's choreographers staged enormous demonstrations of thousands doing the same thing. A number of choreographers who have been horrified by regimentation of any kind have created choreography wherein unison is the expression of that horror.

Lovers sometimes move in sweet unison, as in walking, but rarely otherwise. Almost all acts of loving are complementary, not identical. Thus, when choreographers give dancers prolonged dancing in unison as a metaphor for love, they impose a test of credibility and a difficult problem for the performers to justify. Communities that have traditional dances expect unison, but usually there is allowance for individual style and attitude to the given moves. Hence being precisely together is not an issue or even desirable. The individual joins in, joyously or not, and that opens the door to an individual performance within a unison dance. For many unison can be an ecstasy. Witness the madly intense involvement of high-school girls' movement teams, with their tough guy moves, sprinkled with bits of hip-hop and accented with pumping, fisted gestures.

What of the army of swans hopping across stage in arabesque? If Olga has an impossibly high lift of the leg, should she permitted to show it off? No. No. Cut her down if she tries that again. What should be her specific inner image? What is her justification? She is fulfilling someone's ideal of a flock of fragile, exquisite creatures, each one subservient to that someone's specific vision. An individual variation on the theme of being a "fragile exquisite creature" would not be acceptable. Even though their legs are not bared to the hip and they are not smiling cheerfully and the music is Tchaikovsky not Ferde Grofé, their performing thrust is quite the same as the Rockettes. Both try within the realm of their own style and aesthetic to "dance beautifully," whatever that means. We are treading close to a problem in choreography which is not the province of this book. How many choreographers resort unthinkingly to unison? Face it, it's an easy way to keep a mass of dancers busy and fill out the music. Also, a significant portion of audiences like it. It's as easy to look at as it is to choreograph. If the dancers are really together, we are looking at a form of virtuosity. It *is* difficult for two or more dancers to do exactly the same thing on the same beat. A question to consider: is unison choreography hard to perform with fullness and integrity?

And now, a contradiction: by its very nature, we must assume that all unison dance is either a recurrence or a ritual, that is, that all the moves have been rehearsed prior to the time that we observe it. We have identified an event as something that occurs for the first time. Of course, Fred Astaire denied this reality every time he danced with a woman he just met—and we loved him for it. So where does that leave us?

WORKBOOK
EXERCISES

Performing in Unison

To Project or Not to Project?

My first modern dance study was in the technique of Martha Graham and my teacher was Ray Moses. She was truly a magnificent teacher and I was excited to be cast in a work she was choreographing for a concert at the New School for Social Research, a major event for me. I had been studying dance for all of half a year! It was a brutal anti-war dance (this was 1936) in which we marched off to war from down right to up center, to down left to be shot down, to roll away across the apron to stage right to rise and to resume marching in an unending triangle of death. It was certainly not complex but it was strong and effective. We all knew what we were doing and why, bringing much passion to the wild and dangerous falls we had just learned. The hall was small, seating probably fewer than three hundred, and yet, added to the intensity of our dancing, Ray gave us the fierce injunction to "Project!" Every period and every grouplet gets tied up in the prison of its buzzwords. "Project!" was such a one, particularly in the Graham camp.

Being green, enthusiastic and learning all the time, from then on, I projected like hell whenever I was let loose on a stage. In a few years, I was dancing professionally. Like so many ideas absorbed early, I probably carried that injunction with me wherever I was—unthinkingly. Later in my career, I was asked by one of the most fluent choreographers of her time, Sophie Maslow, to dance the lead in a Madison Square Garden pageant staged as a benefit for Bonds for Israel. She made an amazingly simple and lovely solo for me to a lyric 5/4 section of Aram Khachaturian's *Gayne Ballet Suite*. It depicted David Ben Gurion's first night in Israel (he was to become the first prime minister of the state of Israel). He is so moved that he cannot sleep, and he walks out to breathe the ancient night air of Palestine. I loved doing it, but when it was finally choreographed, I asked, "Sophie, how am I going to dance such a quiet, lyric dance in a barn like Madison Square Garden? I'll have to project like crazy otherwise, I'll disappear." (This was the old Garden, and it seated twenty-two thousand.) Sophie, an optimist, probably said, "Don't worry, it'll be fine," I let it go, continued to enjoy polishing the dance and the work with the other two soloists, Beatrice Seckler and Ethel Winter.

Came the night and there I was at the foot of about ten steps leading up to a fifty-by-seventy foot platform stage, backed up by a seventy-piece symphony orchestra and lit by eight giant arc spotlights poised to follow me wherever I went. My entrance was a minute away. I began filling my lungs getting ready to project as I never had in my life. On the fifth exhalation, I looked around and up at the blur of all those faces (I am very near-sighted), and from nowhere came these thoughts: "It's like a giant bowl. All those people way up there in those balcony seats will be leaning forward looking down toward me. They'll want to touch me and perhaps put comforting arms around me." The music for my entrance began, and I ascended the steps with a serene ease, stood quietly at the edge of the stage and then slid my foot forward in the idle 5/4 walk Sophie had made for me, looking up at the stars of the night. I did the dance. I projected nothing, I simply did David Ben Gurion walking out into the night air exulting that at last he had come home.

In my memory that was one of the richest and the fullest audience response I have ever had, before or since. I never tried to project again. I seriously think the idea of projecting contains a false premise: it says that, in addition to the work of realizing what you are doing onstage, you also have to send it out into the audience; projecting suggests using force to that end. There is no question that without projection, no musical comedy performer is going to succeed, but our field of concert dance, ballet or modern, does not need that extra force. If what you dance onstage has the conviction and force it needs, the audience will come onstage and be dancing with you. You do your work and the audience will do theirs.

Backing off and considering the matter objectively, how do you project your performance if you decide to do so? There are many devices available: an extra strong and vivid makeup; making all the movements given in the choreography broader and more energetic; staying consistently ahead of the musical beat to convey a heightened energy; facing front at every opportunity to create a more obvious audience contact (I won't include smiling because we all know that is a bit vulgar and belongs to Vegas and Broadway). Question: what happens to the choreography? Every one of these devices is legitimate if that is what the choreographer desires. To project or not to project, that is the choreographer's question and only he.she has the prerogative to make a decision.

One more example: Emmett Kelly was the world-famous clown of the Ringling Brothers, Barnum and Bailey Circus. Carrying a broom and costumed in a shabby, patched, loose-fitting suit, unshaven, with the classic white face and red nose, he never acknowledged the presence of the audience. Performing in such huge spaces as Madison Square Garden, he found for himself futile little tasks like trying to sweep up the spotlight that followed him about. His gestures weren't broad and his tasks were simple. The entire audience held its breath while he carefully swept the edges of the light into his little pail until it was a tiny spot.

And now a minor contradiction. In a previous section I discussed Brechtian consciousness and Stanislavski involvement. The "in your face" confrontation that marks performing with a Brechtian consciousness literally calls for a form of projection. It is one that I have used on occasion, specifically in *The Peloponnesian War*.

Project if you must but consider leaving that problem on the shelf, unless the nature of the work asks you to engage the audience directly.

The Two Dances

As an experiment, you might perform either of the two dances concentrating on projecting and then ask yourself, "What did that additional focus do to the dance?" Who knows? You might decide that is the way for you.

So much for more work on the role. Now to finally get out of the studio and on to the stage, that electric confrontation of doers and watchers who together create the art of dance.

5 *Performing*

The act of performing has a built-in audacity. Few of us are quite as laid-back as Ethel Merman. We were on the train from Philadelphia to New York to open *Annie Get Your Gun*. Returning from the dining car, I passed Merman and dropped into an empty seat beside her. We rambled a bit and then I asked her, "Are you nervous about the opening?"

"Why should I be nervous? If they could do what I do, they'd be up there."

She was a rock, a skilled, hard working rock. Most of us, no matter how skilled we are, are nervous before we go on and that's not bad, in spite of Ethel. The performing state is a fragile, difficult thing to maintain, a tightrope—and all too easy to fall off. The nervousness charges us up, heightens our energy and brings all the work into focus. Nervousness is only bad when it chokes the flow of expression. Ideally, all that has gone before should carry us on a free-flowing tide of energy and expression. To finally arrive onstage, in the glare of the lights and the fierce gaze of all those people out there is what all of this is about. All the pliés, all the rehearsals, all the tenderly healed wounds, all the costume fittings, all the thinking, all the tears, all the hopes are but steps to that step out on the stage. Once you are there, everything is different and everything you left behind is there too, visibly and invisibly, felt and not felt. What follows in this chapter are the multiple details that keep us going on that high-wire act called "performance."

Lining Up Your Energies

Lose the Self

In a way, this phrase, "lose the self," is unfortunate. It is a negative way of referring to one of the most positive acts we can perform: becoming "the other" onstage. All the preceding pages of this book lead to this action of becoming the other. It reaches its peak when we actually do lose ourselves in what we are doing (discussed in chapter 1).

Years ago, I wrote for myself a litany which I hoped would help keep my mind clear and close to the work. It often did. As time went by, I began to pass copies of it to my students and friends:

A Way

One way of many ways:
    To find the self,
        lose the self,
        find the object.

Not a table, this table.
Not a minute, this minute.
Not a person, this person.
Words mark the place only,
    eyes speak dark light,
    words conceal, bodies reveal.
Walk into eyes, look inside bodies,
    very difficult,
    often painful,
    even dangerous,
But at least wet with life.

Another time, I visited the dance department of a nearby university with some of our dance majors. As all assembled, I noticed a certain wariness among the host dancers—exactly the kind of thing that will provoke me to crash head-on into a surmised resistance. From nowhere, I began to talk:

When I say, "OK," leave the studio, go outside and find a quiet spot. Clear your mind and resolve to leave yourself outside. It's not unlike when you go shopping and you tie your dog's leash to a post and reassure the animal, "Worry not. I'll be back," and then you go into the store. Do the same here, to yourself. Just leave yourself outside and when you have done that, return and we will go to work. "OK."

My people, used to the unexpected, listened and, with a few grins, left as asked. The host dancers seemed slightly paralyzed but finally when the studio was emptied of our dancers, they very carefully rose and left. In less time than I expected, almost everyone returned, except for four of the host dancers who I later learned never stopped going—away. The returnees were peculiarly somber and thoughtful but the subsequent work, improvisation, was quite wonderful. At odd intervals, when it seems the thing to do, I throw out Leave Yourself Outside (see Workbook, chapter 8). For an unexpected number of dancers it seems to make great sense. It's a naive and simplistic way of preparing for total devotion to the task at hand—becoming the other—that other that will come to life on the stage. That other is not quite you. It is what you create out of yourself.

Another story, one that Tamiris told me. She was choreographing a musical called *Flahooley*. The plot was too complicated for its own good, and certainly for these pages. Suffice to say that Flahooley, the original doll, and the Genie are kept prisoner in a hospital room by the evil manufacturers who want to make millions selling copies of Flahooley dolls. The Genie discovers that he can get the window open and they will be able to get away down the fire escape. As he goes through the window, he calls back to Flahooley, "The lamp! Take the lamp!" Flahooley, the doll, grabs the table lamp instead of the magic lantern that plays a pivotal role in the play. Just before dress rehearsal, the young actress who played Flahooley came to the director with tears in her eyes. "Do I really have to take the wrong lamp? People are going to think I am awfully stupid."

Even among the most sophisticated, this confusion of self and "the other" is more alive than is good for dance and the theatre. In any number of jazz classes, I have found highly skilled dancers who were unable to do the simple pelvic undulations of a good boogie step because it was something "they wouldn't do." Even though I say, "This is a period style. This is them, not you," the pelvis, for some, remains locked and frozen.

WORKBOOK EXERCISES

Every Workbook exercise is an exercise in shifting the focus away from the self.

Leave Yourself Outside[†]
Gifts
Medicine Ball
Outrageous Travel
Passing Through a Physical Object[†] (sense memory)
Dedicate Your Motion[†]
A Duet
Who or What Is Alive in the Music?[†]
Seeing Through the Eyes of Another[†]
Walk Behind Another[†]
The Duet as a Structure
Lose Your Head[†]

A Mind-Wash

Before engaging upon any complex activity, many people benefit from a time to deliberately clear out the mind. Meditation is worth a try, particularly if there is difficulty in concentrating all the energies needed.

WORKBOOK
EXERCISES The Rhythm Series[†]

Though Breath Rhythm and Pulse Rhythm are leads into Inner Rhythm, you may find them just what you need.

Spinning[†]
The Mind-Wash[†]
From Now[†]

Centering

What in a day is relevant to the night's work in the theatre? Profoundly, everything is connected but for us, we need to unload the details of the day—what we were and did—to become what we will be for a few hours. There are as many ways of doing this as there are theatre artists. For me, the ritual begins with washing my face and putting on makeup. I've never been enamored of my face, and my makeup subtly alters it in the direction of how I would love to look. In the process of creating the "new" face, I begin to unload a good part of what is irrelevant to the night's work. With every subsequent element of the preperformance ritual, I get deeper into the frame of mind I need to do the dance: a warm-up, a light run-through of a couple of the dances, working over some worrisome passages, getting into costume, prancing about waiting for the curtain to rise. "Centering" may be a buzzword, and yet it precisely describes the process necessary for any performer to line up all the energies needed to dance on that tightrope.

There are as many approaches to performing as there are dancers, and if you're serious about it, you learn by watching others, by chasing it yourself, by succeeding and by failing, by keeping a journal, by preparing for the performance itself and by thinking about it all. (I think every artist can use a friend, one whose taste is trusted. It is good fortune to have one like that in the audience and later giving feedback.) The night of the performance is so personal that there's nothing anyone can say about how you're supposed to do it except that if you know you need a certain kind of preparation and you don't leave yourself the time to do it, you're dumb. You have to learn who you are, what you need and then give yourself some elbow room. It's hard to be an artist in our country, and if the environment in which we work doesn't make it easy for us, the least we can do is make it easy for ourselves.

There is always too much to do. "I must get my hair cut." "I must get that gift for

Uncle Mort." "This is the last day of the sale on dance shoes." By the time you get to the stage, you're half gone, not ready and all the beautiful work is blunted. The world is seductive, food is seductive, drink is seductive, love is seductive, and then there is the devastating world news and also the Olympics or the tennis match that demands watching. It is an extraordinarily demanding thing that we do, and it contains a pretension. We work, work, work and then we announce to the public, "Now!" We ask a mass of people to leave their homes, run the risks of driving in an automobile, pay money, sit patiently in a room all facing in the same direction—all to look at us. Pretentious? Not if we're good.

I had the good fortune to work with one of the loveliest and best dancers of my generation, Pearl Lang. We were in a sweet little revue by Walter and Jean Kerr, *Touch and Go,* with fine choreography by Helen Tamiris. Pearl and I did duets in a couple of the dance numbers. We warmed up at the same time in the same backstage area. Pearl, doing her barre, was usually like a lark at dawn, almost chirping with joy, happy and bounding with energy. I, in my workout, was a container of several dozen anxieties, fiercely trying to free my tight body, recapture that barely controlled balance, reviewing the triple pirouette I should never have agreed to do. Came the performance, we usually both glowed and meshed to make good dance together. The joke was that if all went well, I left the stage happy as that bird while Pearl, being a perfectionist, would often be in a high rage because of a slow tempo or a ragged light cue. The slam of her dressing room door would shake the theatre.

Losing the self, meditation, centering—they each hover around the same action of getting into the work and the role clean and unencumbered with irrelevant tensions. It is a tradition among some Asian artists to find time for a prolonged meditation before engaging in the work. Unless you are a soloist, privacy, quiet and a bit of solitude are hard to come by backstage. Worse, there are those who will for their own stupid reasons resent your strange behavior. I knew a man who would seat himself on a deserted iron plate landing, cross his legs in the lotus position and meditate. He was not popular, which was a wretched excuse for the occasional brute in the chorus sneaking up behind him with an iron stage weight and slamming it into the floor. The poor man jumped up in fright, facing a group of laughing men. A solution? If you really need to do something, find a way to do it. Find your space and place out of sight of the beasts.

WORKBOOK   The Rhythm Series[†]
EXERCISES   True Repetition[†]
Evolving Repetition[†]
Dedicate Your Motion[†]

Doing this while keeping in focus someone or something that fills you with peace or high energy or a sense of power—whatever you need—may get you into the mind-set you seek for the night's work.

This too, like Dedicate Your Motion, can feed the moment that will bring you onstage in just the right frame of mind.

Find the Inner Rhythm of the Role

The role or the character has an inner rhythm. It relates to the music and the rhythm of the choreography, but it is not the same. As you wait for your entrance, find it, do it, become it. Are you ready for your entrance? I think that many performers do this in the wings as they rev up without being conscious of it. I have seen it. I have done it myself, and in many of my workshops, dancers have experimented with the inner rhythm as a preparation and then performed the dance, discovering an immediate and effortless identity with the role and its inherent energy.

Becoming X, Assuming the Metaphoric Identity

This is the goal. This is what all the work leads up to. Once the premise is accepted that the person standing in the wings is transformed the moment she.he enters the stage, the focus of all the dancer's energy becomes clear and uncluttered by irrelevant vanity or self-hate, inhibitions and fears of personal exposure.

How you step into the role is an individual matter. There are no rules. Some in the Stanislavski tradition are very fond of citing the great actors who came into the theatre four hours before curtain time. Others, equally great, come in at the half hour, put on their make-up and go! Actors have been known to sniff at a handkerchief with a special scent because it draws them into the milieu of the world they are about to enter. All of this is an individual matter. Just get there. Pick a method and try it. And, what may work for one role may not work for another role. Hang loose.

In the early years of my career, I was either in musical comedies or participating in concerts with other artists. More to the point, I was not onstage all the time. I had time to prepare, and prepare I did. Having studied acting with Miriam Goldina and Sanford

Meisner, preparation was enshrined as a sacred part of the stage ritual. For *Strange Hero* I would imagine the space and the people I was about to encounter. Similarly, for *Spanish Dance,* as I waited there onstage for the work lights to go out, the curtain, the music prelude in the dark—I would mentally find myself where the man in the dance was and why he was there. *Man of Action* provided its own perfect preparation. Every detail of the costume had to be just so—the hat at a precise angle, some buttons fastened and some not. Fussing about each item provided just the right amount of hysteria that made the dance what it was.

When I shifted gears and began to do solo programs, there was barely enough time to get onstage from one dance to the other. Deliberate and careful preparation was out. Having just spent fifteen years in the commercial theatre, I was sensitive to the matter of timing. At innumerable dance concerts, I had writhed with impatience and indignation as long minutes crawled by between dances. My rule was, get back onstage—fast— and I was good at that. Extended mental preparations were an impossibility. Was I thus in trouble? Not at all. I could slip into a role as fast as I could get into a costume—faster. Why? Because the long hours making the material in the studio were available the instant I turned my face toward each dance. Martha Graham said she needed no preparation. The moment she hit the stage, she entered into who and what she was supposed to be. Would this work for anyone else? I don't know.

If X is who or what you become when you step onstage, you cannot play X and simultaneously judge X. Your inner life as X should have no more objectivity about X than X would have. You cannot play Iago thinking he is an evil man. Iago believes himself to be innocent and wronged, not evil. Similarly, you cannot be X and make judgments upon yourself as a dancer while you are dancing. Later, yes. The next day a rehearsal might be in order, but during the performance, every mishap, every error, every disaster must be something that has happened to X, and only X can be permitted to reflect on or cope with the problem.

The Hub Meditation[†]

This really belongs to the period of working on and creating the role long before performance time.

Who or What Is Alive in the Music?[†]

This too belong to the preparation time.

Gesture Rondo[†]

This is a fun and crazy game and may be a fertile way of warming up, seizing on a key gesture of X and doing a rondo with it.

Each Alone[†]

If there is the time, the space and the atmosphere that would encourage this as a way of entering into the role or character, I think it would produce staggeringly wonderful results.

Rhythm Portrait[†]

This is a more modest, restrained and less conspicuous way of getting into the character. Is there a difference between the Inner Rhythm of a role and a Rhythm Portrait? Yes. An inner rhythm is more basic, fundamental and repetitive. A portrait rhythm could evolve and be more complex.

Inside the Outside[†]

This also belongs to the creative period rather than to performance time.

Rivers of Energy Pouring Into Each Moment of Performance

The Six Questions

Anyone who couples physical preparation with acting techniques for dance performance will arrive onstage alive inside and out with the power to probe the mystery of the role to be danced.

The Six Questions[†]

They are there, waiting to be tested, used, or discarded.

Controlling the Given Motions

The prerequisite to all art is the craft, the technique, the ability to execute what is given, the bones of the choreography. Without that foundation, all the rest is spindrift without a wave. Once the moves are mastered physically and musically, then the work of bringing them to life begins. Can the two processes proceed simultaneously? They do and they don't. Most good learners are pretty cool dealing with new choreography, gradually bringing to bear their deeper understanding until they reach performance quality. They simply take note of everything that the choreographer gives out, verbally or physically. Choreographers who demand blazing performances too quickly risk making a nervous company that delivers shallow solutions to their roles.

Is the motion passive or an act of will? Is the source of energy the trunk of the body willing the arms and legs to reach out, or are the arms and legs leading and shaping all that transpires? Is there complete control wherein all the muscles spring simultaneously to the beat and all cut on the same beat? Do we need the exotic successions? Is the rhythmic attack on the beat, after it or ahead? These are the choices that must be made in rehearsals. How deliberate are these choices made during a living performance? There is no clean answer to this because the mind oscillates in performance between precise control and voluptuous abandon. Both ways are active and present when the work of preparation has been pursued in depth.

How Does Your Tree Dance?[†]
Before, After and On[†]

And a damn solid dance technique.

Balancing the Apparent Focus and the Hidden Intention

There are times when both the apparent focus and the hidden intention are leaping about in the consciousness, and times when only one is in the forefront. Getting lost in either one for too long a time will oversimplify what should be complex if the dance is to be alive. How long is "too long a time"? The subtlest and most elusive yardstick of all is *taste*.

Bringing this consciousness to bear on the creation of any role is the secret to a performance with depth and mystery.

The Two Dances
Justification[†]
Dedicate Your Motion[†]
Who or What Is Alive in the Music?[†]
The Inner Rhythm of the Role[†]
Emotion Memory[†]
Each Alone[†]
Inside the Outside[†]

Performing the Metaphoric Action

It could be said that there is only one kind of action possible onstage: a metaphoric action. The opposite could be and has been said: the best use of the stage is to strip it of pretense and the imaginary, to create and perform moves that are no more or less than what we see. About twenty-five years of dance has had a profusion of work based on this latter view. Elsewhere in this volume this debate has been highlighted (see chapter 5, "Working on the Role"). In this book I align myself with Homer, Shakespeare, Gary Snyder (a contemporary American poet) and all those who suspect that everything is really a metaphor for something else.

The metaphor works for a dancer if it is appropriate to what is being danced and communicated; if it is meaningful to the dancer; if it ignites the energy of the dancer; if the dancer can make it as real as the floor upon which the dance lives. That is asking a great deal. Sometimes the metaphor is just there, shimmering in the air, and the stage is afire. Sometimes it loses its heat after a while. It becomes elusive or just "doesn't work." What to do? Don't wait for it to flare up again. Go back to the studio or get to the theatre early and start digging for what will work. Without a strong connection with a metaphor, the dance becomes mechanical.

Every one of these can carry you into the metaphoric action, but they aren't easy to do backstage as preparation for a performance. If one works for you, find a way to do it.

Justification[†]
Dedicate Your Motion[†]
Who or What Is Alive in the Music?[†]
The Inner Rhythm of the Role[†]
An Event, a Recurrence, a Ritual[†]
How Does Your Tree Dance?[†]
The Hub Meditation[†]
Each Alone[†]
Before, After and On[†]
The Spine of Style[†]
Inside the Outside[†]

Whom Are You Addressing?

Sooner or later this ought to be confronted, both in relation to how you feel about the act of performing and what you believe is the nature of each specific dance role. Some choreographies are directed quite precisely: to a particular audience, to bookers, to your elusive dance partner, to your own insides, to a deity, to . . . ?

This is essentially a mind trip. When do you do it? In rehearsal? Just before you fall asleep? While making up and getting into costume? Warming up? Peeking through a hole in the curtain? (Very unprofessional!) On the crest of the last breath you take before entering the stage? Or do you take six months off on a mountaintop to meditate on the matter? Find what works for you and do it.

Accommodating to the Physical Environment of the Stage

Touring presents the obvious hazards of unfamiliar stages, particularly for a near-sighted person like myself. My routine was the same, wherever I went. I made certain to leave time to walk through every movement backstage that I could anticipate—with my eye-glasses on. I hunted for every obstacle: electrical cables, props, flats, light towers or shin-busters. I developed such a precise memory that once I was betrayed by it. In the year I met Tamiris, I became her partner and was fortunate enough to appear with her in the glamorous Rainbow Room atop New York's Radio City. The performing space was tricky, being the famous circular dance floor that revolved when the customers took to dancing. I carefully mapped out every move, including the bows. Opening night was smashing, until those very bows. As I bent fully at the waist, my rear butted into something that catapulted me forward as if I had been kicked. What? It was a little piano that Billy de Wolfe, the comedian who shared the bill, had put into place *after* our rehearsal.

Nothing can be taken for granted, even on a familiar stage. One can never know when Billy de Wolfe will move a piano, a prop, a cable or a flat to a different place. Comes the performance, one is moving too quickly making crossovers and entrances to deal with the unexpected. Once, in St. Louis, I was dancing in the small theatre of the Kiel Auditorium that lay back to back with an enormous stage. I had carefully traced an insane crossover that meant going down into a basement, up again to cross the rear of the big stage, down on the other side and up to our smaller stage. That night, as I dashed up the stairs to arrive at the backstage area of the big stage, I could see through the wings dozens of berobed ones on the stage looking up to Christ on the mount, and in my path, staring at me through lidded eyes, a squatting camel. Without a pause, I cleared the camel and made for the other side of the stage. Best to look around.

There's another element to all this. There is little onstage and backstage that is not vibrant, in and of itself. The sets, curtains, light poles, the lights that resemble nothing so much as artillery are all loaded and potent and *yet most of it has nothing to do with what is being danced.* Even sets seen up close are merely dabs of paint with little or nothing of the illusion that they project to the audience. The rehearsal studio tends to be neutral. The stage and backstage are never that for me. I find every part and particle of them charged and potentially unnerving. They all say, "This is it—the real thing. You're not in the studio, where a miss needs only to be corrected. Here there are no excuses and you have to deliver." How many times have I walked onto an empty stage with one worklight and the black hole of an empty house? Each time I felt a chill at the back of my neck, swayed by the silent space and thought, "I'm home." Yes, but this home is an unforgiving place.

What to do? The imagination can link and relate any two objects no matter how divergent they might be. Find anything onstage or backstage that can feed and support what you will be doing in the dance. I get some of my strongest jolts from the lights— from the subtle colors of the gels, the shafts of light and the mysterious blackness hovering above in the flies.

Possibly the most critical physical aspect of the stage for dancers is the floor—its resilience and its surface. Some are floors for dance and some are floors against dance. I would equate the perfect floor surface with the Holy Grail. Unattainable. Within the same dance there are moments when one needs traction and other moments when a bit of slide would be just right.

Hard, unresilient floors are discouraging and literally dangerous. Though this is a book on acting technique for dancers, never pretend to yourself, in the interest of doing a glowing performance, that you are dancing on a perfect dance floor. If it's a hard, ungiving floor, make a deliberate adjustment by softening all landings, pull back on any stamping actions and be particularly careful with all falls.

Nourished by the Ambience of Attention

I have had an experience while teaching that always saddens me. I see a student do something both personal and brilliant. With excitement, I stop the class and ask this wonder child to demonstrate how it should be done. What happens? Any number of times, the lustre turns dim and the dancer fades into mediocrity. I am confused and usually turn to the dancer with wonder: "What happened to that blaze of glory I saw a moment ago? You are investing all these years of work in dance and the moment people look at you, you diminish your talent and withdraw under a cloud. Do you think you can reverse the process and learn to dance even better *because* we are looking at you?" Anyone who has taught dance has had similar dismaying experiences. Any number of people who are gorgeous in class or rehearsal disappear onstage. It's as if the eyes of the audience are drains that suck away their energy. They may be beautiful dancers, but they have yet to find this key to performance. A realized performer goes out into that space, and when the people turn the searchlight of their eyes on them, they begin to glow and become more intelligent than ever. A performer bathes voluptuously in the attention. Attention is like rain on a forest. The attention of the audience is a nourishing atmosphere for the creative theatre artist; it is a threat for someone who has a problem to solve and lacks the will to confront it.

Suppose there is that fear? Let us assume a dancer who has the talent, craft and capacity to deliver really good dance and, at the same time, becomes choked by terror when exposed to the audience. Will psychotherapy help? Perhaps. But we have within the craft of our work the wherewithal to cope with the fear. We can summon the discipline of turning the attention away from the self to concentrate on the reality of what is there on the stage. We have Benno Schneider's pronunciamento, "The shortest distance to the audience is through the other actor!" (Change that to "dancer.") We can also reevaluate who and what the audience is. They *want* the artist to be beautiful. Their hearts hunger to be quickened. They are not waiting for the dancer to fall down; they're waiting to see the dancer fly for them.

You either go out there feeling that you're going to be shot down, or you go out there knowing that you can get stronger because the eyes are not looking *at* you but *to* you. Know it, but don't focus on it, no more than you focus on the rain or the sun. It might be raining but after a while you continue talking, walking and running. The air you breathe as a performer is attention. Let that air invigorate you. Your sensitivities should sparkle, your strength should flow and the audacity of the risks you take should grow. Your audience wants to be moved and changed by you. Above all, don't demand perfection of yourself. Mistakes dot the greatest performances. Midori, interviewed at the start of her career as a violinist: "Do you ever make mistakes?" "Of course. Everybody makes mistakes."

Lawrence Johnson is a young pole vaulter. He won the collegiate indoor championship in March 1994 and set his goal to one day being the first to clear twenty-one feet, beating the world record of twenty feet. Interviewed before the 1994 Penn Relays he said, "The Penn Relays is an emotional meet for me. I really enjoy crowds. A crowd of people gets me going more than anything else" (*New York Times,* April 28, 1994).

Stage Concentration Versus Oscillation

I discussed the "Game of Oscillation" in chapter 4, making the point that pure concentration is a perfection useless to pursue and not even ideal. The flame of total absorption takes place intermittently within the reality of the stage space and its demands. On occasion, people will cough quite loudly in the theatre, and if your hearing is functioning you will hear it. The heart of the game is to keep the focus within the action and to use every distraction to shed more light on the central focus.

If you go through entire performances knowing that you're here and they're out there; if that awareness never leaves you, whatever you're doing, you're on your way out of the theatre. In *The Actor Prepares,* Stanislavski tells a story about one of the acting students who has had his ego badly battered in the first few weeks by a director who will not accept his grandiloquent grandstanding, his noble clichés or vocal acrobatics. He is learning the hard way by committing every sin in acting. On this day, he is assigned to get the student stage ready for an important showing. There is insufficient time and, in his haste, he spills a box of carpet tacks on the forestage. Some of the actors will be wearing ballet slippers or soft shoes. In a panic, he falls to his knees to gather up every last one. He is at this task for several minutes when he happens to raise his head for a moment and, with a start, realizes this is the first time that he has been onstage without any consciousness of being in the theatre, on a stage in front of a room full of chairs all facing in the same direction. All his attention was focused on the simple and crucial task of gathering up those vicious little tacks. He would be an artist if the tacks were spilled on the carpet eight times a week in front of an audience and he were to gather up every one without the consciousness of their presence or of his effect upon them. The task would become a metaphor and he, an honest actor.

Could it be that a continuous awareness of the audience, of being on the stage, of self-consciousness is a form of vanity? The audience is not interested in *you;* it is fascinated by who or what you are supposed to be and do. Stage concentration is the central task, and yet it exists as an island within an awareness of the existing envelope of audience, critics, friends, enemies, the stage, the lights, the wings and the treacherous shin-busters. You know they are there and you turn your back on them to dance the task of X in the world of X. All intrusions are accepted and allowed to slip in and out of focus. With every distraction, you simply burrow more deeply into the life of the stage.

WORKBOOK
EXERCISES
All the improvisations that call for a focus on the other act as a training ground for stage concentration.

The Six Questions[†]
Pursuing each of these will make stage concentration an integral part of your craft.

Dealing with What Is, Not with What Was

I once had a glorious performance that seemed to come out of a new insight about performing. A few nights later, I had another concert and took that same kicker—and nothing happened. I was like ice, self-conscious and watching myself. That performance was wretched until I let go of the previous night and just dealt with what was at hand.

In my own experience, I have never been able to predict what my energy or my frame of mind will be when I hit the space in the lights. My warmup can be ideal; I can feel like a powerhouse and damn! When the music starts, I am mysteriously under and realize I have some serious problems to bring that performance to life. Conversely, I can feel like a limp rag as I get ready, and then I'm out there and everything is flowing. My ground rule is simple. Never expect to repeat a performance. Go out curious. What will you find there and how will you deal with it?

It is an iron law of the stage that no two performances are alike (see "The Intolerance of Uncertainty" in chapter 2). Mishaps do occur, raising the question: "Who deals with the obstacle, the accident?" You are really in the theatre and in the role when it is X who deals with whatever goes wrong in terms of who X is and what X is doing and can do. If you, the dancer, cope with a problem as yourself, that is an admission of failure and the mishap remains just that, a mishap. The error will be apparent to the audience. But if X deals with the obstacle, the odds are that no one in the audience will be aware that anything went wrong. It will be an integral part of the dance.

WORKBOOK   *The best groundwork for this facility is any and all the improvisation exercises.*[†]
EXERCISES

Interacting with the Others and the Environment

Each element of performing connects to all the others. The vibrant performer gains strength from the cast and from everything encountered out onstage—the lights, the music, the sets, the props and all. Though not about a literal performance, this story is very much to the point. Deep into the run of *Plain and Fancy,* a 1956 musical in which I danced, we were all stirred up by the news that Morton Da Costa, our director, had invited Marlene Dietrich and Noel Coward to the show. Even more exciting, at the end of the performance came the news that Dietrich and Coward wanted to come backstage and meet us.

We all assembled in the wide square space in front of our dressing rooms. They arrived, and the woman in life was breathtaking. The talk was carried on mostly by Coward and our director. Dietrich literally hung back, leaning up against a pillar. I looked at her and thought, "Here is *the* glamour woman of our time. What is glamour? What is the excitement that radiates from her? What is *she* doing?" It took a moment or two for me to get to it. *She was fascinated by us.* She couldn't get enough of us. Her eyes were devouring us one by one.

Those who have electricity in life as well as in the theatre are what they are because of their passionate interest and amazement at all they encounter.

WORKBOOK
EXERCISES

Any and all of the improvisation exercises.[†]

Energy: Too Much/Too Little/Just Enough

There is a certain kind of success that is very difficult to deal with, at least in my own experience; success on Broadway. It's glorious at first—the great reviews, the enthusiastic audiences, the good money and the chance to dance and dance and dance. But after several months, one begins to encounter a resistance to doing the same thing eight times a week. In my day, the matinees were on Wednesday and Saturday. Now, it's even worse. Four performances are bunched together on Saturday and Sunday. What art form has ever asked its participants to do the same inspired performance eight times a week for months and yes, years on end? (*Annie Get Your Gun* ran for more than two years.) The "same thing" means not just giving change for a twenty, it is giving your all—your intense brilliant and dazzling expression—*eight times a week!*

You learn a few things about energy. One of the things that earned me my status as a principal dancer was my high energy, and therein lay a danger. I am certain that when I began, I tended to do too much. In the early days of the run of a show, there is rarely a question of "enough" energy, but after a while, there come the low days, the days of working through an injury, or a cold or getting stuck on a matinee day with late service in a restaurant and coming back to the theatre with a full stomach. These are the times when there is not enough energy or strength to do a proper show, but doing anything less is out of the question. After all, I was dancing in front of a "chorus" line made up of modern dance soloists, former members of the leading ballet companies, *and a Broadway audience.* What happens? You make choices. You seize those moments when you can lean back and float in order to get a bit of your breath and strength back. You poise yourself for that phrase that *must* be way up there, and then, you go for it—because you have to. Before you know it, that becomes the way you dance, even if you come into the theatre with an ocean of power. It's called "taste." You stop being a young whirlwind slamming into every phrase, and you graduate to the sophistication of choosing your highs and relishing the subtlety of the soft moments.

A strange experience was the trigger that really clarified this reevaluation of my dance energy. Early in the run of *Annie Get Your Gun,* I saw a performance by the German soloist Harold Kreutzberg. I had first seen him in 1936, when I was writing dance reviews for the paper at City College, where I was a first-year undergraduate. I

101   *Performing*

had been dancing for about three or four months, which of course gave me the right to judge professional dancers, in print, and, to be sure, I was not easily impressed. I dismissed his work as *mitteleurope kitsch,* prettiness, cuteness. The second time I saw him was in 1946. I still thought he did *mitteleurope kitsch,* but I saw what I had not seen ten years earlier: he was a magnificent dancer. I saw him on a Sunday; Monday night I was back in the theatre to do my Indian Dance. As I started into it, I sensed something radically different. I wasn't dancing the same way. It was as if someone else was dancing, not me. It was Kreutzberg, his body, his understanding and the way he worked had taken possession of me like a demon. It was all about energy—about how much force I was letting out. Some things were much lighter and easier than I had ever danced them. Others were fierce and climactic. I was witnessing myself dance. I thought, well, let it happen. It felt strange, but good, and I let it ride. For a couple of nights running, I came into the theater curious about what would happen, determined not to control or check the dance of this dybbuk. (In Jewish folklore, a dybbuk is the soul of a deceased person who enters into a living body and controls it. This was a living artist, but he *was* controlling me.) In time, it became clear. He/I were dancing long arcs of energy. He/I never just did a fabulous move and then another wonderful move. Now, every move was part of a phrase, and most of the phrases were quite long. For a few parts of the dance, his way did not feel right, but for most of the run we had a very successful collaboration. I should have sought him out and spoken to him, but at the time I did not realize how open most dancers are and how pleased he would have been that I was affected by his style. For all I know, he might have been in the Majestic Theatre that Monday night and spooking me from his seat—or envying me. I did have a better jump than he and a steady job in a successful Broadway show. Whatever, I learned to phrase. My body learned to sing in longer phrases rather than chopping up the choreography into powerful separate bits. (See also "Too Much and Not Enough" in chapter 1.)

WORKBOOK EXERCISES The Two Dances

It is too easy and simplistic to find phrasing on a purely physical level. If you were to analyze one or both of the two dances in the framework of the six questions and also a bits analysis, you would find the overall drive and the units of inner action that drive the role from moment to moment to shape and sustain the major arcs of energy.

Competition

I'm not good on this point. I'd be lying if I said I did not experience waves of envy of dancers of my generation who accomplished more and achieved more prominence and renown in the field. On the other hand, I never set out to be better than anyone—to jump higher than another. I had a clear-drawn battle with what I considered my own limitations, and that is what fired my ambition and the intensity of all my work. In performance, it was inconceivable that I upstage another, trying to draw the attention away from them to me. It's an ugly ploy but it happens. What to do when it is done? (1) Don't try to outdo the upstager. (2) "Level" with the culprit. (3) At worst, turn to the director for help. A distasteful business but what choice do you have? Of course, if you have to be liked by everybody, including your tormentor, you have a real problem. No, you definitely cannot accept this kind of bullying. What you do is being stolen from you, and the integrity of your concentration on your role is being invaded.

The Stage Space

Everyone learns in her.his own way, sometimes unconsciously. I never had trouble finding the light onstage, getting into the heat of a lit area. It took me a while to recognize how I did it. Perhaps because I am near-sighted and do not see much at a distance, I sense the intensity of the light I am in from my eyelashes. Can others do that? I don't know. However, if you're supposed to be in the center of a lit area, puzzle out your own way to be sure, without ineptly looking up into the light source or down to find your spike mark.

The other necessary spatial awareness is how close you can get to the wings (be they flats or drapes), the front edge of the stage, the cyclorama or the rear traveler. If you stand before a mirror and hold your hand as far away as possible and slowly bring it toward your face, there will come a moment when your hand will "invade" the space of your face. Try it and then come back to the book.

A few inches away and your hand is "in your face." Similarly, if you stand within a certain number of inches of another person, you will create discomfort, you will be "invading her.his space." In the convention of the theatre, we, at least in Western cultures, think of the stage space as a kind of infinity. Agnes de Mille's cowboys can romp for miles in a space that, at best can't be wider than fifty feet. Let one dancer get less than about three feet from a wing and that wing becomes a part of the dance. Worse, the stage illusion of space is diminished and made to be what it actually is: a dancer, not a cowboy; a stage, not the open plains; and a flat, not a tree.

Of course, there are those choreographers who want the dancer to be a dancer, the stage to be a stage and all stage illusions to be dispelled, and that is perfectly legitimate. The prevailing aesthetic determines the use of the space.

Dealing with Failure or Negative Criticism

Two characteristics of artists who endure: their toughness regarding negative reviews and criticism of all kinds—from friends, lovers, enemies, colleagues and critics, and the clarity and ferocity of their self-criticism. Having recognized a weakness, a miscalculation, a wrong tack, they are ready to make the next move. They know to whom to listen. They know that most criticism contains a portrait of the critic. They can spot criticism that misses the point and yet inadvertently identifies a flaw which only they recognize. When I did the first performances of my play adaptation of Albert Camus' *The Fall* in my studio, I invited a few prospective backers. After the second showing, a woman, reputed to be a brilliant economist—and rich—was introduced to me. Without being asked, she said, "It's very impressive, but it is much too long. You must cut it." I didn't cut it, of course. It was too long for the simple reason that I was being very careful with an hour-and-a-half monologue, trying to remember all the words. As I continued to work on the role, I gained fluency and security and cut over twelve minutes simply by speaking more quickly.

There is only one rule in regard to criticism. Listen to whom you value and respect, but make all your own decisions. Do absolutely nothing because another said so. If you are to claim the title of an artist, there can be only one final decider—you yourself. Criticism from the director or choreographer is another matter. There, the professionalism of the dancer is challenged to the utmost: you must find a way to incorporate that criticism into your own conception of the role.

In evaluating my own performances, I had one clue which told me more than any comments, written or spoken. Whenever people came backstage elated and seemingly pleased with themselves, I felt truly successful. Their congratulations meant less than the glow that emanated from them.

WORKBOOK   I Dare You[†]
EXERCISES
This is a subtle form of criticism from your fellow students that can be of great value, or working alone with the capacity for a ruthless self-criticism could be a challenge of even greater value.

Success Is a Serious Problem

It's a problem that should happen to all of us. The real trick is not to let it be a problem. How? Just accept the premise that with every new role, you're always back at the beginning, taking nothing for granted. Whatever worked sheer magic the last time might work again, but don't assume it.

Taking Risks

There comes a time when the focus on craft, the rules of the art, the passion for success and the fear of failure have to be shunted aside and out of sight. A raw, unfinished artist can on occasion take this risk but until the craft is firm, the rules are known, accepted or rejected and one is ripe for the major career steps, this audacity is best held in reserve. An artist has to earn the right to take risks. Implicit in that course is the very good chance of being wounded. A green artist may find recovery from a failure or an attack a slow or an irreversible process.

In the appendix to this book is an essay by Federico Garcia Lorca dissecting a word and a concept that does not exist in our culture: *duende*. For several years now, in my Acting Technique for Dance Performance classes, I have asked my students to read it. Despite Lorca's occasional obscurity and his references to artists unknown to most of us, I believe its total impact represents the ultimate challenge to anyone who dares to take that step out upon the stage. Any artist in any field can make a connection with the concept of *duende*. It is a statement without parallel.

The Next Step

What you have read up to this point are the basic theories that shape and drive a way of dancing. If you have found it interesting but of no relevance to how you choose to work, this is a good a place to stop and think, "Oh, so that is his process. Not for me," and go on to the Appendix. If, however, you see value in all—or some—of what you have read, the Workbook that follows is a compendium of about eighty exercises designed to help you develop an acting technique for dance performance. If you are focused on a particular problem, there is no reason not to leap forward and work out of the given sequence.

Good luck!

She spoke eloquently about acting. "The camera taught you what not to do. I used to hang a mirror on the side of the camera, because at first I was making faces. And then I found that you should start with the curtain down, your face in repose, and then whatever you had in mind, you thought it and the camera got it. If you were caught acting they didn't believe it." (Lillian Gish, *New York Times,* March 2, 1997)

The dancers illustrated here are among those who brought a living presence to their physical virtuosity.

Virginia Zucchi (1849–1930) was one of the most influential and inspirational dancers of the late nineteenth century. The first and greatest of a series of Italian ballerinas who dominated Russian ballet for some fifteen years, she raised the Imperial Ballet out of a state of torpor and growing public indifference, "virtually single-handed and almost overnight" (Ivor Guest, *The Divine Virginia* [New York: Marcel Dekker, 1977], p. 3). Stanislavski was one of the many Russian artists and intellectuals upon whom she made a deep impression. She struck a chord similar to the effect of Tomasso Salvini, the great Italian actor who brought clarity and direction to Stanislavski's search for truthful performances devoid of brilliant though shallow theatrical effects. Zucchi was a great actress who danced; her work inspired many dancers of her generation.

Dance Collection of the New York Public Library for the Performing Arts; used by permission of Museo Teatrale alla Scala.

Isadora Duncan (1877–1927).

Photograph by Arnold Genthe. *Billy Rose Theatre Collection, The New York Public Library for the Performing Arts—Astor, Lenox and Tilden Foundations.*

Vaslav Nijinsky (1890–1950).
Nijinsky Archives.

Martha Graham (1894–1991).
Library of Congress.

Doris Humphrey (1895–1958) and Charles Weidman (1900–1975).
Collection of Charles H. Woodford.

Helen Tamiris (1902–1966).

Collection of Daniel Nagrin.

Anthony Tudor (1908–1987). Starting late, he was never a great technician, but he was a convincing and moving performer. As a choreographer, he elicited from his dancers vibrant performances lit by an inner life.

Photograph by Gordon Anthony. *Used by permission of the Theatre Museum, London.*

Galina Ulanova (1910–).

*Billy Rose Theatre Collection, The New York Public Library for the Performing Arts—
Astor, Lenox and Tilden Foundations.*

Anna Sokolow (1910–).

Photograph by Barbara Morgan © 1980. *From the collection of Lloyd Morgan.*

Nora Kaye (1920–1987) and Hugh Laing (1911–1988).

Billy Rose Theatre Collection, The New York Public Library for the Performing Arts—Astor, Lenox and Tilden Foundations.

Valerie Bettis (1919–1982).
Library of Congress.

Merce Cunningham (1919–).
Photograph by Terry Stevenson. *Used by permission of Charles Atlas.*

Jean Babilée (1923–).

Paul Taylor (1930–).
Photograph by Z. Freyman. *Used by permission of Paul Taylor.*

Rudolph Nureyev (1938–1993).

*Billy Rose Theatre Collection, The New York Public Library for the Performing Arts—
Astor, Lenox and Tilden Foundations.*

Meredith Monk (1942–).
Photograph by Dona Ann McAdams. *Used by permission of Dona Ann McAdams.*

Bill T. Jones (1952–).
Photograph by Michael O'Neill. *Used by permission.*

Part Two *THE WORKBOOK*

———————————————————————————————

6 *Introduction and Outline*

The following chapters present a sequence of exercises that allows the logic of the work to emerge. It can lead dancers over a period of time from simpler to more complex structures and, most important, to a deeper involvement of self in the act of dance. The sequence begins with a few assignments that can provide the backbone for the work of a group or class. The order in which the exercises are described is but a suggestion for how they might best be experienced or taught. For anyone who is focused on a particular problem of performance, there is no reason not to leap forward and work out of the sequence.

An intensive exploration of all the exercises in this book could take a considerable amount of time. About eighty are described, half of which are emphasized as more critical than the others. If an actor with little or no movement training were to ask a dance teacher how much time she.he would need to acquire a movement facility that would fully augment her.his craft as an actor, the answer would probably be about two years and a minimum of one year. How much time should a group of dancers new to this way of working expend in order to acquire this acting technique for dance performance? How much time do you have?

Actually, working actors should try to keep dancing throughout their careers, and working dancers should be digging continually into the problems and craft of performance. In the academic world of dance, at least a year would be appropriate and half a year would be barely enough. Outside the ivy campuses, you're on your own. Recognizing that there is never enough time, try at first to accept the suggestions about what is crucial to an understanding of the process, and as you continue getting the feel of the task at hand, begin to be more selective according to your needs and taste.

Many of these exercises were first described in *Dance and the Specific Image;* they have been adapted for use in this book. In the text of the exercise, the indented sections are written in the voice of a teacher addressing a group of students.

Outline

In this outline of the sequence presented in chapters 7 through 13, an asterisk indicates a "miscellaneous" exercise and a superscript dagger indicates an exercise that can be done by a single dancer.

Chapter 7: First Assignments

The Two Dances
What Quickened You?†
Read a Book†
A Reading List†
Keep a Journal†
Your First Performance Instructions†

Chapter 8: Level 1

Gifts
Medicine Ball
Outrageous Travel
Goldfish Bowl
Blind Journey†
*Solo Dancer
*Solo Singer
*The Obstacle†
*Passing Through a Physical Object†
*Slalom†
*The Conductor
*The Schizoid Little Fishes of the
    Bering Sea
*Leave Yourself Outside†
*Ambient Sound†

Chapter 9: Level 2

Justification†
The Rhythm Series†
    Breath Rhythm†
    Pulse Rhythm†
    Inner Rhythm†
Go Visiting
True Repetition†
Evolving Repetition†
Dedicate Your Motion†
Spinning†
The Mind-Wash†
Not Naming†
The Other
A Duet
Who or What Is Alive in the Music?†
The Inner Rhythm of the Role†
Seeing Through the Eyes of Another†
*Walk Behind Another†
*Take a Walk in Your Own World
*Your Familiar†
*Possessed by a Mannerism†
*An Event, a Recurrence, a Ritual†
*How Does Your Tree Dance?†

Chapter 10: Level 3

Circles†
Each Alone
Hot to Cold to Hot I†
Hot to Cold to Hot II†
Backdoor†
The Hub Meditation†
Visualization†
Gesture Permutations†
Gesture Rondo†
The Duet as a Structure
Emotion Memory†
*From Now†
*Rhythm Portrait†

Chapter 11: Level 4

*Before, After and On†
*Why Do You Dance?†
*What Happened?†
*The Spine of Style†
*Making Faces

Chapter 12: Level 5

Faces†
I Dare You†
Inside the Outside†
*Lose Your Head†
*Go 1-2-3
*Recognition Ritual

Chapter 13: Level 6

Make a Phrase
Rituals of Power
Props Fantasy†
Processional†
Ping Pong
Adam and Eve
The Minnesota Duet
Prison†
*Focusing
*Ariadne's Dance†
*Whatever Happens, Happens†
*Tandem Solo
*Relay Solo
*Performing in Unison
*Ham and Clove
*Signs of the Time†
*Become a Public Figure†

7 *First Assignments*

The Two Dances

For any teacher or group planning to work through the logic of this book, this first assignment, pursued in depth, will touch upon every one of the principles and techniques of acting technique for dance performance.

Every student or member of the group should prepare two different dance pieces that he.she has previously performed. Each should be at least two minutes and less than ten minutes in length: one was performed in a manner that felt right for the dancer, the other never felt right in performance. It matters not whether either was successfully received. Neither dance need be a solo, nor need it have been choreographed by the dancer. Both should be well rehearsed, technically under control and danced to the appropriate music. If the original was danced in silence, then the inherent musicality of its performance should be present. At least one of the dances must have been choreographed with music and be performed to that score.

Allow whatever time is necessary to prepare the two dances. In the interim, work can be commenced on the exercises given below. When the dancers are ready to perform their two works, the group can give a portion of each meeting to viewing and critiquing two or three showings. Whoever dances chooses either the role that felt right or the one that didn't, never indicating which one is being danced that day. Before dancing, limited information should be given by the dancer to the group: the title, the music, the choreographer, a rough indication of the costume and the lights. Never, at any time, should the dancer verbally elucidate what the dance is about or what it purports to mean. After the information is given, the dancer asks all present to shut their eyes, indicating that they are to be opened when the music starts or by saying "curtain" or "lights." Similarly, the conclusion is indicated by saying, "end," "curtain" or "lights out." The showing done, the dancer places him.herself before the group for criticism, which proceeds in this fashion:

1. The viewers tell the dancer what it is that they saw and felt; what they felt the dancer was trying to be and convey. At no time should any attention be paid to the choreography. What is at stake is performance, not choreography.

2. They point out where they were drawn into the life of the dance and where they seemed to be looking at it from a distance.

3. They make note regarding the quality and continuity of the dance life of the performance and call attention to any point at which this dance life was torn.

4. They observe and comment on how well the dancer related to the music.

These comments have great value if they are specific, but tend to be unhelpful when they are generalized. All the viewers should ask themselves, "If I were the director what would I tell this dancer to make her.his work even better?"

Finally, the teacher or group leader gives his.her critique. Then the dancer is asked to do the dance again, bearing in mind the critique and directions he.she has just heard. The group then considers the difference between the first performance and the performance that followed the discussion. As the group becomes more sophisticated about the elements that enter into a performing life, the teacher/leader can ask one of the viewers, "Would you like to give the dancer some direction?"

At this juncture, I will state my predilection. When I worked as a dancer or as an actor I would always move out of earshot when the director began to give my partner a direction. I did not want to know what the director was expecting, because when we danced the sequence again, instead of dealing with what my partner was doing, part of my mind would be focused on how she.he was carrying out the direction. Thus, when I want to help a student's work by adding a new direction, I usually draw the student aside and we speak privately. The class does not know what to expect and must deal only with what they see. After the dancer performs, I ask them, "Did you see a difference? What was the difference? Did it make it a better, more truthful performance?" Only after this discussion is the content of my direction revealed. A weird note which I find difficult to explain: if a student has taken the direction so well that the performance is astonishingly different and better, and I ask her.him to tell the group what the direction was, she.he is often inarticulate and can barely recall what it was I said!

The dancer can at any time volunteer to perform either of the two dances from a new perspective. At a later date, the dancers should return to one or both of the two dances to do a syntactical analysis that would consciously use all of the six questions.

What Quickened You?[†]	If you are really going to work on the material given in this book, on the earliest weekend make it a point to observe, observe and observe until something you see quickens you, makes a change in you, makes you breathe a bit faster. Then really observe and remember, and at the first opportunity *become* what you observed. This can be anything: another human, an animal, a "thing." Be able to come into class or the studio and become what quickened you, imitating not only its outside but its "insides." The challenge will be to do this without any comment, without glorifying it or satirizing it.
Read a Book[†]	Dance is a profession that yields best to an early start plus consistent, continuous and intensive training. This doesn't leave much time for "reading a book." (However, as I glance through the program notes of major dance companies today—mostly modern ones—the biographies of many brilliant dancers do mention a college degree, even a master's degree.) To the generation of young dancers now entering the field who are nurtured by television, books are in danger of becoming exotic antiques. I recently concluded ten years of teaching in a major university where I encountered an alarming amount of cultural illiteracy. At the same time, I recall all through my tours, both in the commercial theatre and in the concert field, observing dancers digging out the precious books deep in their practice bags to be read in the first quiet moment after takeoff.

A dancer is an artist, or should be. A dance artist in our world will be little more than an attractive physical machine, unless he.she knows who Voltaire was, has decided whether or not to read any more of Rainer Maria Rilke, knows whether the Sung Dynasty preceded or followed the Tang Dynasty and is aware of what it is that we owe to the ancient Greeks who shaped us, helped create the world we live in and pointed to the life we have failed to live. To survive as an artist you have to "read a book."

A Reading List[†]	While we are on the subject of reading there are two books that cut right to the heart of our concern: Constantin Stanislavski's *My Life in Art* and the essay "The Duende: Theory and Divertissement," by Federico Garcia Lorca. Personally, I think every artist, in any field, should read the Lorca once a month in the first year that they encounter it and then at least once every year for the rest of their productive lives. It is the ultimate challenge for all artists. ("The Duende" is reprinted in the appendix.)

The list that follows covers many different points of view. Even those written for actors will charge the mind of a dancer on this matter of performance.

Artaud, Antonin, *The Theatre and Its Double*

Boleslavsky, Richard, *Acting: The First Six Lessons*

Brook, Peter, *The Empty Space*

Bowers, Faubion, *Theatre in the East*

Carnovsky, Morris, *The Actor's Eye*

Chaikin, Joseph, *The Presence of the Actor*

Chekhov, Michael, *To the Actor*

Cole, Toby, *Actors on Acting*

Craig, Gordon, *On the Theatre Advancing*

Grotowski, Jerzy, *Towards a Poor Theatre*

Guthrie, Tyrone, *Tyrone Guthrie on Acting*

Hagen, Uta, *Respect for Acting*

Kirkland, Gelsey, and Lawrence, Greg, *Dancing on My Grave; The Shape of Love*

Le Gallienne, Eva, *Eleanor Duse*

Lewis, Robert, *Method or Madness*

Meisner, Sanford, *On Acting*

Moore, Sonia, *The Stanislavski Method*

Olivier, Lawrence, *On Acting*

Passolli, Robert, *A Book on the Open Theatre*

Redgrave, Michael, *The Actor's Ways and Means*

Spolin, Viola, *Improvisation for the Theatre*

Stanislavski, Constantin, *An Actor Prepares; Building a Character; Creating a Role*

Keep a Journal[†]   Here's a story I first told in *How to Dance Forever* (pp. 213–14). In the early 1970s, I spent a summer in Vermont at Johnson State College with the Workgroup, the improvisation dance company I was directing at the time. Early on, I gave a solo concert. A young man, a recently graduated architect who did not seem to have any work, became a fan and spent much time hanging around our group. Wherever he went, he had one of those black notebooks favored by artists for sketching, only I discovered he wasn't sketching. He was taking down what I was saying! Never having bowed to a master, whenever I realize someone is shoving a pedestal under my feet, I kick it away. I snorted at him, "Man, you want a guru? You got a guru. You. You're the only real guru you're ever going to get." Because I have a resistance to anyone listening with a non-critical mind even though they're listening to me, I found myself constantly mocking him. Gently of course, for he wasn't a fool by any means—and I was flattered, in spite of myself. He attached himself to me again the next summer, carefully noting down my words in his black sketchbook.

A few years later, needing a vacation badly, having little money for it and loving that area, I rang Jon, the architect, to ask whether he knew of an inexpensive place for rent. Unbelievably, he offered his home, saying that he could spend the week happily with friends. I accepted gratefully. The place was wonderful: an apartment over a four-car garage on an elegant estate with a little pond for swimming. It was spacious, comfortably furnished and stuffed with art books and records. But to this day, what I remember most are two towers of black sketchbooks. Each stood three feet high on one side of his desk. They were all identical with the one he had lugged about those two summers.

I found myself shifting from my mocking memory of his note-taking to a secret envy. I thought of those thousands of thoughts, mine and others, which I had jotted down on thousands of scraps of paper. Where were they? Terrible to relate, I have them somewhere, since I throw nothing away. They're never available, except by accident or an episodic housecleaning. Too bad. There have been times when I was going through some creative turmoil that was clarified by the good luck of finding and rereading notes of the previous year. Here this man had his entire intellectual and artistic history; questions, quotes and musings within reach. I admired what I saw and wished I had done likewise.

A journal is a good thing for an artist. A day doesn't pass that doesn't contain something worth noting: an event, a passing thought, a teacher's trenchant remark or an astonishing newspaper clipping. These things are gold and should not be lost.

> Find a sturdy notebook that transports easily in your practice bag. Use it to catch and preserve observations, incidents, strong stuff from teachers and especially your own thoughts, ideas and questions.

Your First Performance Instructions[†]

> Recall and write the instructions you received for your first performance. Take any dance phrase or dance and perform it, to the full, exactly as you were instructed at that first performance.

8 Exercises

Level 1

Gifts

The first necessity in any session is to ensure the safety and freedom of the dancers' bodies. The easiest way out is to say, "Take ten or fifteen minutes to warm up." A terrible idea: the time is too short, too few dancers know how to do this well and too many will fill the time with chatting. Another way is to conduct a quick warmup: walking, then faster and faster, breaking into a run, slowing down to easy stretches, slow big body moves, extended arm motions, pliés, shallow and deep, and so on. Strategically conducted, this works. I found another way, Gifts:

> Pick a partner and face each other. The exercise is called Gifts. One will lead and the other will follow as in a mirror game. The leader has but one mission in mind: to get the other warmed up and on the way to dancing. That is the "gift," to free the body of the other. The challenge is to fully take in who the follower is. "What does she.he need to get started? What is unique to this person, this body before me? Is there a nervousness? Would a bit of silliness be the right beginning? Would a formal, symmetrical opening center this person best? Is there a fragility or vulnerability that should make me cautious about what I give her.him? Are the shoulders lifted in a tense manner? Perhaps some easy shoulder rolls, lifts and drops would ease and lengthen his.her neck?"

> Take your time to sense the specific needs of the person before you. Don't do what you think all dancers need—only what *this* dancer needs. You literally are trying to think yourself into his.her body. Can you really do this? Never for certain, but you can guess on the basis of what you are seeing and sensing. All of us, whether we are self-aware or not, are constantly sending signals out to the world about ourselves. If you want to know about the other, the information is there right in front of you, and if you really have to know, you will develop the skill, for it is just that—a skill open to those who yearn for it.

133

When the leader has done a modest chunk of warmup work, she.he cues the other to take over the role of leader, and so Gifts proceeds, the roles changing from one to the other. It is vital that one of you does not dominate by hogging the role of leader.

There are two negatives that should be respected. If any of you, in the role of follower is given a motion or sequence that you sense is beyond your capacity, that in fact might be dangerous for you, *do not do it,* and signal your reluctance to execute the move. The leader must respect this and go on to something else. The second negative says that the leader cannot do any move that loses eye contact with the follower for more than a moment. Any prolonged motions of turning away or bending far down or far back are oxymorons—a total contradiction to the whole point of Gifts. If the leader cannot see the follower, neither can the follower see the leader to follow. Facing the follower can be just as disconcerting if the leader continuously casts his.her gaze to the ground, elsewhere or subtly, internally. Losing eye contact loses contact and the information needed to know what is happening with the other—the sacred other person. The leader's paramount responsibility is to be constantly aware of every change, even the facial expression of the follower, to know how to proceed.

The rules of a good and a safe warmup are well known but worth repeating now:

Early stretches are wakeup stretches and not for limberness.

Go from slow to fast.

Go from simple to complex.

Feet, legs, pelvis, torso, neck, arms, hands all need attention.

Grandes pliés, deep knee bends—whatever, should be controlled, slow, limited in number and not introduced too early.

Introduce elevation late in the sequence.

Introduce little jumps before big ones.

Cool down should be followed by stretches for limberness.

Decide who will be the leader and start when you hear music. Use the music as you use the space you have for working. Find your freedom within your respect for the configuration of the space and for the contours of the music. Be sure to continue if there are breaks in the music or if you hear me call out suggestions. If the leader chooses to cover space, travel abreast, not "follow the leader," thus keeping eye contact alive all the time.

Go!

I find it necessary to monitor this exercise closely. Every group has its own predilections, strengths and weaknesses. Sometimes I note a plethora of waving arms and have to call out, "Consider some big body motions." Or I suggest, "Think of getting to demi-pliés." I sense when they are ready to move ahead and call out, "If you haven't done big leg motions, now's the time," or "Time for little jumps," or "Time to travel, to cover space," and then "Whenever you are ready, cool down and stretch." (I never speak out when dancers are improvising unless the structure requires calling out the time for the next stage. The less aware the dancers are of the teacher while moving, the better.) All through Gifts, I stay *en garde* for injudicious choices such as violent jouncing of hams on heels, ballistic leg swings, jumps too early in the warmup, and so on, and will immediately enter the work space to talk quietly to the dancers concerned. If it is apparent that one of the leaders is losing focus on her.his partner, it will help to move close enough to give the quiet suggestion that eye contact should be maintained. Sometimes, I end it by saying:

> Whenever you are ready, cool down, stretch down and then take a moment to discuss with your partner what happened. What worked for you? Where did your partner really locate your need? Where was a need ignored?

When time is tight, I say:

> When you are both warmed up, ready to dance, let go of the leader-follower relationship and keep moving easily to the music on your own motivation as you both turn to face front. We are ready to move on when all are facing front.

I find that Gifts is easily the best initial exercise for either a group totally innocent of improvisation or a company that has been doing it for years. First, it is rare at the beginning of a session that all the dancers are safely warmed up and ready to dance. It does need dancey music, such as Renaissance dances, Bach's *Well Tempered Clavier* (book 1), Brazilian carnival music, Flamenco singers with guitar, Louis Armstrong; choose your own, sensing who and where your dancers are. The wonder of *Gifts* is that it is perhaps the fastest and the safest warmup I've ever encountered. I've been initiating workshops in this manner since 1974 and have never witnessed a serious injury.

A more subtle value is implemented because in this very first exercise, the central focus is *the other,* the sacred other person. Reaching into the needs of the body before them, each dancer who is leading is learning to pay attention to the other and possibly to forget the self. It is an ideal introduction to what may become not only a new way of performing but a liberating one.

This is a good place to mention an apparently minor point that is not minor. All students participating in improvisation should wear knee pads. In my classes, those without knee pads may watch but not dance. Without such protection, students may unconsciously avoid a whole range of excitements and virtuosities.

Medicine Ball	Make circles of six to eight. In days long before the frisbee, it was the custom on beaches everywhere to stand in a circle like this and pass around a large, leather ball made heavy with stuffed rags. The game would start easily and slowly and, as it speeded up, part of the fun was to throw the ball in unexpected directions.

We are going to "throw" sound-motions. One person starts by "throwing" a short, impulsive sound and motion in the direction of any one in the circle. This direction must be unequivocally clear to the intended receiver. The receiver, without pause to reflect or evaluate, immediately repeats what was "thrown" back to the sender and then, without any hesitation or pause, "throws" his.her own impulsive sound and motion to another in the circle. That person repeats the ritual of reflecting what was given to the giver and sending immediately out a personal sound motion to a new person. In the act of reflecting, the goal is to truly mirror the sender, not diminishing what was given or augmenting it in volume or gesture. Never move closer to the receiver than half the distance between you. If you were correctly mirrored, you would be knocked down. This receiving and giving continues until you hear, "OK, Let it wind down."

You should perform the two acts of reflecting and sending as one without any pause to reflect, to be "creative" or to reconsider any gesture or sound. The faster the exchanges go the better. Start slowly to get the flow and sequence of the actions, and as you get more certain, build speed until you are all going as fast as you can. One person in each circle volunteer to start. Wait for the "Go!"

Medicine Ball is much more difficult to do well than it must appear in these pages. Initially, few find the flow easily. The ritual of returning to one and then giving to another without pause is very confusing and even unsettling to some. The ideal is an uncritical and immediate acceptance of what was given and an impulsive, unplanned and uncontrolled release of a sound-motion, both rendered as a seamless whole. It is necessary for the director or teacher to catch the cautious evasions as they crop up and also to pick out mannered and controlled sound-motions. Few are aware of the lack of spontaneity or the hesitations, even hairline hesitations, that slip in between receiving and reflecting or between reflecting and sending. I have to demonstrate what they do for them to recognize the flaws. I also call out cues to speed up. If there is a large number of dancers and they really get into it, the din will be such that it will be a trick to be heard.

Outrageous Travel	Form yourselves into parallel lines of six to eight, one in front of the other at one end of the studio and facing the opposite end. The first person (First Person) in line crosses the space doing the most outrageous sound-motion travel possible. The others in that line observe First Person. Then the next person in line crosses the space, "becoming" the First Person. This means not only duplicating what was

visible—the appearance and motions of First Person—but finding the impulse behind the motions and the sounds. Then, one at a time, everyone in that line does the same. If what was originally done appears to be beyond your technical ability or strength to the degree that it might be physically dangerous for you, don't even try. Otherwise, throw yourself into it. Above all, do not attempt to be more outrageous, sillier or funnier than First Person; just slip into her.his skin and become her.him.

First Person observes all, seeking the one who comes closest to what was originally done. When the last person has crossed the space, First Person awards an accolade to the best one. The accolade is a gentle double tap on the top of the head, and this person becomes the new First Person, who now performs the most outrageous possible sound-motion travel with the others one by one attempting to "become" what they observe. If no one has come really close to what was done, First Person puts hands on hips and says, "Tough," gives no one the accolade and makes, in the opposite direction, a new outrageous sound-motion travel for the others to study and slip into.

The game continues for as long as the director chooses. In setting up Outrageous Travel, I start with one line doing it and the others observing. Wanting full energy from the dancers, I pick a First Person who from previous observation appears to be lively and uninhibited.

Sound-motion exercises are used by many directors and teachers to get actors to explore movement. Most actors not only have a skill and freedom vocally—they like to sound off. Moving about terrifies and confuses many of them. Coupling motion with sound peels away their inhibitions. The effect on dancers is a mirror image of what happens with the actors. For them, injecting sound into motion is disorderly, and by that token it suddenly becomes possible to indulge in messy, even wild motions—nothing like the neat, controlled actions which are the spine of their training and their ideal. Sound-motion for dancers is like being on a holiday, or being a bit bad. They break down the narrow inhibiting walls of what is permissible. It is not wrong for a dancer to pour out neat, controlled actions in an improvisation, just so long as the moment cries out for neat, controlled motions. To really improvise, the dancer stands ready to do anything in any style.

Goldfish Bowl

When I first began to explore improvisation, I felt the need to deal with the mountain of excess baggage dancers always seemed to bring into the studio. They came loaded with their self-defenses, their vanities, their expectations, their desire to please, their hostilities and what not, and still do. I needed something to help them shed the clutter of what they dragged in and to bring them quickly into flesh contact with the moment at hand. I wanted what was present to be paramount in their minds. I hit upon the following sequence:

> Sit in circles of six to eight. Close your eyes and clean out your head with your breath. In a while, I will say, "OK, go," and you will open your eyes, rise and whenever you are ready, walk to the center of your circle. The moment your body comes in contact with another body, close your eyes and you will become a goldfish in a very small bowl. You love to slither and slide among your fellows and, above all, you like finding yourself in the middle of all the others; but, because you are gentle by nature, you would never force your way in. You only hope and wait for the opportunity to slip-slide into the center of all the others. Slithering and sliding is easier with the arms extended over head but that can get tiring.

Blind Journey[†]

After Goldfish Bowl has progressed for a while, I will say:

> Go on a Blind Journey of curiosity. Leaving your goldfish bowl, pause, taking a moment to decide what it is in this space among the people and the objects that you would never really experience with your eyes open. When you know what that is, embark on this Blind Journey of curiosity. Of course, move cautiously. A swift or violent move could injure you or another. After a while, I will say, "Return to your goldfish bowl." With your eyes still closed, you will attempt to locate the others with whom you shared a small space and resume what you love to do, slithering and sliding deep in the midst of the others. Is it important that you return to your original bowl? You decide that.
>
> After a time at this, you will hear me say, "Go find a private place." When you get there, sit, and with your eyes still closed, let your mind rove over what you just experienced.

At this juncture, most groups will be in a wide-open state and receptive to the next step, The Rhythm Series (chapter 9, level 2).

The reader has probably noticed that the dancers are being asked to keep their eyes closed throughout this sequence. Most dancers find it strangely liberating; a few have difficulty with it. Those who wear contact lenses may experience a burning of the eyes. I tell them that they should open and shut their eyes a couple of times whenever there is an irritation. Some others just don't like dancing blind. I don't probe into their why. I tell them to open their eyes whenever they want, for as long as they want. I also tell them that when the eyes are open, the enormous flood of information and sensations coming through their eyes are distractions and dilutions of the work at hand.

With our eyes open, we are *en garde*, more deliberate and more aware of how we appear to other people, even if *their* eyes are closed. Ridiculous, but if we can't see, we tend to lose consciousness of being seen. Eyes open tends to be inhibiting. Eyes closed, we enter a space where the odd, the unexpected and the hidden that live inside us have the courage to venture forth. Most of us become less self-conscious and freer—creatively. A wider range of possibilities and images becomes accessible. "Eyes closed" and "working blind" will be used often throughout.

Moving about with eyes closed intensifies all the neglected senses and kicks off a sense of danger and adventure. The usual protective self-focus is diluted by the sheer necessity of finding others and touching the environment. Bodies bumping, as in Goldfish Bowl, set up an intimacy and sense of community with the other dancers without the watchful mentality that haunts most human relations. Usually, the first time a group does Goldfish Bowl, at least one person will introduce an aggressive or rough energy that confuses and disturbs the others. Almost always, when the dancers return to the Goldfish Bowl, they are gentler and more sensitive to each other, having learned tentativeness in the Blind Journey. I'm sure there are occasional faint erotic flurries which are, in the context of the exercise, just that and nothing more—just part of the tapestry of life. The Blind Journey raises the awareness of every motion and passage through space to heightened level. Taking nothing for granted is not only a ground rule for a Blind Journey but for art. Not seeing, all the sensitivities are honed.

*Solo Dancer   Arrange all the dancers (any number is fine) in a circle. The first few times around pick a dancer who improvises freely and with variety. (Later, you might choose a dancer for whom this would be a challenge; or ask for a volunteer.) Instruct him.her to let it fly when you give the "Go!" Impulses can come from within, from what the other dancers are doing or from the impulse to affect what the circle is doing. Stop whenever you feel the improvisation has had its full measure. To the circle:

> Whatever the dancer is doing will provoke sounds from you—any sounds—singing, shouting, clapping, stamping, anything but words. All your sounds will live off the dancer: about, to, for or against him.her, supporting, teasing, frustrating or at times harmonizing with him.her.

*Solo Singer   This is the mirror image of Solo Dancer. Pick anyone you know to have vocal freedom and audacity. Instruct him.her to let go with a river of sound when you give the "Go!" Impulses can come from within, from the motions of the dancers or from the impulse to affect what the circle is doing. Stop whenever. To the circle:

> Whatever the singer is doing will provoke motion from you. All your moves will live off the singer: about, to, for or against her.him, supporting, teasing, frustrating or even at times harmonizing with her.him.

*The Obstacle[†]

Put a folding chair into the middle of the space. Pick a dancer for whom appearance and charm are the *ne plus ultra* of dance, and of life. Tell him.her that you would like very much to see whether he.she can pass under the chair—without moving it. Or devise any task that will be so demanding that the dancer will for once think only of *doing* without appearing to be doing.

*Passing Through a Physical Object[†]

This works best for a group of six to fifteen people.

> Form a big circle. When I tap any one of you on the shoulder, go to the center of the circle and on the impulse of the moment take any position—standing, sitting or lying down. The next person in the circle does the same, only some part of her.his body must touch the first person's body. Person after person, going around the circle, adds his.her body to the structure of bodies until one person is left. This one positions her.himself at the point where the diameter of the group is the greatest and must now walk, wend, crawl, wriggle her.his way through—never around—the group *without disturbing or forcing anyone to change her.his position.* Coming out on the other side, she.he taps a dancer who rises, permitting the first person to take his.her place, and now this second person takes on the same task of passing through the widest part of the conglomerate of bodies without disturbing or changing anyone's position. If any of you is tapped and has already made the "journey," convey that fact by not responding, which tells the person to try another.
>
> After everyone has traversed the structure, I will call out: "Find a private area for yourself." Now alone, do what you did working your way through the others. Do exactly what you did with only the *memory* of the other bodies to guide you. Do it once alone, then find a partner and do it for her.him to critique, and then observe your partner critically, thus both helping each other learn to make the imaginary tangible.

An alternative is for the leader/teacher to assemble the entire group and call out the dancers, one by one, to do the imaginary traversal through the group and then giving or calling for a critique of the sense memory displayed. Many elements went into making this exercise. It opens up the possibility of body contact, without which improvisation is impoverished. It relates to the challenge of The Obstacle, a task that is so demanding that self-preoccupation and self-decorativeness are improbable. It is an ideal sense-memory exercise for dancers because it uses the whole body. The usual actors' exercises, like sewing on a button or putting on a garment, place the strongest emphasis on the hands—which are physically the smartest part of the body. Though sense-memory exercises are a staple of the actor's training and a skill, no dancer can afford to neglect them. It means what it says: having a vivid, sensual memory of actions with a real object and the ability to re-create those actions without the object. In the exercise, or in performance, the real object is imagined—remembered, sensed—whatever, just so long as the motion of the performer is determined by truth of the remembering. It is the essence of the theatre—pretending what is not *is*.

*Slalom[†]

This is a more athletic version of Passing Through a Physical Object and is exactly what it sounds like:

> Everyone picks an observer-partner. All the observers stand aside to observe. The others, one by one, form a single line, all spaced one to two yards apart. This line can be arrow straight or chaotically crooked, it matters not. When the last person is in place, I will shout "Go!," and this last person will run full tilt, slalom style, to the other end of the line, letting out a shout upon arriving. This is the signal for the next person to do the same. When the last person has performed the run, all gather around the point where the line started. One by one, run from where you started, duplicating the slalom run as if all those dancers were still standing there. When the running group has done this, find your observer-partner and learn how vividly and accurately you repeated your run. The critique concluded, the second group repeats the ritual. Finally, repeat the entire sequence a second time, the running and the critiques.

As Picasso was so found of iterating, "Art is a lie." There is so little onstage that is real, that without a rich and continuous infusion of imagination, the whole edifice of credibility collapses. Passing Through a Physical Object and Slalom, two highly physical sense-memory exercises, are essentially exercises in imagination. The muscles of imagination always need exercising.

*The Conductor

Form groups of three deciding which of you is A, which is B and C. On my "Go!", A becomes the conductor and starts an impulse rhythmic action, in place or travelling. The action of B and C is to live off whatever A is doing. Your impulses in moving are for, against or to A. Doing the same motion as the conductor is only one of ten thousand possibilities. You never lose sight of the conductor. The conductor never loses sight of the orchestra.

After a time, I will call out, "Change!" and B becomes the conductor with A and C the orchestra; a bit later, I will call out "Change!" and C will become the conductor. Finally, you will hear, "All!" and then all dance for, to and about the other two. There will come a moment when you will all know you have done it and you will bring it to a close.

This was originally an exercise of the Open Theatre and I suspect that the name, The Conductor, is not really helpful because it implies following, harmonizing, and even copying the actions and dynamic of the conductor. I prefer that the options be wider, also allowing for competitiveness, mockery, and even hostility—as long as it is about what the conductor is doing and what the dancer is feeling at that moment. Call it The Spark Plug?

At the American Dance Festival, during a class in Acting Technique for Dance Performance, on an impulse, sometime after I had called out "All," I shouted, "All! All in the entire room!" The room swelled with energy and interactions that went on for at least an hour or more. Groups of three, four, five, and solo figures, filled the space, oblivious to time and my presence. Was it the moment or was it something that is inherent in The Conductor? Try it.

*The Schizoid Little Fishes of the Bering Sea

If the leader/teacher wants to diminish the degree of his.her control over the group, this version of Goldfish Bowl would help. It incorporates Blind Journey and the return to the bowl without direction. To a group that is seated, eyes closed, waiting for the description of a new exercise:

> When I say, "Go!", rise to your feet, your eyes still closed, and become a little blind, schizoid fish in the Bering Sea. You are conflicted because there is nothing you like so much as to be swimming deep within the pack of your fellow fishes. It fulfills a profound instinct that incidentally protects you from the big voracious squid who thinks the pack of you is a giant dangerous fish. You also have a contradictory need to swim about freely and unencumbered by the presence of others, and when you feel crowded or hungry, you venture forth to freedom and food. But, after a while, your tiny presence alone in the wide sea is frightening, and you seek the others to find security and ease. But then, the crowding pressures you to swim out alone and free of the others. Go where your instinct propels you!

The eyes remain closed throughout. The beauty of this setup is that it gives the dancers the freedom to clump with the others or to venture out alone without direction. This too can lead directly into The Rhythm Series (see chapter 9). The leader/ teacher picks the moment to call out, "Find a private place, sit with your eyes closed, and let your mind rove over what just happened. Is there anything that you should remember?" When all are in place, The Rhythm Series (chapter 9) can be introduced.

*Leave Yourself Outside[†]	On the signal, "OK," leave the studio, go outside and find a quiet spot. Clear your mind and resolve to leave yourself outside. When you have done that, return and we will go to work. "OK" (chapter 5).
*Ambient Sound[†]	Sit erect and listen. Take whatever you hear and become that sound; let that sound take over your entire body.

9 *Exercises*

Level 2

Justification[†] Here are three ways of approaching this. One poses a problem for the entire group; the other two are individual assignments. As a group problem: have the group learn a moderately extended technical passage with a couple of physical challenges embedded in it. When the dancers have mastered it, ask them to perform the dance phrase fully with each of the following images in turn:

> You just won a big lottery prize. Celebrate, using the dance phrase you just learned.
>
> You are auditioning for the choreographer you dream of working with.
>
> You are a leaf in a quiet wind.
>
> You are a piece of seaweed on the ocean bottom, torn from your roots.
>
> You are offering all of what you are to one whom you love.
>
> Your body is a steel weapon and you are sharpening it for tomorrow's battle.

The possible list is endless, just as the ways to bring this or any technical phrase to life are endless. Make your own images. As an individual assignment:

> Here is a technical phrase. Find your own reason for doing it that will reveal the full beauty of its particular movements. Be prepared to demonstrate what you have done for the group.

The group and then the leader/teacher critique the performances—and these are to be considered as performances, not merely technical executions. Another individual assignment:

> In your technique classes, whenever you are in complete technical command of any sequence, justify what you are dancing, fill it out with a precise and specific image and intent.

Breath Rhythm[†]

This exercise and the next two—Pulse Rhythm and Inner Rhythm—comprise The Rhythm Series. The three flow directly out of the early work in chapter 8: starting with Goldfish Bowl, going to Blind Journey, back to Goldfish Bowl, to find a private place and the readiness to embark on The Rhythm Series. To lay the ground for fuller energy, start each of The Rhythm Series exercises from a standing position rather than sitting or lying down.

> When you find your private place, remain standing with your eyes still closed. When everyone has found her.his private place, listen to the next sequence:
>
> With your eyes still closed clear out your head with your breath. I am going to ask you to observe something that is delicate and easily altered. Odds are, the act of observing it will change it. Make an effort to observe without changing.
>
> Observe your breath. Note its duration, rhythm, depth, texture, intensity. Note everything about your breath. When you are convinced that you have it, *become* your breath. Let your breath take full possession of your body. Let your body become the metaphor for your breath. Neither think nor imagine what your body will look like as you do this. Only do it. Become your breath. If what you become needs to cover space, open your eyes. Otherwise, all through this work keep your eyes closed.

There is no way to indicate precisely how long any particular exercise should go. My principles are: I give the dancers all the time they need to get into the problem, all the time they need to get fully wet with it and time enough so that something happens. What is "something"? "Something" is a change, no matter how subtle. A change should be enough of a cue to move on. Whenever possible, I respect the timing of the "slowest" person in the group. A few times I am pushed beyond my limit by the rare ones who seem to have dialed eternity. All these principles are shattered by workshops and classes hemmed in by unreal tight schedules. When I sense that the group has "done" Breath Rhythm, I will say,

> "Continue what you are doing. Without losing any part of your rhythm, neither its intensity nor its intent, continuously narrow the range of your movement. Every move will be smaller than the previous movement. A time may come when you will appear to be still—but you will know that you are still moving."

Pulse Rhythm[†]

When the group comes to an apparent halt, I continue:

> Now observe another rhythm in your body. This one is harder to detect. Sometimes when you are very quiet, you can actually become aware of your pulse at the base of your neck, or the tip of your nose, or your fingers. Try to sense that. If it doesn't work, try the usual technique of pressing the finger tips to the artery above

the big bone in your wrist. Study your pulse: its tempo, rhythm, force, texture, intensity, intent. When you think you have it, study it a bit more because unlike Breath Rhythm, once you begin to move, you will not be able to keep observing your pulse. You will have to keep it alive in your memory. As with the Breath Rhythm, become your Pulse Rhythm. Let it take possession of your body. Let your body become a metaphor for your pulse.

When the dancers have "done" Pulse Rhythm, sometimes, rather than suggesting diminishing the range of movements, I will simply say,

Taking all the time you need, let your Pulse Rhythm wind down.

Inner Rhythm†

When there is stillness, I continue:

You contain still another rhythm. Go into the space within you and in that silence, feel, sense, hear what you can. You may find a rhythm. You may sense the rhythm that drives you, that governs your eating, walking, talking, your doing. Your internal motor has similarities with what it was when you were ten and it is in someway different than it was ten minutes ago. Seek out your Inner Rhythm. If you don't find it, do not make one up. You will find a value in listening to the silence. Sometimes, just shifting your position may help you feel it.

When you find the Inner Rhythm, study it. When you feel saturated with what you have found, let it take possession of your body. Let your body become that rhythm. If it is complex, fine. Do it. If it is simple. Fine. Do it. If it isn't interesting. Fine. Do it, without trying to make it "interesting."

But what if it is too much, frightening or dangerous; a rhythm so violent, you might hurt yourself attempting to realize it? Here, you have no choice. You cannot walk away from it. If you can't deal with all of it, deal with a part of it. Do its echo. Do its reverberation. Do what it feels like to observe it from the distance but don't walk away from it. Make nothing up. Only deal with what you find and with what you can.

In the matter of finding the Inner Rhythm, the point is to go beyond the surface. Be suspicious of what comes easily. It may be on the mark, but check it out, test it. Try the following with any group of dancers.

With your eyes closed, raise your arms. On my "Go," let your arms slip into a repetitive rhythmic pattern. "Go." (After a bit.) Continue what you're doing, open your eyes and look at the others. Call it an Impulse Rhythm.

You can get that from yourself or anyone at any time. You can say to a group of children, "Make up a rhythm," and everybody will do something. It is not without value. It has been used to good advantage in The Conductor (chapter 8). An Impulse

Rhythm is easy—too easy to be of use in any venture to touch the core of your concerns. An Inner Rhythm is further down the hallway. It's not the first thing you encounter. You may have to go into the basement, the attic or just get out of the house. It's not on the surface. Look at water. It glints, it reflects and it's lively. Chances are that what you're looking for is underwater. At the bottom? How deep is the bottom? You wont know unless you dive down. Whether it's found in the deep or in the shallow and whether it's found quickly or after a long search, you arrive at a point when you say, "This is it."

I've said that your inner rhythm is not on the surface, but in fact it may be. Our shelves are crowded with what's on the surface in terms of movement, answers, rhythms and solutions. And surprise! Sometimes what's on the surface is precisely what is needed. But unless you go to the bottom, you won't know what's there, and you will not have earned the right to choose what was there floating in front of you on the surface. Whether you are searching for the specific image or the internal rhythm, you will never know for sure what "it" is. All you have to depend upon is the intensity of your search and your sense of rightness.

Dedicate Your Motion[†]

I have used this exercise while the dancers are deep into Inner Rhythm. It jolts the dancers out of the premise that movement is motion is movement and nothing else. It is a deceptively simple ploy. I will call out:

> Dedicate your motion to someone who is not present.

In the summation after the first time I throw out Dedicate Your Motion, I add the following:

> This can be a private exercise to be performed in your own time at your own discretion. Dedicate a whole class to someone who is not there. Or, as deliberately as you can, try to get someone's attention in class. Why? Just so that you might recognize that is what you may have been doing. Perhaps you're doing it all the time. What does it do to the texture and the tone of your body? In rehearsal, you might try to find the "audience" that will bring out the best way for you to do your role. In some of these attempts, you might be quite obnoxious and in others you may discover a most lovely way of dancing. As much as possible, do this exercise in rehearsal or in class. If in rehearsal, the choreographer calls out, "And just what are you doing?" you know you have made an inappropriate dedication. A stage performance could be wrecked unless such a focus had been carefully thought out, chosen and rehearsed.

> You can dedicate your motion at any time: in class, in rehearsal, in performance, in creating a dance. Rather than "someone," it can be "to an animal of which you are in awe," or to a "place of great beauty." Infinite variations are possible.

Go Visiting   After five to ten minutes of Inner Rhythm (the timing is a function of taste, style and a sensitivity to the moment), I say:

> Continue what you are doing as I speak to you. When you hear me say, "OK, go," without losing one bit of your Inner Rhythm, go traveling, Go Visiting, and see what the others are doing. You must not lose one bit of your identity—the rhythm that is carrying you along—as you move among the others observing them. OK, go!

After the dancers seem to have had a good tour of each other, I add:

> Continue what you are doing and now have a question in the forefront of your mind. Who in this group interests you, positively or negatively? Either will do. Enter into the working area of that person and deepen your observation. After awhile, you will become aware of one of several impulses. You may want to be influenced by that person or oppositely want to change him.her in a specific way or just want to be in their area as you do your rhythm. Accept the possibility that the person who interests you may be focused on another. That should not alter your purpose. If and when you succeed in absorbing what you wanted to take away or in altering the other, or had your enjoyment, you can leave the floor. If you fail, (you are left alone), recognize that in movement and then leave the floor.

In all of this work, some people have difficulty finding an inner rhythm and, as a consequence, might feel ashamed because they seem to lack an essential talent or will become defensively hostile to the whole "stupid" idea. Almost always, these unhappy ones come out of the second or third session with shining faces, "I found it!"

Most groups being given Inner Rhythm for the first time approach it with uncertainty, and a few, with apprehension. Of late, when I sense a self-protective tension in the room, I have adopted a devious ploy. Instead of asking them to find their own rhythm, I take a side road:

> Is there someone with whom you are now dealing who rouses conflicting feelings in you? Is there a person who has qualities you admire, while at the same time he.she ticks you off in an unpleasant way. You admire *and* dislike this person. If there is such a one let's call him.her X. Now see X in your mind's eye. Take a good look from the distance. Then come as close as you dare and study X carefully. Walk all around X, observing thoroughly. Now, look deep into X, sense what it going on inside and try to feel the rhythm in his.her body. Can you hear X's inner motor? What is the rhythm that dominates his.her walking, talking, eating?
>
> When you find X's inner rhythm, study it. When you feel saturated with what you have found, let it take possession of your body. Let your body become that rhythm. If it is complex, fine. Do it. If it is simple. Fine. Do it. If it isn't interesting. Fine. Do it, without trying to make it "interesting," without exaggerating and without getting judgmental. Just do the rhythm you found in X.

Amazing. This exercise almost invariably gets quick and strong involvement from all, not infrequently tinged with caricature. The movement pours out freely. There doesn't seem to be any question that another person has a rhythm that dominates his.her every move. Having done this, it becomes a much easier leap to "do yourself."

True Repetition[†]

The complete Rhythm Series is given only once. It has but one aim: to set the stage for Inner Rhythm, an exercise and process that functions as a meditation—a movement meditation, a way of getting into the body, getting it going, cutting loose from the mess of the outside, relaxing the militant control of the mind and, best of all, connecting with where you are at the moment. When Inner Rhythm is incorporated into the improvisation sessions, its form is more precisely defined in either of two forms of repetition, True Repetition and Evolving Repetition.

> Go to the perimeter of the room. There is a place in this space that belongs to you. On the word "Go," roam the room until you find that spot. When you find it, stand on it, clean out your head with your breath and listen for, sense, find your inner rhythm. If and when you find it, let it take possession of your body. Take all the time you need. It may appear bit by bit, like a chick cutting its way out of an eggshell. When you know it is complete, that it is being fully stated by your body, commit yourself to doing that phrase from that point on *and that phrase only* with no changes for a hunk of time—plus or minus ten minutes. Change only if you sense continuing will cause you physical harm or experience a fatigue that is threatening. Otherwise, no changes—at all.

Evolving Repetition[†]

> Start off exactly like True Repetition. When the rhythm finally emerges fully in the body, the intent is to do the rhythm as found. If a change happens, *allow* it to happen. If no change happens, no change is forced on the phrase. It is allowed to continue as it was. Radical or abrupt changes would be suspect because they would not be rooted in the rhythm that was originally found.

True Repetition acts like a movement meditation and draws dancers into an open, receptive and relaxed state. It is ideal for starting work sessions. Evolving Repetition is a more "athletic" and adventurous structure and certainly more interesting to watch. The Workgroup often opened programs with an Evolving Repetition. Whenever the dancers do not need the Gifts because they are warmed up and ready to dance, I have set up a ritual in which, as they enter the studio, they go in their own time into the space, clear their heads, find their own inner rhythm and slip directly into either a True or an Evolving Repetition for at least ten minutes.

Spinning[†]   Another classic and ancient way of clearing the mind for work is Spinning. Members of a sect of Muslim Sufis use whirling as a way of achieving an ecstatic trance. For dancers, it acts like an emotional and intellectual centrifuge, throwing off distractions and leaving a clean center from which to begin the work of improvising. It can be used to precede Inner Rhythm:

> Spin in place, at any tempo, for as long as you can. Pause, and then spin in the opposite direction for as long as you can. Then, in the stillness, find your internal rhythm. Those of you who know the secret of spinning interminably without getting dizzy may be interrupted by my asking you to bring it to a close.

The Mind-Wash[†]   This, and the three exercises that follow, should be introduced singly, but later they work best flowing one into the other. (See The Duet as a Structure in chapter 10).

> Start seated, cross-legged and facing a partner with your knees two or three inches apart. Close your eyes and clean out your head. Whenever you are ready, open your eyes to look at the tip of your nose. Unlike the classic yogis who spent a lifetime doing that only, whenever you've had enough of looking at the tip of your nose, let your gaze drop to high on your chest and gradually allow your eyes to travel down your body, across the floor, across the ankles, across the floor between you and your partner, across your partner's ankles, another bit of floor, and then travel up the body of your partner, across the face, over her.his head, to the wall beyond, the eyes climbing in a path as wide as your eyes, up the wall until they find the ceiling. Then traveling across the ceiling and finally as far back and behind as you can, without falling over backward. Take as much or as little time as you need for this visual journey.

Any number of dancers have told me that The Mind-Wash has served them as a meditation technique. I have used it myself innumerable times when my head was too turbulent to move on to the next step.

Not Naming[†]   You can add a Taoist touch to The Mind-Wash. Not Naming is a lovely challenge which some dancers find quite helpful:

> In the course of the eye-journey, as your gaze travels down and up, devote your mind to seeing *without naming what you see.*

Most find this difficult, but some are able to achieve it intermittently and find it a transporting experience. To make it work, when setting this exercise, instead of saying, "Your eyes go down to your chest, then to the floor, across to your partner's body, . . . " I simply pantomime with the tips of the fingers where the eyes should focus, from the tip of the nose to the upper part of the chest, and so on, thus indicating the eye journey without naming anything.

The Other

When the Mind-Wash is complete, return to look upon the face of your partner, and when your partner meets your gaze begin The Other. Its title defines it. You are looking at this other to see what you can see. This is a rare moment when your bare face is exposed to another whose face is there before you. What is there to see other than eyes, lips, hair, etc.? If you have the patience and the desire, you will begin to see things you never noticed, no matter how long you have known this other. Why do we go into this? Shortly you will be dancing with, to, for and about this other. More knowing of the other allows for more sensitivity.

A Duet

Some of my first explorations into improvisation took place in 1969 at the University of Texas in Austin. During a lull in the second week of the workshop, I asked whether anyone had a form along the lines of the work we were doing. My best dancer spoke up: "Back home in Connecticut, I have a big basement in which my friend and I would practice whenever we could, and one of the things we loved to do best was to put on a piece of music we both liked and then we danced looking at each other. It was as if I was dancing about her and she was dancing about me. I don't mean 'about' as 'around.' I mean that she and what she was doing was the subject of my dance and vice-versa. We could do this all afternoon."

It sounded good—if not sensational. I said, "Fine," and asked her to explain once again to everyone what they were to do. People paired off and I put on my then favorite piece of music for an extended improvisation, Stravinsky's *Sacre du Printemps*. It turned out quite well. Not only did the energy flow right through its entire length, but the actors and the dancers appeared to lose self-consciousness with a full absorption in each other. They were playful, teasing and serious in turn. This was a useful form. It involved everyone, built up a good dance heat, and, best of all, it asked for and seemed to get exactly the frame of mind I was seeking: a loss of focus upon self, replaced by focus on the task at hand and/or the other—the other person.

Everyone pair off. (If there is an odd number, there can be either a trio or one person can drop out to observe.) When the music starts, you dance looking at your partner and dancing about your partner, about his.her motions, hair, clothing, personality traits, eyes—anything that gets your attention. Synchronous movement is only one of an infinite number of choices. Along the way, try to make something happen, either to you or your partner or both. When it happens, leave the floor. If your partner leaves first, dance a recognition of being left and then leave.

To create a flowing sequence, begin with The Mind-Wash, weaving into it the mind-set of Not Naming. When the arc of The Mind-Wash is completed, contemplate your partner, The Other. When you hear music, begin A Duet with your partner. Finish it as before.

Who or What Is Alive in the Music?[†]	The teacher/leader selects a piece of music:
	All sit and listen. When you can see who or what is alive in the music, rise and become what you saw in your mind.
The Inner Rhythm of the Role[†]	Choose a dance role you are working on now. Locate the specific who or what that is at the heart of it. What is its rhythm? What is the internal motor that drives it? When you can link up with it, let it take possession of your body and stay with it until you are physically drenched by that rhythm. Rest for a moment and then dance the role. If your choreographer permits it, try this during a rehearsal.

You might also try this with a dance role that has eluded you in the past. Did any new doors open?

Seeing Through the Eyes of Another[†]	Any number of dancers sit in a circle. Rotate in any direction and at any speed on your bottom. What you are really doing is observing the others in the circle with a view to pinning down who it is that interests you the most, positively or negatively. When you make this decision, learn all you can about this person while you continue the circling. During all this observation, you never let anyone catch your eye, particularly the one upon whom your full attention finally settles. Your observation remains covert. When you think you have absorbed all you can from this person, stop the rotation at any point, close your eyes and continue to observe and absorb what you see of that person—in your mind. When all stop, I will give the next direction.
	(All have stopped rotating.) When I say, "Go," open your eyes, rise and find another place to sit in the circle, but not in the place of the person in your mind. (They do so.) Now, close your eyes to mentally recapture that person. When you do, open your eyes and look out at everyone *through the eyes of that person*. Again, begin the rotation on your bottom and, through the eyes of that person, observe all the others with a view to pinning down who is the person who that person would find the most interesting, positively or negatively. When the person is found, observe her.him closely and covertly. Repeat the rest of the sequence: ceasing to rotate when the person is absorbed, closing the eyes to continue the study of that person, rising when you hear "Go" to find a new place in the circle, sitting, closing the eyes to recapture the person and then opening the eyes to look through the eyes of this person.

A brief summary of the above: (1) Find and observe the one who takes your interest. (2) Go to another place and look at rest of room as she.he would do. (3) Pick out someone else as she.he would do and take that person's place.

When does one call a halt to this process? Two or three times should be sufficient to underline the creative possibilities gained by "seeing through the eyes of another." Hidden within this simple and subtle little game is the possibility of a giant moral-ethical leap, but that is something for the reader to pursue in his.her own time—not here in this book. (Note: An individual can perform this exercise in any assemblage of people where a close scrutiny can be carried on unobtrusively—a subway car, a restaurant, a dance class, and so on.)

*Walk Behind Another[†]

Walk behind another, fall in step and become that one, accepting into your body the length of stride, the carriage of the head, any idiosyncratic, asymmetrical motions, the hip motions and the energy. Do this without caricature or comment and you will have the strangest sensation. You will no longer be feeling quite like yourself. This is a form of physical observation which will make you more aware of the infinite range of differences among humans.

Incidentally, there is a hazard in this. The followed may become aware of what you are doing and resent it. If you keep your distance, the danger will be diminished.

*Take a Walk in Your Own World

This is a safer but more complex way to fall into the walk of another. It is ideal for those times when a very large group shows up at a brief or one-time workshop.

All sit and listen with your eyes closed. When you hear music, that will be the "Go." You will rise and go for a walk in your own world—whatever that phrase means to you. That is stage one.

Stage two: When you hear me call out "stage two," look out from the walking in your own world to the others walking in their own world, observing as many as you can. But be certain that you lose nothing of the quality and the action of your walk in your own world.

"Stage three!" will be the signal to pick, among all the walkers you have observed, the one who interests you the most for any reason, positive or negative. When you have decided, carry your walk close to that person (but not in front), all the while observing very closely. There is only one restriction: you cannot pick anyone who picks you. One of you will have to give way and find someone else.

"Stage four" will be the cue to "become" the walker you have been observing. This will be tricky. That person's walk and motions will change at the same time because she.he is doing what you are doing, becoming another person. So your task will be to remain close to the one who interests you, imitating what she.he *was* doing, not what *is* being done. You will have to remember what you saw. By "becoming," I mean you take on for yourself, not only what you saw the person doing but what you sense is the impulse that shaped her.his motions.

"Stage five." Do what you see that person is doing *now*. This is easier and will lead to small or large circles of people doing similar motions. If a pair is facing each other and doing the same motion, they broke the ground rule by picking each other. If there is a "follow the leader" line with one at the head imitating no one, that one broke a rule by not picking an "interesting" person.

"Stage six." Still observing your "interesting" person, do what it feels like to be that person. This is not an imitation; this is not what it *looks* like to be that person but what it *feels* like to be that person.

"Stage seven." Gradually and slowly modulate your motions until you are back walking in your own world.

This exercise is best done to a piece of music, at least twenty minutes in length, that has a driving rhythmic pulse, a continuous flow and without strong dynamic changes. Consider the minimalist composers Terry Riley, Steve Reich and Philip Glass.

*Your Familiar[†]

Since it is the whole person of the dancer that will be out there under the lights in front of all those people, some degree of self-awareness sooner or later, and better sooner, becomes an integral part of the performer's preparation. The next three exercises raise to the surface—to consciousness—what should be known.

If working alone, choose several tracks of your favorite moving music. If working with a group, find something infectious enough to move almost everyone. During the first selection, have a good time, get loose and easy. Launched into the second piece, be on the watch for a position that is all too familiar, and freeze. What is the feeling of that position? What does it want to do or become? Stay with that position for a long time, until it is impossible not to move, and then—go. The movement that follows should take its impetus from what is felt and implied by that same "familiar." When that plays itself out, return to the "familiar" and again hold the position for as long as you can, allowing all of its implications and all the feelings it provokes fill you until you must move once again. Keep this up until the music runs out or you run out of energy or, better still, until you have wrung that "familiar" dry. That will be the time to leave the floor. In the rest time that follows, let your mind run over what happened and what it means to you.

A variation of Your Familiar starts the same way: you halt at encountering a "familiar" and finally releasing the hold to continue improvising. But you stop when you encounter another and different "familiar," freezing there until that one boils over into a further improvisation and so on. Question: was there a connection between the different "familiars"?

In seeking the answers to these questions, there is no crying need that you be able to verbalize them clearly. In our business, some things are known even though they are never neatly wrapped up in words. Knowing without words and knowing with words are equally valuable.

*Possessed by a Mannerism†

Some dancers are haunted by criticisms of one or more of their mannerisms: a Baroque arching of the hand, constantly gazing at the ground, a worried frown that accompanies every technical difficulty, hyperextending the lower spine in turns—the list can be endless. Actually, most of us have one or more mannerisms that cling to us like barnacles. They are irrelevant and attract attention precisely because they usually are not at all pertinent to what we are doing. They are just there most of the time.

> While seated, close your eyes. Clear your head with your breath. In the empty space that ensues, ask the question, "What do I always do in dance, regardless of the occasion? What is my mannerism? Do I have one?" If the answer is no, open your eyes and leave the floor. If yes, see yourself performing the mannerism in your mind's eye. When it appears clearly and vividly, open your eyes, rise to do it and, whenever you are ready, travel among the others to find one to whom you will show this mannerism. If there are an odd number of you on the floor, the last person can go to one of the dancers who has chosen to leave the floor or join a pair to make a trio.
>
> There will be four stages for this exercise.
>
> Stage one: Each of you in turn, demonstrate to your partner the mannerism you just visualized for yourself.
>
> Stage two: Separate and find your own space where you will again "see" the mannerism and, as you do this, begin to sense its inner rhythm, the motor that drives it. Once the rhythm is established, let it flood your body, let it move your body. Now, with this base, improvise a dance about the mannerism. Do it fully and consciously; do it in different ways, in parts of the body where it is never done; do it to show it to the world like a flag; conceal it while still doing it; sense what the mannerism is trying to say or do. Dance to, for, about and against your mannerism. The only music for this exercise will be the inner rhythm you found.

Stage three: When you have done this improvisation, and you will know when you are done, find your partner, and if necessary, wait until he.she is finished. Now, taking turns, improvise for your partner the dance you did in private.

Stage four: When both have danced for each other, rest and talk to each other about what you saw in the other and what you learned about your mannerism and, if it is not too private, what you learned about yourself.

When you are next alone in a studio, do Possessed by a Mannerism again. In this private space and time, you may be able to delve deeper into what is really going on, where the mannerism came from and what it is really about. Habits need conscious attention without undue pressure or tension. They are potentially fertile, for they signal something that is important to you.

*An Event, a Recurrence, a Ritual[†]

During Inner Rhythm the teacher/leader can call out any one of the following:

1. "This is the very first time you are doing what you are doing." (An Event)

2. "What you are doing now, you have done before." (A Recurrence)

3. "Every motion you make has been done by generations of others like you. All of it is traditional and it must be done precisely as you learned it and as it always has been done. It is a ritual performed for reasons known to you. Mistakes and liberties are serious infractions of the rules you live by." (A Ritual)

Individually, dancers can take this exercise into technique classes, either going through an entire class with one of the three perspectives or shifting from one to another during the course of a class. Every dance role will be enriched when this aspect is clarified and identified. The Two Dances should be understood and analyzed in the light of these distinctions.

*How Does Your Tree Dance?[†]

In working on The Two Dances, knowing X, which is the appropriate tree metaphor? Is the trunk the source of the movement? Or does X lead with leaves and branches? Or is the whole tree dancing? Or, is there a moment when a succession is called for?

Choose a favorite technical sequence from any one of your classes. Practice it fully in the four different ways. Then find a partner and each of you dance the four ways for each other. Which way gave the dance sequence its fullest expression?

10 *Exercises*

Level 3

Each of the following exercises introduces important principles and ways of working that pave the way for more complex exercises and performance pieces. The first two are circles and its variant, Each Alone.

Circles†

With your eyes closed, listen to the sequence of the next exercise. You will hear better with your eyes closed. First, you will hear music. After a while, I will say, "Someone or something is doing something." I may choose any verb: flying, loving, hunting, planting, destroying, shielding, ad infinitum. Picking an example at random, let us say, "Someone or something is running to or from someone or something." The "someone or something" can come from any part of your mind: books you have read, films, history, TV, friends, your own life. When you know who or what that someone or something is, with your eyes still closed, stand. Be certain that the someone or something is a specific. Is the runner a woman? a lion? a bird? a raindrop running down a window pane? If it is a woman, what is the color of her hair? Does she have a name? Do you know her? In other words you must find in your mind a specific running man or woman or bird or lion or whatever, and never, ever, the general idea of a man, a woman or a bird.

When every one is standing, we will go on to the next step. While you are standing, waiting for the others, use your time to learn all you can about X. X is what we will call the someone or something known only to you. Look at X from all sides, from close up and far away. Does an odor come off X? The more specifics you learn about X, the richer and more personal will be the movement that emerges from this work.

157

The images may range from the literal, like the time you broke your nasty neighbor's window and fled the scene, to the metaphoric, like the memory of a raindrop running down a window pane last week. You might recall the Greek myth of Atalanta, the princess who would only marry the man who could beat her in a foot race. If he lost, he also lost his head. A crafty suitor, Hippomenes, hid three golden apples in his tunic, throwing them in her path one by one. He thus won the race and married the princess. You may choose anything—yourself fleeing, a raindrop, Atalanta or Hippomenes—so long as it is a specific and not a generalization or an abstraction.

When everyone is standing, I will stop the music and rewind the tape to the beginning. As I am doing this, each of you should sit, stand, kneel or lie down, whichever is an appropriate place from which to become X. Above all, know that it is you who are taking this position and not X. Do not for a moment try at this stage to "become" or look like your X. It is too soon because there is too little you know of X. To do so will shape all you do into a chain of clichés. When you finish Circles you may be surprised by all you have discovered about X.

When you hear the music, something that may appear strange will be asked of you: let your scalp, your ears, your brows, your eyes become X running. Do not question the logic or the feasibility of brows running. At the center of what we do as dancers is the use of the body and its parts as metaphors for the whole world. If running is the action of X, then run with your scalp, your ears, your brow and your eyes. If it is appropriate to X that your eyes remain closed, fine. If open is true to this moment for X, then open let them be.

After a while, I will say, "Whenever you are ready, become X running with your jaw, your nose, your lips, your tongue." If you are still deeply involved with the first action, finish it before going on to the mouth. When you do go on, *do not lose what you have done.* That continues.

In time, I will continue, saying, "Whenever you are ready, with your neck, become X running."

Then "... with your chest become X running."

Then "... with your shoulders become X running."

Then "... with your elbows become X running."

Then "... with your hands become X running," and as you go on, lose nothing of what you have been doing. You are constantly accumulating, though at each stage your action is being led by that new part of the body."

Then "... with your waist, belly, voice, become X running."

Then ". . . with your pelvis become X running."

Then ". . . with your thighs, knees become X running."

Then ". . . with your feet become X running."

Then "Whenever you are ready with all of you, with your totality become X running."

In this last stage, a time will come when you will have "become" X. When you sense that transformation, celebrate it and then leave the floor.

Two negatives: (1) This is not an exercise in isolations, but rather, the entire body supports the action of the individual part of the body. (2) This is not an exercise in exploring the range of movement that is possible, say, of your mouth or your hands. The motions are governed strictly by the image and action being fulfilled. Sticking to the specific action of a specific someone or something will create rich movement. Isolations or variation games will convert the entire exercise into an academic excursion irrelevant to our work and intention.

Because Circles is more complex than the previous exercises, it would be well to give a quick summary and then open the space to questions before actually starting.

Timing the intervals between calling out the parts of the body is a delicate matter ideally done by feel and not by the clock. A section can be a minute, two or three. The conductor of the exercise needs only to pay close attention to the flow of energy in the group.

Inviting the use of the voice is a risky choice that may work best with a small group. If the group is large, and heated up, the din may be such that the subsequent directions will be inaudible and for some will be violently intrusive.

Each Alone   Whenever a group was ready to work on the ritual of becoming someone or something, I would first introduce circles, making it clear that it would be done only once and that thereafter we would do its variant, Each Alone. When that time came, I would say:

Each Alone begins exactly the same as Circles. From a seated position, you will hear music and then I will give you, "Someone or something is doing something." When that someone or something arrives in your mind, stand. When everyone is standing, I will stop the music and rewind the tape to the beginning. As I am doing this, each of you should sit, stand, kneel, or lie down as before.

The variation begins here: When the music starts up again from its beginning, call up the vision of X doing what X does *and immediately, without plan,* allow the impulse for *any* part of your body to perform that act—as X. In time, you will feel as if you "have done" that part—that it has become X doing what X does and you will be ready to move on. Without planning or thinking, another part will have the impulse to do this. Taking all the time that is needed, you will proceed in whatever sequence your body tells you. Try to retain what you have done as Each Alone evolves. Symmetry is possible but not necessary: the focus of activity might be the shoulders or only the right shoulder. Discard the rigorous logic of Circles and instead follow the dictates of your body. Sequence and timing are yours to control. You may never get to body parts mentioned in Circles, and you may become absorbed in an area untouched by Circles. There will come a moment when all the pieces come together and you will be X doing what X does. Celebrate that becoming and then leave the floor.

Without the constant intrusion and interruptions from me and with the concentration of permitting the action of X to flow through the body undirected, the dancers were able to go much more deeply into the life of X, discovering surprising movement metaphors and, best of all, moving in an imagined context with conviction and freedom. If anything could describe the goal of all performance, "moving in an imagined context with conviction and freedom" certainly touches the center. Each Alone became the key to the powerful rituals that developed out of The Duet. One had to *become* another in order to be, think, act, and dance as another.

I created Circles and Each Alone for the Workgroup because I believed they would accomplish two things. First, it was the simplest way to introduce, in a way that dancers would understand, a source of creative movement which I had learned in the Stanislavski technique of acting and from Helen Tamiris. In these two exercises, one never asks for an emotion or a mood. That is the direct highway to banality. One always asks for an *action* on the assumption that the specific "who" doing a specific action in a specific context will arrive at a truthful emotion or mood. To ask parts of your body to become in turn a fine-boned, young, red, female fox fleeing the hounds in a driving rain would in time produce a gut emotion of unquestioned intensity, a genuine feeling in the body of the dancer and some fascinating movement.

The second value is that they became profound lessons in the metaphoric possibilities of the various parts of the body. Without this awareness and a mastery of poetic dance metaphors, the entire way of working that is presented here would degenerate into one continuous flow of literal movement, which is the last thing we want from dancers. In dance, a strategic moment of literal movement has been the strongest part of some of our best dance works and the key to some ostensibly abstract dances. As an extended mode of expression, the literal becomes acting and negates the meaning and point of the dance art.

One both unexpected and yet obvious note: in at least one of the various stages of Circles or Each Alone, the dancer may come across a part of the body which translates into a literal action. Say the image is the man in the myth, racing the princess for her hand in marriage. Comes the moment when the focus is on the feet, the dancer may find her.himself dashing through the studio. It may prove to be not only "literal" but "uninteresting" or, conversely, the most exhilarating of all the segments. More, if most of what had gone before was retained, the running may be like no running that had ever been done since this literal movement is an island within a circle of metaphors for the same action.

You never know anything until it happens. It is very important in all improvisation not to look ahead, not to anticipate. Anticipation and, even worse, planning cut out the heart and meaning of improvisation. Improvisation starts with a set of givens, rules and wishes, and from then on, one deals with the immediate present, never knowing what will happen until it does happen. By its open-ended nature, improvisation is an ideal tool to discover fresh and personal movement expression.

I felt that performing an action one part of the body at a time would be a way of freeing it imaginatively—and it did. The improvisations were full of surprises both to me the viewer and more importantly, to the dancers in the workshop. In the little talks we would have after a session, time and again, a dancer would say, "I never did anything like that." "I never moved like that." "I was completely into that." "I forgot the studio— all the others." "I didn't know I was dancing."

Hot to Cold to Hot I[†]

When a group finishes either one of these two, I sometimes ask:

> Was there some part of the body that felt remarkably free? Was there some part of the body that felt frozen, almost incapable of moving? I will play the music again. Take all the time you need to get back into X. When you are there, let that part of the body that was freest take the lead. When it is flowing and hot and whenever you are ready, shift to that frozen part as the lead while thinking, feeling, sensing the fluidity of the free part. Keep shifting back and forth to thaw out what resists the action. Thus, one part of the body can lead the more timid part into a freer and more expressive mode of moving.

Hot to Cold to Hot II[†]

The same exercise can turn its focus on one part of the body that may want attention or study. The hands of most dancers, for example, are trapped in a mannerism that they acquire early and rarely lose.

> Begin with any image that interests you and perform the action with your hands. Then, in your own time, shift the same action to any body part, say the lower back. Then go back to the hands, retaining some of the texture and power of the back. After that, find another body part, say the mouth. Again, returning to the hands, what can be gleaned from the motions of the mouth? The exercise proceeds in this manner, sandwiching a time with hands and differing body parts, constantly drawing differing qualities from each section of the body.

Backdoor[†]   Everything up to this point moves dancers into deeper levels of consciousness, but by that very token, a protectiveness of old ways can lead to shallow and impersonal choices that are clichéd, obvious or, worst of all, evasive. Backdoor and the following Hub Meditation are mind trips that open up the most unexpected doors to many dancers.

> With your breath, empty your head. (Pause.) In a little while I am going to say a word or short phrase. The moment you hear the word or phrase allow a smell, a sound, an image, a word, anything, to appear in the center of your mind. With the next breath, or sooner, whatever is in the focus of your mind must change to something else. This process is continuous: a change in your mind with every breath, or sooner. Continuous change is the only control you are to exert on the process. Above all, don't try to impose any overall conception of how one thing should follow the other. You don't try to make a logical flow or, conversely, try to create surrealist or strange connections. You simply attempt to observe passively whatever will emerge, logically, or illogically. There is only one compulsion: whatever occupies your mind must change with every breath or sooner.

After about five minutes, I ask people to let it wind down, and when it has, to open their eyes. When everyone's eyes are open, I ask:

> Is there anything remarkable, special, unusual, confusing, or interesting about what took place? I am not asking about your specific sensations and images, which I am sure are interesting. I am really curious about what, if anything, you found interesting in the structure or the process of it.

Sooner or later, what emerges in any group of ten or more people is the following pattern: a large number of them had a recurring image. Some find that image logical, and others find it rather unexpected and surprising. To some the image was rather attractive and interesting; others didn't like it. Not a few experience a strong image they had never seen before. Almost everyone answers affirmatively upon being asked, "Is there some image that even now stands out beyond all the others?"

The Hub   Immediately after giving, doing and discussing Backdoor:
Meditation[†]

> Close your eyes and clean your head out with your breath. In a little while I will say, "Someone or something is *doing* something." It will be a simple verb, such as, "Someone or something is rising and falling." From here on, let your mind roam and search for everything in your experience of rising and falling. Rising and falling in nature, in history, in films, TV, the people you know, your own life; a piece of bleached driftwood in the surf, a child on a pogo stick, a red autumn leaf in a cold wind, a close relation's struggle with an addiction, a graph of a sine wave, the breast of the woman who has just been crowned Miss America, a white line of paint

running across a Jackson Pollock painting, the sound of the waves one evening when you were in Maui. The list can and should feel endless. Each of these will be for a moment in the center of your mind, at the very hub of your consciousness.

After a while, you may discover that regardless of what you come up with, *the hub of your mind is occupied with one thing,* even though you continue to raise up new images: there you are on that frightened horse being bounced up and down in the saddle as he gallops off the road into the desert away from the blaring horn of that monster white trailer truck.

Note that in this example everything was specific. Don't reach for anything as general and grandiose as the rise and fall of the Roman Empire. Avoid unspecific feelings like going from gaiety to sadness to gaiety. These will land you neck-deep in stereotypes and stencils, to steal a word from Stanislavski.

When you know that the hub of your mind is occupied by one image regardless of whatever other images come up, accept that and move in to get a close look at what is there. Then open your eyes. You will have just done a Hub Meditation.

At this point I state a ground rule for this way of working in dance. The worst idea for a dance or the conception of a role is a "good" idea. The best idea is one that won't go away, whether you like it or not, like a nettle that sticks to your garments. I accept with a passion the statement by Ben Shahn, in a book which I feel is of great value to anyone interested in the arts and the creative process, *The Shape of Content* (Cambridge: Harvard University Press, 1957): "Whatever crosses the human mind may be fit content for art—in the right hands ... it is the fullness of feeling with which the artist addresses himself to his theme that will determine, finally, its stature or its seriousness" (p. 72).

The revelation that Backdoor and The Hub Meditation bring is that, for most people, given enough time, the mind will find itself occupied with an image that dominates all others. It matters not whether the image is attractive or repulsive, whether the image is fascinating or on its surface quite dull, that is the image to work on and that is the essence of this approach to improvisation.

A relevant story: I had a talented and devoted student who took a number of workshops in choreography with me. She always produced work that was personal, strong and unexpected, but in the improvisation exercises involving imaging, she would resort to literal pantomime and dead-end repetitions. Finally I spoke up: "What gives, Sarah? Every time we get to this, you get lost." "Well, every time you give us a Hub Meditation, I see Archie Bunker." "So, did you ever do Archie Bunker?" "No! Of course not!" Too bad. She missed out on something that was perhaps more important to her than she was willing to realize. For her values and conscious mind, Archie Bunker *was not material worthy of dance or art.* This is precisely the self-inflicted snobbery that defeats many young artists and some mature artists. They keep under covers a passionate connection and knowledge of something that they fear is not "good" enough for "ART"—in favor of what? Better to spell "art" with small letters and learn to respect one's deepest feelings as the source and focus of the work.

The last thing one should do is to hunt for a "good image," a "creative image," an "exciting image" and, worst of all, to try to find an image that the dancer thinks will interest, excite, or please the teacher, the audience or the critics. The basic dictum of the work says, if it isn't personal, it isn't worth working on.

Visualization[†]   There are those people who are unhappy with the many problems that depend on visualization because they are convinced that they can't do it, or can't do it well. When I hear this, I throw out to the group:

> Close your eyes and see the departure area of an airport with taxicabs, buses and limousines zipping by. A man is standing near the curb looking about. Can you see him? How is he dressed? Is he wearing a hat? Step up close to him and study his face. Walk around him and view him from the rear. Walk off to the side, still looking at him. Have you ever seen him before?

A suggestion to the reader: reread the above paragraph and then take the time to do what it suggests. . . .

Have you ever seen that man before? In the many times I have given this simple setting, almost everyone created a man they had never seen. You, too, probably created a man unknown to you. Your life of observation was the raw material—the encyclopedia from which he was shaped. Your memory, sense memory, and imagination were your tools and they worked for you without your control or supervision. The vision of that man did not just happen. Imagination stirs up the great soup of the accumulation of your many observations to create a man standing at an airport curb or a poem, a song, or a dance. I have yet to find one of those "I-can't-visualize" people who did not see that man on the departure curb. Something about that airport scene proves that they can.

Gesture Permutations[†]   It is a given in the modern dance that being literal is a no-no, and with justification. If our intention is to be specific and to have a specific identity at all times, what is to guard us against falling into this trap of the literal? The strongest substance has a vulnerability. An ancient vase of Venetian glass can gleam in its glory for centuries. One light tap of a metal hammer and we have a mess of shards. The plastic wrapping on four little cheese and peanut butter crackers will frustrate all efforts to tear it open until stabbed by the point of a nail file. Getting caught in the literal and the linear is the Achilles heel of our way of working.

What can shield us from the devastating question, "Why are you dancing? Why aren't you actors in a play and just speaking what you have on your mind?" There is an answer. *Never flee the literal, but never get stuck in it.* Learn to bend it, stretch it, squeeze it, quicken it, transmute it to another body part, alter the "who." All of which is to say, learn to make the literal a springboard to a metaphor—and in so doing make motion poems—which could easily be another name for dancing. The next two exercises contain strategies for transforming the literal into dance metaphors.

Pair off. If there is an odd number, make one a trio. Now, talk about what you really think about Arizona. (Any place will do, the closer the better. After several minutes): Continue your discussion, but make no sound. Communicate only with gestures. (After several minutes): Now pause and between you cull a short sequence of the silent gestures you exchanged, six to be exact. Person A makes a gesture. B replies, A replies, B replies, A replies and B replies. Period. If you are a trio, keep it to six: A, then B, then C, then A, then B and then C. Once you have decided on the six gestures face me. (When all are finished and facing me):

Now go through the sequence of the six gestures three times, and each time you make your gesture do it as if it were the first time you ever did it. Do it with the same conviction that you had before I stopped you.

Now do the six gestures three times, as fast as you possibly can.

Now do the six gestures one time, moving slower than you have ever moved in your life.

You are a mammoth human made of lead and concrete. Do the six gestures.

You are actors in a silent movie. Do the six gestures.

You are underwater. Do the six gestures.

You are an ambitious courtier in the court of Louis XIV. The monarch favors anyone who appears to be an elegant dancer.

You are clowns in a circus.

Do the six gestures in waltz time.

You stammer and stutter painfully.

You have no hands and no arms. Communicate the meaning of the six gestures with your torso.

You communicate only with your shoulders.

Only with your feet.

All your gestures are made of porcelain. They have been dropped, broken and glued together this way and that but not logically. Communicate as best you can.

Don't do any of the six gestures. Rather do what they feel like.

Manifestly, this list is potentially endless.

Gesture Rondo†

Leave your partner or your trio and in your own space and in your own mind, go over the gestures you have been doing. Decide which one you want to continue working with, for whatever reason. When I give you the "Go," you will do that gesture with as much truth and conviction as you did the first time and then, with no premeditation, allow *anything* to happen out of it, from the most obvious, literal banal association to the most esoteric muscular association. You may start on a physical impulse, that leads to dramatic one, that leads to whatever. Just let it flow and above all avoid "good taste." Just go. If and when the energy runs down, come to a pause and repeat the original gesture as simply and honestly as possible, allowing anything to flow for as long as it does until it stops. Then again do the original gesture. Continue until I call out for this Gesture Rondo to end. Go!

After doing this sequence most dancers, instead of living in terror of the literal gesture by either sedulously avoiding it or feeling guilty of bad taste if they do it, discover that the literal gesture is a gold mine. The literal gesture becomes a source of a limitless range of movement. The infinitely small island of classroom moves which most dancers think contains the whole world of dance movement becomes one rich and useful area among many. If one were to total a lexicon of any one dance technique—flamenco, ballet, modern, tap, Hawaiian—it would reveal a small number of moves compared to all that the human body is capable of. Whatever we do and have done in our lives, from early morning to sleep and dreams and from the earliest remembered days to this morning, is waiting there to be used in our dances: bent, twisted, turned inside out, stretched, shrunk and magnified. Every part of our lives has value for us as dancers and artists.

The Duet as a Structure

This sequence is the centerpiece of all the improvisations in this book. (Note that it includes four exercises given previously: The Mind-Wash and The Other, both in chapter 9, and The Hub Meditation and Each Alone in this chapter.) From it can flow an understanding of self, the other, a way of dancing, a way of improvising, a way of creating choreography and for our purpose here, of performing dance. It is ideal for studio work. Inevitably, on the first reading, The Duet as a Structure may appear to be overwhelmingly complex, but it is bound together by an internal logic. Approach it step-by-step and clarity will emerge. The Duet as a Structure can be mastered bit by bit, solidifying each part before attempting to put it all together. Once that happens, the dancer, the student, the teacher, the choreographer will have at hand a tool to practice this matter of becoming another and performing the metaphoric task that ignites the inner powers and sensibilities of the dancer.

For The Duet as a Structure it is well to have twenty to twenty-five minutes of music, preferably a single composition that does not have radical changes. Shorter pieces will work if they are bound together with a single, coherent style.

> Sit cross-legged, facing your partner, knees a few inches apart, close your eyes and clear a space in your head with your breath. (Pause.)
>
> First you will hear music. After a while, you will hear me say, "Someone or something is doing something to or with or for someone or something." Put this statement on a shelf of your mind to be dealt with later.

Should you, the reader, wish to follow this sequence with a specific image in mind, make one up now or choose one from the following:

Someone always has to have his.her own way. You are that person or you are dealing with the person.

Someone needs to live in a neat, orderly, predictable world. You are that person or you are dealing with that person.

Someone is a protector, shielding another from anything potentially dangerous or negative. You are that person or you are dealing with that person.

Someone is leaving. You are leaving or you are being left.

Someone is always busy and in a hurry and the other is laid back.

Someone is always on the lookout for funning, joking, and clowning. You are that person or dealing with that person.

> Now do The Mind-Wash, followed by The Other. Your partner is now "the other," the person with whom you are going to enter a world made by both of you. It may be the first time you have worked together or the twentieth, there will always be something new to be observed. What can you glean just by looking, and looking?
>
> The moment will come when you have learned what you can for now and you are ready to take the "Someone . . . something . . ." statement off the shelf of your mind and do a Hub Meditation with it. You let your mind roam through literature, films, TV, your own life, until one image dominates. All this time, you are looking at your partner. These two actions, looking at your partner and looking for what will occupy the hub of your mind may seem too far apart. Wait. You may find that they reenforce each other. If and when you find the specific someone-something, you have a decision to make. Which role will you play?
>
> After knowing which one, ask yourself: If you are So-and-so, *what is your task?* What do you need to do with, to or for this other person? Once you know your task, you need to find a movement metaphor for this task. It is here that your

imagination has its greatest challenge: finding a poetic movement metaphor rather than a literal action. One way you will be dancing, whatever that elusive word means, the other way you might just as well speak like an actor rather than go through the motions of an inefficient dumb-show. A degree of patience will serve here. Allow for "near misses" or "failures" the first few times you do The Duet as a Structure. In time, finding the movement metaphor that charges your dance energy and communicates to your partner will become a part of your craft in this work.

Once you have determined your role and your task, you are ready for the next phase of The Duet as a Structure. When you are ready, indicate that to your partner by turning your palms up and resting your hands on your knees. When the other is ready, he.she clasps the upturned palms and both rise and separate, each to find a private place. Here you will prepare your self to become X, the person you found in your Hub Meditation, and to be geared up to accomplish the task you have chosen. You do this through the structure called Each Alone. This is the development of Circles in which the entire structure becomes open-ended, with each dancer deciding the order, when and how long to work on the body parts.

Once in your private place, you will begin Each Alone, on your own. Call up the vision of X doing what X does and immediately allow one part of your body to perform that act, as X. When you feel as if that part has become X doing what X does, you will be ready to move on. Taking all the time that is needed, you will continue in whatever sequence your body tells you, body part by body part. As you do this, try to retain what you have done. Symmetry is possible but not necessary: the focus of activity might be the shoulders or only the right shoulder. Discard the rigorous logic of Circles and follow instead the dictates of your body and your feelings. Let them control sequence and timing. You may never get to body parts mentioned in Circles and you may become absorbed in an area untouched by Circles. There will come a moment when all the body parts will become a unity and you will be X doing what X does.

You are now ready to engage with your partner, with the other. Without losing any of the character you have become, and deep within the danced truth of X, approach the other person who, for simplicity's sake, we will dub Y. Here you may face a decision. If Y is ready to engage, then each of you will proceed to do what you have to do—in dance. If Y is not ready, would X wait or barge right in? Would Y be pliant or resist by continuing with Circles until finished? This is the beginning of making choices as the person each of you has become.

Whatever the outcome, sooner or later the two of you will engage in the attempt to make something happen. There should be no terror of the literal, only of getting stuck in it. The literal can be welcomed but only as a springboard to a danced metaphor.

By now the questions arise: "How does each know what role the other has taken?" Neither knows, no more than we do in "real life." If this is true in life, then why should it not be so here in this duet?

Second question: "What if both take the same role—the same side of the implied dichotomy?" How many times are two united in a power struggle, each determined to dominate or each longing to find someone to lean upon? The complementary relationship of opposites is not a necessary condition. It probably happens as often as similar types try to relate.

If, as the duet progresses, you are having difficulty realizing your goal, be as flexible and resourceful as X is—or as rigid, depending on who X is. It may even make sense to change your intent because of what you are experiencing as X.

If you achieve your task, celebrate that and leave the floor. If your partner does this before you, then dance out your recognition of failure and leave the floor. If nothing you do brings you any closer to success, you, still as X, may give up and dance your acceptance of that failure and leave.

As noted earlier, anyone coming across this material for the first time may groan, "How complex! How can anyone follow such a detailed and torturous path—and dance?" Answer: It is constructed out of a series of exercises, each of which should be known and practiced separately before being drawn into this shape.

A summary of The Duet as a Structure would go like this: Sitting facing your partner, you will hear "Someone . . . something. . . ." Do nothing about it except to save it on the shelf of your mind. Do The Mind-Wash and when finished, contemplate your partner (The Other). When you have done that, return to the "Someone . . . something . . ." and do a Hub Meditation. When you have found the dominating image decide on your role and your task. When you and your partner are both ready, you find separate areas in which you will do Each Alone. When you have become X through Each Alone, find and engage with your partner. If you succeed in your task, celebrate that and leave the floor. If you fail, recognize that—in dance—and leave the floor. If after many different attempts you are convinced it is futile, recognize that—in dance—and leave.

Even reading this condensed version may still be confusing. Perhaps it would help to review the mental process I went through in a duet with Ara Fitzgerald, a member of the Workgroup. What was given:

Someone is favored in almost every way: looks, health, wealth, position—the works. You are that person or someone dealing with that person.

As I sat there looking at the sweet, clear-browed face of Ara, she became very wealthy and I became very ugly and poor. I found, out of the blue, a very powerful man—physically powerful—who had spent time in jail for theft and assault. A resentful man with a violent temper. I had achieved a notoriety by writing of my childhood and history of violence. I was now a minor literary celebrity and Ara and I were guests at a country estate. I was determined that she should come to love me and because of that love, let me push her about and dominate her. Once she accepted my treatment of her, I would have all I wanted and could leave. I would have a victory over a "rich bitch."

Ara had found her role and task sooner than I did, and her palms lay up and open, waiting for my grasp—for my decisions. She sat there gazing simply and directly into my face. Finally, when I was clear, I grasped her hands and we went off to separate parts of the studio.

When I found my "private place," I realized, as I stood there, that it was a cell—a prison cell. The first place in my body that became active was my lower abdominal muscles which seemed to be writhing with all their power as I was pacing the cell. It was as if I were being led by those muscles up and down a brief length of my space. In my mind, my feet were bare, though I was dancing with shoes. My attention then shifted to my feet which worked harshly into the cold, damp concrete as if they held the angry claws of a predatory animal. That action slowly flowed into the thighs, which bulged with the muscles of a weight lifter. The power allowed me to perform sudden squats to a stillness as if waiting to spring. All this time, I was intermittently pacing my cramped space like a caged animal. Without warning, my mouth became alive—a stretched gash across my face which I constantly tried to make smaller by turning my lips inward. This, in time, activated my whole face which was always on the verge of exploding out of control as I kept trying to keep it in rein, all the while pacing the cell. Then the attention shifted to the shoulders, which felt massive and writhing like the abdominals. This action gradually flowed down the arms to the hands, which wanted to flail about but were always caught by fisting and lowering the arms so that they would be quiet for a while. Lastly, the back came into play, and its wish was to crouch, to duck, to avoid blows from somewhere—but the wish had to be concealed, so the crouch was spasmodically evident but mostly suppressed.

I had "become X." As I looked over to where Ara was dancing, lightly flinging her arms about as if they were little flags pressed into the wind, I realized that I had to put on a tweed suit over my anger and my ugliness. I did everything I had been doing, but one could barely see what I was doing except that I was walking toward her with a slow held step followed by quick ones that were almost out of control. It resembled an erratic rhumba. The moment I approached Ara, she turned to me and circled me as if to observe me on all sides and to be observed by me on all of her sides. Pretending a cool, I alternately observed her closely and looked away as if there were other items of interest to me. There was a slide almost to the ground which I stopped with some show-off pushups into a sudden squat and then came erect, trying to tower above her.

Ara moved close to me. "This was going to be easy!" Looking away, I reached to her, pulling her to me into a ballroom stance and, leading with definite power, guided her about the floor as if on a dance floor. She followed as if we had done this many times before, once releasing herself from my grasp to do the circling back into my arms. The more we danced, the more brutal I became until I was sweeping her down to the floor, pushing her away and pulling her back, each time going further and further from her, pretending an interest elsewhere, not unlike the way cats will play with a cricket or a mouse.

Finally, I went to the far end of the studio, confident that she would be waiting for me, so sure was I of my power. I was ready to leave the floor after "celebrating" my success, the achievement of my task. While I was strutting my power, I glanced back at Ara, and instead of that flighty arm-flinging, she was pacing back and forth in a limited space with a strangely familiar contorted body. *It was as if she was going through the same agony I had suffered.* The similarity was so great, I was shocked into the most unexpected compassion and concern for her. Uncertain, I wavered there, not knowing my next move, and found myself falling in love with her. Confused, I approached her cautiously and slowly began a dance of protection and cradling and loving—which Ara accepted and reciprocated. We ended with a fierce, yet tender love duet which finally settled into a moment of emotional exhaustion and we left the floor together.

I have no idea whether Ara had achieved the task she found during her Hub Meditation or whether it had changed as the dance progressed. What shook me was that for the first time I had set out in an improvisation with a clear direction and because of what I had experienced, I not only took an entirely unexpected path, but went through a profound change in character. This duet first occurred during studio work and because it came out so richly, we did it again and again until we were sure it could be performed for the public—which we did, many times, because it "worked." For that very reason, we never spoke of it. In spite of doing this duet many times in the studio and in performance, we never discussed it. It always started from the same place, the same premises, but it always came out differently.

To sum up these last few pages, The Duet is the most fertile, challenging and exciting structure of all. Even when performing it in public, there is that long period in the beginning when we, in the Workgroup, were "doing nothing," just sitting cross-legged and staring at each other. Nonetheless, the audience was mesmerized, glued to what was highly intense activity, albeit mental. Once again, I learned that if there is an active, honest, inner life, an audience will go all the way with the performer.

Emotion Memory[†] Choose a dance role that calls on an emotion that you find difficult to summon. Isolate the emotion and think over your own life, your deepest personal experiences. Is there a time and a place when you felt something parallel? If and when you find that time and place, re-create it in your mind. What do you see? What is the color of the sky? Is there an odor filling the air? Is there a face in front of you? Do you hear a particular piece of music? As part of your preparation to perform the role, use anything from your past that will summon up that feeling.

As I noted earlier, I, personally, have a resistance to this as a technique for performance. Try it. It may be your magic key to it all.

*From Now[†]   This is Evolving Repetition (chapter 9) with a slightly different beginning.

> Gather at the edge of the work space, entering one by one. Find your place, close your eyes and breathe deeply. Wait until an internal rhythm emerges. Each of you takes off in your own time. Ten minutes is an optimum time span. If you find it useful as a way to get into work sessions, set a timer to ring or create a ten-minute tape of ambient sound and record a voice counting the minutes as they go by.

*Rhythm Portrait[†]

> Prowl around each other, observing everyone covertly, but never let anyone catch you looking at them. You are looking for the person in the group who interests you the most, positively or negatively. Once you have made your decision, concentrate your powers of observation on that person only, learning all you can by the simple act of looking—still never allowing that person to know it is he.she in whom you are interested. Ultimately what you are trying to sense is her.his internal rhythm in the form of a repeated phrase.
>
> When I call out, "the rhythm," start to physically beat out, with your hands, the rhythm you have unearthed—but do it silently. When I call out, "Now!" make the rhythm audible and as loud as is true of the character of "that person." Allow what motions are needed to support the rhythm.
>
> Stage two: One by one, take the center of the space and beat out for all to hear the rhythm you have discovered, moving and covering space at the same time. All the others learn the rhythm and follow the motion of the dancer in the center.
>
> Stage three: When all have taken center in their turn, I ask each to find a private place in the studio. Once there I ask, "Which one of the rhythms you learned felt good? Made you feel strong? Made you want to dance? Try to recapture that rhythm. Once you have a handle on it, improvise with that rhythm at the center of your focus.

If one looks deeply into another, one may discover a powerful piece of music, a rhythm that is arresting without being arbitrarily inventive. The goal is not to *make* a rhythm, but to *find* it.

11 *Exercises*

Level 4

*Before, After and On†

This exercises addresses (1) the technical mastery of being able to dance, at will, before, after and on the beat; (2) the individual proclivity of the dancer in relation to rhythmic music; (3) the organic rhythmic relation to the music in the context of the six questions, the who or the what doing what.

> Problem 1: Find some infectious walking music: a paso doble, a Sousa march, a Dixieland march. To walking music do the simplest of walking step phrases: one step on each beat. "Strutting" would be a better designation than "walking." I will call out, "Strut square on the beat." Then, "Strut a hair ahead of the beat." Then, "Strut a hair behind the beat." When you have done that a few times, gather in groups of three. One of you calls out the commands, "Before! . . . After! . . . On the beat!" as one dances. The observers will tell you how successful you are—or not. Then the other two take their turns. Repeat the entire exercise to a moderate tempo waltz: balancé left, right, left; step right, left, right; then balancé right, left, right; step left, right, left; and repeat.

This is not an idle exercise, and if it is proffered to professionals, they should forego sneering at such childishness. For all the world to see, there is a video of Rudolf Nureyev accompanied by a highly skilled woman who is usually behind the beat, sometimes on the beat, and never quickens when he so brilliantly chooses to. If you are good at this and do know what you are doing musically, congratulations—enjoy the exercise. Your help will be needed.

> Problem 2: A highly rhythmic piece of music will be played. Go off by yourself and design an eight-count module of movement that can be repeated many times. It is more important that you be sure of it than that you create a complex masterpiece. When you have it under control, get off the floor.

When all of you are off the floor, reassemble in groups of three. The music will again be played. One by one, dance for each other and observe each other with a view to characterizing each dancer's tendency—if there is one. You can challenge each other to go before, after or on.

The first exercise may cover this ground but I think something extra would be revealed because each dancer would be creating her.his own phrase, thus revealing a more personal inclination.

Problem 3: Choose a phrase from one of The Two Dances that uses music. Because of the nature of X and what X is doing, is X ahead, on or behind the beat?

*Why Do You Dance?[†]

Answer the question without words. Try this alone and with an audience. It is not a bad idea to repeat this exercise over the years. You may find that the answers change and that most times your own answer will, in some respect, surprise you.

*What Happened?[†]

When the Workgroup met for the first time after a late summer break, on a hunch I threw out a question that went back to elementary school days:

Jung Jung, go into the space. What did you do on your summer vacation? No words.

It actually turned into a delightful afternoon as one by one we rose to tell—with no words—an exercise in learning to speak in dance.

*The Spine of Style[†]

Someone who lives at the bottom of a society, resents it fiercely and wants the world to know that she.he is actually the equal of anyone, no matter how high. Become that someone.

It becomes the task of every performer to be more than a sausage skin that is stuffed by the choreographer with moves, ideas and inspiration. A dancer with a mind that has experienced history, other cultures, his.her *own* culture and history has the capacity to penetrate beyond the superficial appearance of a lonely prince, an Andalusian Gypsy dancer, a woman from the complexities of Greek mythology, a figure in a world of chance, an embodiment of a Vivaldi concerto, finding who and what lives at the core of these things or people. Such work on the dance role asks for knowledge, observation and imagination. The work of the choreographer is realized when the work of the dancer delves just as deeply.

*Making Faces

I studied with Hanya Holm for a brief period when she had one of the most beautiful studios in New York. It was in the early forties when I was working on Broadway. One afternoon, after a class, I dropped into Hanya's office to ask her something. We spoke for a while and then ran dry, just sitting there. I can't remember who started it but suddenly, there we were, exchanging faces with each other, one more grotesque than the other. It went on for quite some time and then petered out. I gathered up my things, nodded and left. We never spoke of it then or later. I think it can be a fun thing to do with anybody who will enter into the silliness of making faces with a fellow dancer, a lover or a child. It loosens up your face, gives its muscles a workout, provides a little fun and perhaps opens up a facet of your expressive arsenal.

12 Exercises
Level 5

Faces

Will everyone please get to a sink and thoroughly wash your hands? On the way, or returning, choose a partner. When you return, washed, sit facing each other cross-legged, a few inches apart, and close your eyes. When you sit, avoid touching the floor with your clean hands.

The bemused go to wash, return as partners and sit:

With your eyes closed, clear a space in your head with your breath. Anytime after I finish speaking and whenever you are ready, reach your hands forward to touch the face of the person in front of you. With your fingertips study this face—the varied textures of skin and hair, the shapes of bone and muscle. You will study not only to experience but to remember. When you think your hands have the memory of that face, drop your hands in your lap. When your partner's hands leave your face, with your eyes still closed, turn a quarter of a circle away on your bottom. Now reach your hands forward into space *as if that person is still in front of you,* and with your fingers relive the entire experience of touching her.his face, not merely going through the motions of touching but feeling once again the skin, hair, muscle and bone.

Do not be disconcerted if you find areas whose sensory experience you cannot recall. In some places, the most you will have is the idea of moist skin or a hairline, not the sensation. Do not despair. Do as much of the face—in the air—as you can. Then swivel back to face in the original direction, with your eyes still closed, and reach out to once again study to remember the face of your partner.

If you encounter a shoulder instead of a face, your partner is still re-creating in the air. Drop your hands and wait until you sense your partner return to face you. Then resume your exploration, going specifically to the places where your memory failed you. Experience and study with your hands what eluded you, and when you think your hands have it, drop your hands once again. When both you and your partner have lowered your hands, having finished this second study, swivel a quarter turn away and go directly to the blank places and fill them in by experiencing the actual sensation of touching. When you have done all you can, drop your hands to your lap and wait until you hear an, "OK," indicating that all are finished.

I Dare You[†] When dancers work with each other day after day, inevitably they notice each other's style, the strong points and the limitations. I Dare You is all about limitations. It only works with a group that has been working together for some time.

One person leaves the room and the others try to find the key limitation in the way that person has been working. Once there is a consensus on this, the challenge for the group is that the I Dare You has to be couched in a poetically specific and nondestructive way, a way that will stimulate the imagination of that dancer. A literal statement like "Improvise with a flowing, gentle quality," will come off as criticism and beg for a generalized response. Once there is agreement, the dancer is called back and the person who contributed the most to the formulated I Dare You, gives it to the dancer, verbally. Time is left in the session for each to write down the exact wording of the challenge they received. As part of the challenge, an appropriate, though makeshift costume could be helpful to slipping into X.

Allow a week for all the dancers to work on their I Dare You, finding a specific image, a rich movement metaphor and a loose construction around which to improvise. There is no pressure in this exercise to create a piece of choreography, though many have done just that. An improvisation that has been roughly sketched is just fine. The purpose is to encourage the dancer to enter a new room, to experience a new way. A week should be enough, and when the dancers meet again, they each show what they found. At best, this is a quality that was there all the time but was never previously exploited by the dancer. The group helps the dancer by commenting on how closely he.she met the challenge. Here are a few sample challenges from an actual class:

Become a length of lavender silk thread that is being used to crochet a delicate rose. This was given to the strongest dancer of her class, tall and powerfully built. As exciting as she was to observe, these were the only qualities we ever saw her exhibit. Her study-improvisation was gossamer and yet strong as silk. Later, she built a piece of choreography around this study and performed it with success at the student concert.

Become a monstrous, brutal piece of construction machinery used for road building. This was a tall elegant man who had a narrow image of what constituted beauty in movement: fey and floating. I think the I Dare You made him furious, and that only added to the power of an awesome study that was the best and most exciting dance I ever saw him do.

Become a hard-hearted, egotistical, cocky, smart-assed, macho stud who's on the rampage. This was an exceptionally attractive woman who tended to cling fiercely to a trite idea of femininity in all that she did. Her study was a farcical, hilarious and outrageous blast climaxed by making violent love to the floor. She appeared to have a giddy relish in letting go of her girly-girl image, at least for the length of that improvisation.

Humorous challenges can be just as effective as profoundly poetic ones. I Dare You can also help dancers explore the matter of for whom they are dancing: "I dare you to dance for the spirit of José Limon." "I dare you to dance for a Hollywood casting agent." "I dare you to dance for the wild winds."

Can I Dare You be a solitary exercise? All it takes is a ruthless objectivity in self-observation. "What is it that I never do? Am I shying away from it out of fear of my inadequacy or is that completely beyond me? Would a shot at it open a door that I thought was closed to me—even a crack?" If you fail, who would know but you?

Inside the Outside[†]

This exercise requires at least three days of work. The beginning assumes that the dancers are not only physically warm but have achieved a psychic looseness with a Repetition, Spinning or any physical meditation.

Day one: Sit with your hands clasped. Close your eyes. Clean out your head with your breath. When you achieve some clarity, unclasp your hands. (When all unclasp their hands): First you will hear music and then you are going to embark on a Hub Meditation (chapter 10). The question is: What is male? When you find the specific image at the hub of your mind, pause to learn all you can about it. Observe it from all sides. Come up close. When you have finished your observation, go to an initial starting position—sitting, standing, kneeling or lying down—that would be appropriate for you to work at becoming X. (In that initial position, you are you, not X.)

Without planning or anticipating, become X bit by bit, part by part as in Each Alone (chapter 10). After a time, you will hear music. If and when your Each Alone is finished, do Go Visiting (chapter 9) to see who the others are and what they appear to be doing. In time, gravitate toward the person who interests you the most, positively or negatively. What do you want? Do you want to change that person? Be changed by that person? Or just be in their company for a time? When you get what you want, celebrate that and leave the floor. If you fail in what you wish, dance the recognition of that and leave the floor. Take time to absorb what happened.

Day two: Everything is the same except The Hub Meditation is the question, What is female? (Best to leave this question for day two. Having "had their day," the men will more easily accept the adventure of answering the question of "What is female?")

Day three: Yesterday, you did a Hub Meditation on What is female? The day before, you did one on What is male? Recapture the specific images of each in your mind's eye, first one and then the other. Now mesh them into one body and wait to see what will happen. What do you see? Is one image visible and the other present but not visible? Is one on the outside and one on the inside? Are both visible but is one dominant? So many possibilities.

When the male/female structure is clear to you, go to work on whichever is on the inside, using the technique of Each Alone to become that image. When you have finished, you are ready for the second stage. As X, go through another Each Alone, this time putting on the other image *on the outside*. We can call this outside image Y. Y is what X shows to the world.

When you have finished this double task, you are ready again to Go Visiting, look about you and take in the "world" in which you find yourself. You have one more question to answer before you go on. What do you as the complexity of X clothed as Y want to do—need to do—for, to or against the world in which you find yourself? Are there individuals out there with whom you need to interact? To avoid? Do you have a task in relation to that entire community? To one or to a few individuals? Are you a hermit? Once you have answers, retaining the full sense and presence of both X and Y find the *danced metaphors* that contain this action. Now you are ready to do whatever you have to do, with or without others. If you succeed in your task, celebrate that and leave the floor. If you fail, dance the recognition of that and leave the floor.

I did this structure fully only once, at the University of California at San Diego. It covered the three days and it worked. There were many dancers, men and women, attending this workshop and large numbers often make for freedom because the dancers quite accurately assume that they will be less conspicuous among so many. There was no problem from any of the men when the question went out, "What is female?" The dancing was varied, animated and quirky. Duets and trios went on for a long time and *things happened*—people changed as they danced. The talk afterwards was full of a wonderment at how completely they were caught up and how the many emotional and intellectual surprises jolted them.

There's always a risk when the space is opened to deep and often conflicted feelings. Over the years, I've given out these two questions, What is male? and What is female? to about eight different groups. Be warned. This one is, as they say, "heavy." In the appendix of *Dance and the Specific Image: Improvisation*, pages 195–203, there appears a dialogue between some dancers at a University of Hawaii workshop and myself. It was kicked off by some who were upset because they had wept during a Male/Female. The discussion touched upon some of the fundamental attitudes that go to shape art.

Most of the dancers in the workshop were excited that they could be dancing *and* actually dealing with what really mattered to them. How sophisticated and how mature should the dancers be to attempt this? I have no answer. I only know this stuff is dynamite in the bodies and minds of dancers who are open and willing to look at each other and themselves.

*Lose your head[†]

In an early workshop, I hit upon a structure that could involve all. I had an old rock record, so badly worn that at about its third minute it would invariably get stuck in a maddening repetition. Early in one of the sessions I said to the entire group:

> Find a turning movement that meshes with what you hear. Your inner action is to lose your head, whatever that means to you.

*Go 1-2-3

Many of the exercises came out of various kinds of resistance. In the earliest workshop, at the University of Texas in Austin, there was a rhythmic wizard who was something of a leader. He was bright and outspoken, but in every improvisation would get caught in one characterization, regardless of what was being done: a stiff military figure with mannequinlike elegance. I was convinced that this was a gambit to avoid doing anything that was unexpected or revealing. To get him to come loose, I devised this:

> Make a circle of anywhere from six to a dozen or even twenty people. One person goes to the center. When I call out, "Go!" that person begins to dance off the impulses of the moment. The focus of the people making up the circle is to sense, feel and finally determine the inner rhythm that is driving her.him. Finding this underlying, basic, repetitive rhythm that could support the improvisation of the soloist is an individual and silent activity. If it helps, you can soundlessly pat out the rhythm you perceive on your thighs.
>
> After a period of time I will shout, "Go 2!" whereupon everyone in the circle will beat out with hands, feet and/or voice, the rhythm you found individually. Try to be heard by the soloist despite the chaotic sounds of the others and hang on stubbornly to what you believe is the best rhythm to support the soloist—yours.
>
> After a while, I will call out, "Go 3!" Now, listen closely to your neighbors and, retaining the character of your own rhythm, musically blend it with what you hear. Once you are meshing with your neighbors, shift your focus to the soloist. There are many choices open to you at this point. While keeping a musical relationship with your neighbors, your sounds can challenge the soloist, support the soloist, or mock the soloist, and so on. Whatever your attitude toward the soloist and what he.she is doing is what will shape the music and rhythms you and the others are creating.

I asked my rhythm whiz to take the center space. He started as always, with his toy general posturing, but the circle began a combination of a heavy rock beat and a pounding African rhythm. They caught what he apparently wasn't doing. At first he maintained his prim, jerky style, but his endurance was less than theirs and, to catch his breath, he slouched to his knees. They increased the volume and intensity of their rhythms. A bit more of this and he rolled over on his back and, mocking them, began to shake his shoulders. Before he knew it he was swept into a wild thrashing about that resembled a tantrum. Again, driven to exhaustion, he stopped and, in the simplest way, rose to his feet, the circle going with him and relaxing, both going into a quiet, kooky shuffling about, totally unlike anything he had ever done before. Finally, I said, "OK," and everybody fell back, aware that something had really happened; but the peculiar value of this exercise was that the longer it went, the deeper it reached. He got so tired he could barely go on and it didn't seem to matter what he did. The toy general disappeared and a latent fury flared for a bit, followed by a slightly embarrassed self-mockery.

Returning to Go 1-2-3 again and again, I would witness dancers start up mannered and controlled and then, in that sea of sound and past the point of exhaustion, with a new flush of energy the soloist would strike out in forms, gestures and dance that were not only often startlingly beautiful, but almost always a retrospective surprise to the soloist, the dancer. Turning the corner of being too tired to care, motions would pour out that seemed to come from deep, lovely and sometimes dark places. Great excitement can be added by inviting skilled musicians to join in.

Recognition Ritual   The conventional greeting when dancers meet to work is, "How are you?" They may exchange groans and a catalogue of injuries, but in time the greeting becomes a formality. Recognition Ritual is an attempt to bring the exchange into the life we all understand best—dance and learning to speak in dance. It may be preceded by From Now (chapter 10).

> All fill the space in a large circle, pacing about, getting limber and preparing to dance. Whoever is ready and willing, step into the center and dance your answer to the unspoken question, "How are you?" All the others will pay close attention to what you are "saying," having the option of responding to what they "hear" positively, negatively or indifferently. Their responses may range from lifts to touching to circling or dance actions at a distance. There is no proper response. Whenever you are ready to quit, you retire to the edge of the circle and another person will step into the center and "tell" us how he.she is. Each person holds the center for as long as needed. Recognition Ritual ends when the last person steps back to the circle's edge.

13 *Exercises*

Level 6

Make a Phrase

Gather in groups of three. Any one of you, on any impulse, will release from your body a short phrase of dance. The other two learn it. As soon as "the teacher" nods, satisfied that what was given was learned, one of the others repeats the phrase and adds another short phrase of dance which the other two learn, always starting with the first dance phrase. When number two indicates satisfaction, the third person, starting with the first and second dance phrase, adds a third phrase of movement which is learned by the other two.

This flow of learning and adding continues until the dancers feel that they have collectively created a string of moves that are just long enough. How will you know? Worry not. It will feel right, and you will stop adding and begin to really learn to do the entire sequence. The test is to do the complete sequence at least twice without pausing at the repeat.

Having done this, the three of you separate, going to work at mastering what was made. Only one third of the whole phrase was yours. Now you have the problem of making all of it yours. When you feel that you have mastered it, return to the area where you were working together. When all three are finished, go through the entire phrase twice, dancing full out and yet moving in unison. There will be subtle differences and that's fine.

Satisfied that you all can do it, you are ready to embark on an exciting complexity. First, do the entire phrase twice, together. Having done that, each of you is free to improvise with the material with only two restrictions. You can do any one movement as slowly or as quickly as you wish and as often as you wish, with any dynamic—turning it, carrying it into the air or to the floor—*just so long as the order of the moves remains sacrosanct.* The sequence is inviolable; how often or what you do with each move is your choice. The second restriction is that *every move and choice is about, to and for what one or both the others are doing.* You never slide off into a solo preoccupation. This is preeminently a trio. Go at it until I call a halt.

The next problem is to answer a question. Is there, in your dance phrase, an energy trying to become something? The three of you will come to the answer just by talking and agreeing; or, you will dance for another trio and ask them what they think you are trying to become; or the teacher/leader will say what he.she sees. You now have a goal—a place or a state of being that you want to reach. Once that is settled, again follow the structure of doing the long phrase twice and then improvising (still observing the two restrictions), now with the need to arrive at the state of being agreed upon and thus coming to a finish.

Some examples from actual classes will clarify the dynamic of this exercise. One trio seemed possessed by a frenetic intensity. I told them, "You are fiercely resolved to discover serenity together." They did—after a long and frenzied struggle. Another trio looked like karate-style warriors. I told them: "You are gladiators. Only one of you will be left alive by the evening's end. Your long phrase is the ritual warmup that you have been trained to do. In the changing room before you enter the arena, you warm up together, first in the ritual and then in the improvisation. You are studying the style and weakness or strength of the other two, all the while trying to gain a psychological advantage. There is no physical contact. When you are ready, you stop in the pose that best exhibits your power." They were two men and one woman and we hardly breathed as we watched.

In Make a Phrase, I saw quite a few students discover for the first time what it meant to be a person doing something in dance without deliberately carrying that ridiculous sing, "Look Ma, I'm dancing." They were dancing without trying to.

Rituals of Power

The power game involves all of us in one way or another. It is the doorway for most of the pain coming into the world, whether among nations or intimate circles of family or friends, or it is the lever of compassion and love. Rituals of Power needs five to seven dancers sophisticated in the techniques of improvisation that we have been describing. The turmoil of a stage full of egos working for domination or subservience will challenge the ability of all to accommodate to changes and surprises. Rituals of Power can be set anywhere: a business office, a royal court, a military unit, a fraternity house and so on.

All sit in a circle, big enough to observe all. Accept the premise that we are all guests at a luxurious home in the country. First, all do a Mind-Wash (chapter 9). Then, after simply looking at all the others in the circle, ask yourself, "Who are these people sharing this weekend with me?" Everyone will create his.her own secret cast. Who are you, and where do you rank in popularity, talent, power? Who do you think might look up to you? Who is your equal? To whom would you defer? Where do you want to be in the power-prestige structure of this group, and what are you willing you do to get there? What is the dance metaphor, the physical metaphor for the task you have set for yourself? When you have the answers to these questions, turn your palms upward and rest your hands on your knees.

When the last person does this, she.he rises, leaves the circle and goes to find a place in an imaginary line that faces the circle, placing her.himself at what might be the head, middle, or the rear, depending upon where she.he ranks her.himself. Then, clockwise, the next person rises to do the same—and so on until all are in the line, self-ranked. There will be surprises and some gentle jostling as individuals negotiate for "their" position within this group.

When the group has settled into a line with a "leader" at the head, the "leader" walks to one side of the space and faces into the space. The person behind goes to stretch out prone and at right angles at the foot of the leader. Each person in turn does the same, a couple of feet away from the previous person. When all are in place, the leader walks across the bodies of all to find his.her place to do Each Alone (chapter 10). Then the first person to lie down rises, steps across the bodies of the others and finds a place to do Each Alone. In this order, one by one the others rise to do similarly. At this juncture, the taped music will begin.

When you finish Each Alone and have become X, you move to engage one or more of the others with the intent of realizing the task, the ambition you have set for yourself, unless your X is trying to be unnoticed. Your X may have a high-ranking position in the group and yet wish to avoid the responsibility and the exposure it entails. Follow the needs of your X. The development of this stage of Rituals of Power is exactly like The Duet as a Structure (chapter 10), except that now there are more than two people onstage. Depending upon who you are, will determine how many you deal with. One character might try to affect everyone, while another may focus on only one other. If and when you realize your task, you celebrate that in dance and leave the dance floor. Similarly, if you are convinced you cannot succeed, you dance that resignation and leave.

If this exercise works well for the group, try revisiting it a week or so later:

You will sit as before, anywhere in the circle, clear your heads and go back to Rituals of Power, as you experienced it last week. What do you recall? What happened? Did you change? Did you change anyone? Did you succeed? Fail? What was left undone? What did you learn about these people—about yourself? In reality, we have already lived a part of Rituals of Power and this will be a continuation of what happened last week. As you sit in the circle, observing each other, you should ask yourself, "What remains to be done? Having lived through this and that with these others, what am I now going to do? What am I going to try to become?" The order in which you line up and lie down will probably change. Much will be different and some things the same. Find out!

By its very nature, there is no way that anyone can predict how an improvisation will shape up. It may go flat. If so, so be it. A tennis match between the two hottest players in the world may be a bore. How many Super Bowls produced super yawns? Professional wrestling is always exciting (if that's your taste), because it is theatrically plotted and choreographed. When you go to a genuine sporting event, you hope for excitement and may get it—or not. Honest improvisation is no different. As an exercise in acting technique for dancers, Rituals of Power is unparalleled. It takes The Duet as a Structure and carries it to a richer and more demanding level.

Props Fantasy[†]

One can fire up the imagination to find, create and become with a prop or a costume. It really doesn't matter from where you start, just so long as you ultimately plunge in deep enough to get your eyelashes wet with the magic "if."

Set out in the space anything that is available: a wine bottle, chairs, a table, a book, a pillow, etc. Two of you enter the space and begin to deal with what you find there. Beginning on a literal level is fine. Where and when does the literal spin away into fantasy and metaphor?

Processional[†]

Start with a Hub Meditation while all are seated, eyes closed: Out of your past was there someone to whom you never spoke your love? Rise when you can see that person or a person you imagine and go to the perimeter of the room.

For the next section, find some music that can support slow gliding strides. It should have a lyric, a blues or a ballad base.

Cross the space twelve times, each in your own world. Every cross is a poem to a different part of the beloved, a poem that describes, evokes or becomes that body part. The sequence is the same for all the dancers: the hair, the eyes, the mouth, the neck, the chest/bosom, the shoulders, the elbows, the belly/voice, the pelvis, the thighs/knees, the feet and finally the totality, the beloved, entire. Each cross uses that particular part of the body as the focus of the movement, like the pen of the poem. This is not meant to be an isolation sequence. The entire body supports the action of the focal point of each cross. The form of the twelve crosses takes its structural cue from Circles. On the last cross, pause to become the beloved—to become a statue of the beloved in motion.

Ping Pong	Two dancers face each other about twenty feet apart. Either one starts by "throwing" a movement gesture across the space to the other. The receiver accepts the imagined impact of the gesture into his.her body, letting it ride in and out of the body. The body change made by the thrown gesture shapes what is thrown back to the original sender, who continues the game of receiving and sending. The improvisation continues back and forth. The image to think of is the jai alai basket—a scoop that receives the ball only to swoop it out in return. This is not and should not be a mirror exercise in that the receiver returns what was sent. In jai alai, as in racketball and as in life, the receiver's response is a function of three factors: what was thrown, the nature of the receiver and the position of the receiver.

Adam and Eve	This exercise for two dancers is a variation of Ping Pong. It can be adapted for any characters—Hamlet and his mother, Willy Loman and his son, or any characters that you make up together.

> You are Adam, and you are Eve. You are at opposite sides of the space. In the beginning, Eve, who has never yet slept, is looking at Adam, who is asleep for the first time. After a while Adam wakes and discovers Eve for the first time. This is Ping Pong. You cannot come any closer than you are.

The Minnesota Duet	Another exercise for a duet, created by a pair of very good dancers in a workshop in the Minnesota woods. It teaches students not only to act on the basis of observing each other but to anchor that observation in a personal commitment: they are dancing for something they want—for themselves.

> Face each other from opposite corners of the space, your arms crossed on your chest. Contemplate each other, asking, "What is there in that person across the room that I would like to possess for myself?" List all those qualities and wait until one shines out more than all the others. When you know for certain what that one quality is, give the signal by uncrossing your arms to hang at your sides. When the second dancer makes this deciding gesture, both of you approach each other to possess that quality which you are determined to absorb into yourself. Become what you desire. You can use proximity to get what you want but no body contact, no touching, no pointing and no illustrating with the hands. When you have captured or absorbed what you desired, leave.

When this was done the first time, it had all the tension and design of a Western facedown. Possessing the quality of someone else seems like a crazy idea at first but it is the paramount activity of adolescents as they "try on" personalities for size, a perennial activity of some highly impressionable personalities, the professional task of all performers in the theatre but alas, a terrifying prospect for rigid people desperate to keep intact the image they have of themselves.

Prison

For this exercise you will need to construct, in your work space, separate enclosures or cells about six feet by four. Use cushions, chairs—whatever is available.

> Step inside the space furthest from where you are now. When you arrive, you have only one thing to deal with, the word *prison*. Whatever that word means to you and whatever flows from or away from that word, is what happens.

When I did this with the Workgroup, it provoked some of the most profound and complex improvisations I had ever seen. The dancers used that word the way an oyster uses a grain of sand, taking it in internally and growing something significant around it. Make your own setting and try it with any word you choose: drop *forest* into to your mind, let it swim about for a while and odds are you will find yourself in world as dense and active as the forest and possibly as vivid as an actual forest.

*Focusing

One day I observed two dancers engaged in a swirling, twisting, turning duet, remarkable for the fact that they never lost eye contact: on the floor, turning, in the air or running. It had the quality of a good-humored duel.

> Someone, something cannot or will not stop looking into the eyes of another.

The beauty of this fanatical locking into an activity is how often it leads the dancers into virtuosic movement. It follows directly from Tamiris's challenge to "follow through." Make your own task that involves a pair or more dancers and pushes them to the limits.

*Ariadne's Dance†

If there ever was an exercise in sense memory, and of the imagination, this is it. The name comes from the princess who saved Theseus from the Minotaur's deadly labyrinth; he deserted her on the island of Naxos.

> A pair of lovers have just parted. The one who remains freezes like a statue of the deserted Ariadne. Standing there full of longing, bit by bit, particle by particle, the body decays and crumbles. For as long as it takes, the dancer is "gone," dead, as it were, on the floor; but some part resists, and bit by bit and particle by particle, life is regained until erect. There is actually strength—a new strength, not seen before, and this phoenix-figure covers the space to an exit, but not the exit taken by the one who turned away.

*Whatever Happens, | Wherever you are, you are. Whatever happens, happens.

There are any number of places in the country where dancers meet regularly for a few hours a week, people coming and going, dancing, observing, with no supervision or ground rules and no judgment. For any group or class that is engaged in cracking open this matter of acting technique for dance performance, a venture into this open-ended way could deliver some surprises worth the risk. And risk it is, as is all improvisation. Three particulars need to be said: for our purposes here, Whatever Happens, Happens should be done by a group that has been working together for a few months, at the very least. Secondly, one or two people or the teacher/leader should stay out observing and being *en garde* against the actions of people getting too close to the edge. Third, and this is only Daniel speaking, don't make a habit of it.

*Tandem Solo Pick some strong music with a powerful momentum and start off with a good improvisor.

One of you will go to the center of a circle of dancers. As you listen to the opening strains of the music, catch an idea out of what you hear and then take off. After a while, I will call out the name of another dancer who will replace the first one in the center of the circle. The challenge for that second dancer will be to realize what she.he reads as the intent of the first dancer. After a while, I will call out a third dancer, who tries to continue what the second dancer had been doing and so on, until near the end of the music, I would say, "Everyone finish it."

*Relay Solo This is a tricky development of Tandem Solo. Use music or not, as you choose.

Six to nine people sit in a circle, all with eyes closed and all meditating on a specific idea for a dance. Whoever gets one first slaps her.his palm on the floor three times, thereby claiming the space and the right to begin. Call this person A. The floor-slapping opens everyone's eyes. Dancer A rises to enter the circle and, taking all the time he.she needs, begins his.her solo. All observe A closely. Whenever A is ready, he.she says "Now" for all to hear, stops dancing and retires to the circle's edge. All rise and attempt to take off from where A said "Now." Dancer A remains standing and observing; when A sees someone who seems to be following through with what had been started, he.she calls out the name of that person. All the others stop dancing, retire to the circle's edge and observe this second soloist, B. Dancer B continues developing what A started, calls out "Now" when ready and leaves the center for the others to attempt to continue in the direction taken. When the fourth person says "Now," all rise and try to support what D is doing—this now becomes a group dance rather than competing soloists. The cue to bring the dance to a close comes from D, who stops dancing.

You may choose to have more than four soloists.

Tandem Solo and Relay Solo both require strong powers of observation, and that, for all performers, dancers, singers and actors, is precious: the ability to "read" another.

*Performing in Unison

If you have at your disposal any piece of choreography that has an extended passage for two or more dancers moving in unison, rehearse it to achieve not only full technical command but as exact unison as possible. Plan to perform it for the group or class. The problem for both the doers and the watchers: do the dancers just dance the hell out of it, all the while looking out of the corner of their eyes and smiling like crazy, or is it a choreography that demands a more complex justification? Who are you and why are you all doing the same thing at the same time? Can you justify the unison activity? Does the inherent anonymity give you a freedom you don't possess when you are doing a more individual and responsible role? Is there an ecstasy possible when the individual is submerged in the group?

Unison looks so simple, but from my standpoint it is anything but. I can think of no exercise that forms a greater challenge to justification than this. On rare occasions, I have seen dancers pour their hearts out in an ecstasy that is overflowing *because* they are dancing together—in unison.

*Ham and Clove

Paul Zimet, one of the leading members of the Open Theatre, gave occasional acting lessons to the Workgroup. Once, he asked Lee Connor and me to read and work on a scene between Ham and Clove from *Endgame* by Samuel Beckett. The next day, Lee and I were about to go over the scene again and I said, "Why don't we do it our way, as a Duet? Our characters and intentions were clearly defined. All we had to do was follow the exact route of a Duet and we had a dance—and surprise, we did. It proved alive enough to be performed publicly many times and was called Ham and Clove.

> Ham is blind, and limited to a small space (a wheelchair in the play). He depends on Clove and needs a physical hold on him to control him. Clove is young, agile and now finally rebellious, enjoying keeping out of Ham's powerful reach.

Take any pair or group of characters that excites you, from anywhere: the theatre, novels, films, soap operas, your life. It is all out there for the using.

Signs of the Times[†]

For anyone working alone, only the initial phase of this exercise is potentially useful. It can ignite further solo work, either as improvisation or choreography.

> Find your place in the space and seat yourself. With your breath, create a clear space in your mind. (A bit of time.) Wherever you go, wherever you look, there are

signs saying things to you, informing you, ordering you, beseeching you. Do a Hub Meditation on as many signs as you can recall. Which is the one that is there in your mind, regardless of what new ones you recall?

When it is clear that the hub is occupied, rise and begin to say the words of that sign silently, to yourself, at any tempo, until it settles into a definite rhythm. As you are doing this, allow the body to follow the impulses, dictates, undercurrents, the literal and the metaphoric elements of your sign. Gradually shape your motions and your words into a repetitive phrase. When you can do this with authority several times over, stop and go to the perimeter of the floor.

When the last person has left the working area for the floor's edge, from your position, in your own time, you can now utter your sign aloud for the first time—loud enough for all to hear, simultaneously moving through the motions of your sign. After you fully establish the sound-motion presence of your sign, begin to take cognizance of the others. What they are doing and saying? Depending on how they affect you, the you that is bound up in your sign will direct with whom you choose to interact and what you want to do with, for or to that other person/sign.

From here on, do not alter or augment the words, but they can be rephrased rhythmically, intellectually or emotionally, depending upon what happens. The movement phrase can be dealt with in a more fluid way. Body contact, repetitions of single motions, altered dynamics, turning, shifting the phrase to the floor or into the air are all possible, but no radical movement changes should occur. You are finished when your intent in regard to one or more of the others is fulfilled or unequivocally defeated.

Become a Public Figure[†]

This resembles Signs of the Times. It too asks for a Hub Meditation that calls up the contemporary scene. As in Signs of the Times, only the initial phase will serve solo improvisation and/or choreography.

Do a Hub Meditation on figures who are in the public eye. Let a parade of them pass before your mind's eye until one cannot be displaced from the hub of your mind. When that happens proceed to do an Each Alone, that is, becoming your X one part of the body at a time. Taking all the time needed, prepare a full-length portrait of your X. When you have become X, look about you. Do you need to relate to all, some or one of the others? By relating, what do you mean? What do you want to do to, for or against the other(s)? What is your dance metaphor for what you want to do? Having answered these questions, proceed to live out your intentions.

This exercise can use the format of The Duet, Rituals of Power or Inside the Outside. In the few times this exercise was given, the results were audacious, vivid and full of authority. Why? Perhaps, like finding the inner rhythm of someone who attracts your interest even though they rub you negatively, we are freer in our observations than when we are looking within.

APPENDICES AND INDEX

Anecdotal Material

Theory. Theory. Theory. Sometimes the recounting of a few actual events can ground ideas, making them more useful. In a choreography class at the American Dance Festival, Adam Battelstein, a monk praying, strong dance with unusual moves, much energy and a good strong continuous thread of thematic development. I fall asleep. I ask him to do it the next day. I watch and my mind registers a blank.

Class talks. "There's no dynamic buildup." "You're not using the space. You don't move from downstage right." "There's no rhythmic drive or excitement." Then I ask him to do it once more. He does about twenty seconds and I finally get a glimmer of what might be wrong. Not choreography but performance—the inner life. I take him aside. "What you are doing is forbidden. Your superiors consider this ritual sacrilegious. If anyone in the order learns of it, you will be excommunicated, *but you find yourself compelled to do it* in spite of the danger. You know you will have no life outside and yet you persist."

This time the piece is hair-raising. He still has no dynamic buildup; he is still huddling downstage right with his back to the stage area and the rhythm is still tight, restrained and erratic. We are all caught up with his passion and yet the choreography has not been altered. There are some new accents, strange rhythmic breaks, and we are not sure whether he has taken a breath for the entire length of his dance. Some of us also had difficulty breathing. It is not enough to do something. There must be a contradiction, an obstacle, a reason for *not* doing what you are doing.

At Arizona State University, Gregory Nuber presents a lovely and brilliantly danced solo that has elements of greeting to the audience, showing off and having a good time with excellent elevation. The problem: Greg is really happy when he is lusting with pleasure in the movement. He is confused, embarrassed and unconvincing when he is expected to address the audience directly. The piece is difficult and some of the technical challenges dominate his mind, all of which makes for an uneven performance.

Suggestion: "You live in a beautiful city of which you are very proud. Show the beautiful places in your city. Describe and reveal them with your body." It works briefly and unevenly. I try another tack. "You are the music. Your body is creating the music. Your body is singing the music to us." He starts off flying but soon seems more confused than ever. I ask him, "How would Baryshnikov do this stuff?" His eyes light up and he sails into a full-breasted, hungry-for-space version that does not let up until the last few moments. It took more energy than he anticipated and he ran down, but it worked. It is not enough to give what you think is a valid direction. It is futile to demand that your brilliant direction be followed when it doesn't ignite the performer. You have to find the one that works. As a performer, it matters not what own your internal image is if: (1) "it lights your fire," and (2) it looks to the choreographer exactly what was wanted. She.he need not know what is going on inside, only what is seen.

Kathleen Henry: This is an elegant and sensuous study with gentle swaying, tilts and torso thrusts forward and back. The problem: Done in anxiety and uncertainty. I learn that it is a Luigi study. The suggestion: "You are getting lost in a morass of self-focus which has nothing to do with Luigi. You say he is your hero but when you dance you think only of your limitations. Next time there will only be your homage and devotion to every nuance of Luigi's lovely movement." Amazing. She acts relieved. In the most innocent way she accepts the premise that we will not look at her weaknesses as a dancer and only look at Luigi's wonderful study. She looks and dances quite well, a bit unsteady, but her lack of concern about herself carries her and us directly to Luigi.

Kurt Anton: A tall, very strong dancer in the prime of young power and daring, doing commercial work, clubs, industrial shows, and so on. The piece he shows us is new and has been performed once. It is a blast from beginning to end: full of virtuosity, speed, frontal assault, seduction, all vitiated by intermittent tension about the technical displays, some being quite difficult. It is crisscrossed by a shifting focus and no central spine.

My suggestion: "Every move is a breeze. You're dancing on shipboard and there are several devastatingly beautiful women on the cruise. It would delight you if they made a play for you rather than having to make the exertion." He does it to the hilt and the viewers all sense the seduction gambit, saying it was done quite well. The technical work looked more secure and less tense. But I sense he feels uneasy doing this.

I ask him, "Do you like doing this seduction bit?" "Not really." "Do you like these moves?" "Yes, yes!" "Well, glory in them and celebrate your power in doing them. Welcome the audience to share your pleasure in what you are doing." He performs it with happiness and it is very good.

Oraldo Para: A ritualistic dance. The problem: He is young in dance technique and does his best. There is self-consciousness due to this. The suggestion: I ask him to close his eyes.

D: Does this dance take its inspiration from some work of art?

O: Yes.

D: Can you see some of this art in your mind right now?

O: (A bit of time.) Yes.

D: Can your body fill out, no, better, become one of these works of art with all of its strength and style?

O: (His eyes open startled. Thinks a bit more.) Yes, of course.

He danced full out, a little past his technique but it was dancing. At a three-day workshop at the New York University Tisch School of the Arts, there is a session on just this problem—acting technique for dance performance. Weeks ahead, students were told to bring to performance level a dance that will be viewed only for its performance quality and not at all for its choreography. Names have been lost in time.

The first is a lithe, dark-haired dancer who begins upstage left with an insouciant pose, legs crossed. To a deliciously funky boogie-woogie by Meade Lux Lewis he begins to slither in fairly good jazz style in a diagonal toward downstage right. There is an element of teasing seduction which is constantly being sidelined by sudden violent virtuosic falls and turns. No sooner than he reaches downstage right he has shifted his focus to us, the audience (students, faculty and Daniel), dazzling us with his skill and sexy moves.

The response is mild and the comments caught on to the obvious that the focus was messy. Out of hearing by the class, I tell him: "You kept changing your focus. First, a man alone, then vamping someone just past downstage right, and then showing off for us. Is there someone there in that corner that interests you?" "No, no." "Do you have someone who *really* interests you?" "Yeh." "Is that person in this room?" A sigh. "Nope . . . in Chicago." "You are going to be a magician. In that first pose, you re-create X from Chicago in your mind. When you begin to dance that diagonal from upstage left, your moves are going to bring X to life here in this room. Your moves are a portrait of X. They are conjuring up X all the way from Chicago. By the time you finish the diagonal, X has arrived! From then on, you celebrate your achievement and show off for the benefit of X.

He loved the direction, has full fun with it and provoked bits of laughter throughout. The class approved. I asked him to tell the class what I had told him. He stumbled about, embarrassed and inarticulate. "Someone is over there and I'm dancing and showing off." I try to articulate it and am not much better. "He was a magician and his dance could re-create someone." Why was I also embarrassed? It was the kind of metaphor that works and sounds silly when revealed to others.

Another dancer. He is short, red-haired and strongly built. He also begins upstage left. As his music starts, he plunges into it with all his force. It is a rawly sung gospel version of "Were You There When They Crucified My Lord?" He seems utterly transported as he works his way diagonally downstage. In less than two minutes he is confronting us, dancing at us in sequences of violent and daring falls. There are a few leaps and spins. Midway his back is to us and he is working the upstage area with lurching lateral progressions. The dance ends with intensely dramatic poses that compete with the emotionality of the singer. His intensity, physical virtuosity and daring is impressive, but neither I nor his fellow students seem to have been moved. We have been looking at him from a distance and were not caught up in his actions or his emotion. They criticize the strong use of his face. One said the dance had no shape. One dancer loved it. I draw him aside and out of hearing of the students. "Don't answer any of my questions, only nod your head when you have the answer in your own mind. . . . Is the man who is dancing alone? . . . Is there anyone watching him? . . . Does he want something to happen? . . . Is this something important to him? . . . Does he have the power to make it happen? . . . *What would it matter if it did not happen?* . . . Who is he? . . . Don't start until you have the answers to all these questions and you know where you are.

The dancer spends a long time brooding up in his corner of the space. Finally, he takes his place upstage left facing diagonally across the space and nods to the student running the tape recorder. The singer launches full force into the song and the dancer doesn't move for a very long time as he gazes into the distance. Finally, he lowers his head and begins to move in a most deliberate manner in contradiction to the soaring passion of the singer and in the same deliberate manner he begins to accelerate and intensify his moves until he almost reaches the wildness of the climax of the first version, pauses on the crest of the music and is still. This one got more than fierce applause. Some were moved enough for tears. I was shaken.

Aside from the integrity of his performance, there was the brilliant compression of his own choreography. He barely left out anything of the first version, touching upon all the points but using an economy of expression that stood up against the baroque fullness of the singer. The beginning, the "doing nothing," was as compelling as any other part of the dance. It is rare that a direction produces results as full and to the point as this one.

At the American Dance Festival in 1993, I broke one of my sacred rules. In the Acting for Dance Performance class, a dancer rises to show one of her two dances. The technique is astonishing. Really good elevation, high extensions sustained by iron legs, spins that finish in tight, sustained soussus and a vigorous relation to the music beat. The taste indicated in the choreography is sheer display and nothing else. The performance is cursed by a facial tension that speaks of panic—utter terror of making a mistake by one who is making no mistakes. "Don't speak your answers. Just nod your head when you have the answer. What is your favorite holiday? Celebrate your favorite day of the year." Nothing, absolutely nothing. She is as grim as ever. I tried three other set-ups. Nothing. The same tight mouth, the lips disappearing, the large wet eyes that always seem to have just been weeping staring fixedly through her frozen face.

Finally, I give up. "I am going to violate a rule. I don't care how you feel, how nervous you are about performing, I want you to arbitrarily force your face into a smile and dance at the same time. Show me a broad smile." With difficulty she stretches her lips laterally under the staring eyes. "OK, that's the face." She gets into position with tight face, the music starts, she cracks a smile and in the first move loses it all. She is as brilliant as ever technically—and as panic-stricken. Who or what frightened her to the degree that she has a paralyzed face? I am very sad for her and it is apparent that I cannot and should not function as a therapist.

It would appear from the foregoing that I am some kind of whiz at analyzing performance weakness and coming up with magical solutions. I am not, I fail at times, but generally, I am good at this work. I wouldn't have gone to the trouble of writing this book if I did not have good reason to believe that. How does one get to be good at this kind of teaching, direction and analysis? It is all in the mind. It is all in how one looks at things.

Many of my colleagues seem to be caught up in the moving designs created by the dancers. If these are engaging, elegant and inventive that, to them, is a successful dance. They focus more on what the dance looks like and less on what is being done. Do I think my way is a better way of looking? Of course. That's why I wrote this book.

To return to the question that cued this discussion: How does one get to be good at this kind of teaching and direction? If the six questions are present in the mind of the viewer, the teacher, the leader, the director, the choreographer, then what was not noticed before will be there. Perhaps it will not be as clear as a hand before the face, but there will be enough for the leader and the dancer to try this and that as they inch closer and closer to the truth as they both sense it.

A *Beat Analysis of* Dance in the Sun

I am adamantly opposed to ever revealing what my dance works are about and I have never understood it when my colleagues go on at length explaining the inspiration, meaning and intent of what they are doing. But most people in the audience cannot approach the choreographer and ask, "What were you doing? What did you mean? What did you want us to see?" We must learn to deal only with what we see and perceive and not with any explanations from the artist—or from the critics.

The magic of art is that it reaches out to many of us, though not all, in a way that enkindles some part of our own experience and life, and in the light of that flame, we grasp something that quickens us. At the core of that work of art is some part of the artist's experience and life. If the artist reveals the specific of that, our specific is diminished, pushed to the background and probably erased. The exquisite balance that exists in art is lost. On one side is the artist and on the other is the audience. Between them is the object the artist made. They both make that object art. If this were not so, how would it be possible for us to stand so still and shiver a bit as we gaze upon an Apollo carved two thousand years ago, or gasp coming suddenly upon a burgundy red Tang vase from China? The sculptor and the potter are long gone, but the object is there, and so are we, with no artist to explain his.her meaning.

Having said this, I am going to present a beat analysis of *Dance in the Sun,* a dance that has not been in my repertoire for many years. (It does exist in a film by Shirley Clarke and is on videotape in my own videotape library.) Why am I betraying my own principles? I have found in my teaching that the beats proved to be elusive for many, despite the fact that their existence, whether consciously analyzed or created intuitively, are essential to a performance that is alive and evolving every moment of the dance.

The Impetus

I was walking and looking along a country road at the peak of autumn. Turning a bend in the road, my eyes were filled by a young birch tree that seemed to be creating the color yellow for the first time. I stopped, looking for a long time. In the days that followed, the vision of that tree wouldn't leave me. It had to be a dance. In the course of what is described, there is constant reference to "seeing." I *am* seeing—in my mind's eye. I can see the glow of that birch tree even now as I type this sentence. What I describe below is not a barren stage but a breath-taking autumn day on a crest of Mt. Airy Road, in Croton-on-Hudson, New York.

The Outer Action/*The Inner Action*

Entrance, walking slowly from downstage right along the apron looking about.
Looking and looking, never to forget what I am seeing.

Nearing stage left, head turns left, see something upstage left.
My eyes are filled by a young birch tree that seems to have swallowed the sun.

Pause and run up there, reaching right arm up as if to touch . . .
Why do I want to touch the leaves?

Both arms come up as if to embrace.
Seeing it all, tree and sky, I want to embrace it all. . . . Daniel, how pretentious!

Turn while dropping arms and letting sweatshirt fall.
Taking a long breath, still looking about.

Lyric arms flowing in successions starting from torso.
A mess of reaching, receiving and needing to touch the immensity of what I am looking at.

Right leg raises slowly; glide run to downstage right; long, slow relevé; jumps in place; run backward to upstage right; sissonnes into beat run in two circles.
Each single thing I see adds to a tide of energy and power that fills my body until I am pouring it out, trying to fly up out of my skin, and I pound the ground in futility at my limitations.

Glide run to downstage right; jumps in place; run back to do jumping run in circle; glide run to downstage right; jump in place; run back to upstage center and stop to pause.
Repeats what just happened with even more intensity.

The sexy box step; the torso aims to touch the sky; another glide run and everything seems to move from the hips.
Taking a breath, a rest, backing off, the impact of all this takes on a faint erotic overtone.

The legs like a clock or a slow-motion seesaw.
Taking a long breath, sensing a new burst of trying to leave the limits of my skin to merge with the sky and the tree.

Into the waltz and the big leaps; relevé and jumps in place.
I believe I have succeeded and I am flying, floating and hovering.

The flowing, lyric arms; slow pivot turn in place, looking about; finally going, pick up sweatshirt and leave with one glance back.
Energy is spent and all that will be left will be the memory of this moment. Well, remember it!

Susanne K. Langer on Performance
A Critique

In the early fifties, an astonishing event occurred. A professional philosopher wrote several books that regarded dance as a serious focus for study and analysis. These were *Philosophy in a New Key* (New York: New American Library, 1951) and *Feeling and Form: A Theory of Art* (New York: Scribner's, 1953) by Susanne K. Langer. Not until Noverre in the eighteenth century and some of the nineteenth-century aesthetes like Théophile Gautier and later Paul Valéry did any serious thinker spend any significant amount of paper considering the nature and significance of dance in human culture. Philosophers have been probing the meaning of our lives and the arts as far back as the ancient cultures of Greece and Rome and, until recently, dance has not been on their agenda. I am leaving out the cultures of Egypt, Asia, and the Near East because I am ignorant of how their philosophers dealt with dance.

Without entering into the whys of this situation, Langer made a powerful impression on some elements of the dance community, particularly in the academic area. I doubt if any bearer of a Master of Fine Arts in Dance has not struggled through the tangles of her writings. The irony of that awe of this philosopher is how she at significant points denigrates dancers:

> Isadora [Duncan] did not understand music *musically*. . . . Her musical taste as such was undeveloped—not simply poor, but utterly unaccountable. . . . dancers are not particularly discerning critics of music. . . . The writings of most thoughtful dancers are often hard to read because they play so freely across the line between physical fact and artistic significance. . . . to such an extent that their philosophical reflections are apt to be as confused as they are rich. To a careful reader with ordinary common sense they sound nonsensical; to a person philosophically trained they seem, by turns, affected or mystical, until he discovers they are *mythical*. [*Feeling and Form*, 170, 171, 186]

Despite this contempt, her influence among dancers and teachers of dance persists. The question being raised here is what did they take away from their study of Langer and how might that have affected their thinking, teaching and creative work, specifically in relation to the matter of performance? I find myself in disagreement with Langer on many points, but what concerns us most in this book is how she views performance, a matter into which she delves quite deeply.

Before plunging into the quotations from Langer and my disagreements, it would be helpful to go to the dictionaries to draw out their definition of a word that is central to her argument: *virtual. American Heritage:* existing or resulting in essence or effect though not in actual fact, form or name: "the *virtual* extinction of the buffalo." *Webster:* "being is essence of effect, not in fact; not actual, but equivalent, so far as effect is concerned; as, 'he is a *virtual* stranger although we have met.'" In *Problems of Art* (New York: Scribner's, 1957) Langer writes:

> The image in a mirror is a virtual image. A rainbow is a virtual object. It seems to stand on the earth or in the clouds, but it really "stands" nowhere; it is only visible, not tangible. Yet it is a real rainbow, produced by moisture and light for any normal eye looking at it from the right place. . . . if, however, we believe it to have the ordinary properties of a physical thing, we are mistaken; it is an *appearance,* a virtual object, a sun-created image. [P. 5, emphasis added]

Upon reading this paragraph, I lifted the phone and rang the Physics Department at Arizona State University and was put in touch with a professor who does work for NASA. I read him the paragraph and he flat out said, "No, no." A rainbow, he explained is "a physical thing," an electromagnetic phenomena which is as material as your own face. In both cases, we are looking at reflected light, not the object itself. The only time we actually *see* something is a light source such as the sun, the flame of a candle and a light bulb. Everything else is a reflection, *but reflections are material objects because light is a material object—a physical thing.*

Her key words are *virtual* as juxtaposed against *actual.* On page 180 she writes:

> The widely popular doctrine that every work of art takes rise from an emotion which agitates the artist, and which is directly "expressed" in the work, may be found in the literature of every art. . . . Now there is one curious circumstance, which points the way out of this quandary: namely, that the really great experts— choreographers, dancers, aestheticians, and historians—although explicitly they assert the emotive-symptom thesis, implicitly contradict it when they talk about any particular dance or any specified process. No one, to my knowledge, has ever maintained that Pavlova's rendering of slowly ebbing life in *The Dying Swan* was most successful when she actually felt faint and sick, or proposed to put Mary Wigman into the proper mood for her tragic "Evening Dances" by giving her a piece of terrible news a few minutes before she entered on the stage. . . . It is *imagined* feeling that governs the dance, not the real emotional conditions. . . . It is *actual*

movement but virtual *self-expression*. . . . In the dance, the actual and virtual aspects of gesture are mingled in complex ways. The movements, of course, are actual; they spring from an intention, and are in this sense actual gestures but they are not the gestures they seem to be, because they seem to spring from feeling, as indeed they do not. The dancer's actual gestures are used to create a semblance of self-expression, and are thereby transformed into virtual spontaneous movement, or virtual gesture. The emotion in which such gesture begins is virtual, a dance element, that turns the whole movement into dance-gesture.

Part of what she says here is indisputable in that artists having experienced an emotion, go on to make an "if," a magic "if," but on reflection, how many times have I *and you* told stories and experienced the emotion all over again, laughing or weeping? There are times when I've been on the stage where the emotion of the moment and my own emotions were close, and sometimes when I couldn't tell one from the other. One of the best performances of a piece of music that I got out of any composer, came about because Eric Salzman wouldn't record it the way I wanted and in the process of our fight he got very upset and stormed his way through the piece with a conflicted rage, which was exactly what the piece was about.

During an improvisation in a workshop in Hawaii, some of the dancers literally wept as they danced. This weeping—this actual emotion—disturbed them so much that we could not go on with our work until that was discussed. They were certain that something very wrong had occurred. I asked them whether they would have questioned an improvisation in which they had achieved an emotion of great elation and joy.

I have no idea as to whether Susanne K. Langer ever set foot on a stage except to lecture on philosophy. To my mind, she speaks as one who has never performed. She really does not know what she's talking about. She simplifies what is quite complex. She is correct in that artistzs are pretending. They observe, study, think about and reformulate experiences from which they create metaphors for what they feel and believe. Dancers rehearse over and over again choreography which is at times intensely emotional in its content. The rehearsals tend to be businesslike, cool and collected as the motions are learned and mastered. A corner is turned when they *are* learned and mastered. The magic "if" that is the key to the theatre and to Stanislavski's thinking takes over, and then for some dancers there is an inner life wherein there is the *semblance* of an emotion oscillating with *real* emotion.

The emotions of performers are like the waves beating on the shore. The water is there, always, but sometimes it is swarming and flooding the beach and the rocks and then it draws back, leaving the serene sweep of the clear sands. Just so the performer, dancer, singer or actor glides in and out of the emotion that pervades the work. At all times, he.she is immersed in the intent and the action, sometimes with a distance and an objectivity and unexpectedly, with no planning or conscious control *the actual emotion surfaces, sweeping the artist to the highest levels of performance.*

Langer makes the wrong dichotomy. Hers is actual *versus* virtual. Mine is not even a dichotomy but rather the kind of unity seen in channels that border the ocean. The tides rush out, leaving calm and quiet, and then they reverse to pour in the floodtide. We are speaking of a continuity that contains a unity: an ebb and flow of the sea. Always there is water. Onstage there is always the unity created by the choreography and the role continually shaped by the flux within the performer. There are words for this process—this flux: "out of it" and "in it," "objective" and "subjective," "self-conscious" and "unself-conscious," "distanced" and "immersed." In performance, actual performance, not the speculative one described by a philosopher sitting at her desk, performers deliberately and consciously, with radically different techniques, put on the *semblance* of doing and feeling that is appropriate to the role they are playing. I believe that most performers at some entirely unplanned and unexpected moment slip into the role and are no longer pretending because there is no longer the conscious self-awareness of knowing that you are not really doing/feeling but only appearing to do/feel. In this loss of self-awareness, they are actually doing/feeling what is appropriate to the role they have assumed. They become something that cannot be jammed into the definition of what she calls the "virtual gesture."

Ironically, her definition of the virtual gestures is exactly what the Stanislavski technique dubs as "indicating," which is the most heinous act possible for a performer who is dedicated to that technique which is the dominant one for American actors. As an acting teacher would put it, "You *look* like you are doing, you are not *doing*. You are making the *appearance* of doing, not doing." The premise of this school of performing is that by doing, the actor/dancer will begin to feel what the character feels.

As a matter of fact, without this loss of self-consciousness in the act of performing as a *recurrent* experience, not only is the performer not performing well but he.she is miserable. Having this intermittent experience of immersion in the role in class or onstage is the chief reason that draws most actors, singers and dancers into the profession of public performance and staying with it. Losing this capacity, which can happen, becomes discouraging and a reason to quit the stage. This "in it" and "out of it" flow governs the creative process as well. In this matter, either you believe that Susanne K. Langer's thinking is right and useful for you or the position presented here in *The Six Questions* is valid.

This sporadic total absorption is not the secret province of performing artists. It is an experience open to all: to a lawyer researching a case, a greengrocer arranging rows of glistening Granny Smith apples, a teacher introducing the complexities of long division and yes, a philosopher puzzling and probing the mystery of dance performance. Becoming so fully concentrated on the task at hand that for a time there is no awareness of self is the key to a fulfilled life in any line of work.

Consider the "virtual" and the "actual" in "real" life: What about enemies who greet each other with embraces and fond wishes? How many weep at funerals while inwardly celebrating the occasion? What of the mellifluous words of salespeople as they pour out enthusiasm for what they know is a shabby product? If we listen closely to Langer, all good liars and successful prostitutes should be regarded as artists. They are masters of dissembling the virtual gesture. Coming closer to home, have you or I never conveyed the semblance of an emotion?

Yes, artists structure themselves around an imagined world, and a basically symbolic world. Out of her own life she should know that what is imagined and what is a symbol— a metaphor—are all actual phenomena. What is imagined can rip us apart just as profoundly as an earthquake. An unexpected insight after a dark period of confusion can lift us into an exaltation that shakes us to the bone.

It could be asked, "Daniel, why did you drag this lady into your book and why are you going on at such length about your disagreements with her?" My answer to that: She has provided a generation of dancers and teachers of dance with an impressive theoretical justification for dispassionate performance and dispassionate choreography. She glorifies the shell of our art and diminishes its heart. I want and need both.

"The Duende," by Federico García Lorca

Federico Garcia Lorca (1898–1936) was a Spanish poet and dramatist. His plays are often staged in America: Blood Wedding, The House of Bernardo Alba *and* Yerma. *There is less awareness here of his poetry, though one of Doris Humphrey's major works created for José Limon was based on "Lament for Ignacio Mejias."*

Why include this essay in a book about dance performance? Why does it look like prose and read like poetry? It is at times obscure and includes many references to Spanish artists unfamiliar to English speakers. In Spain and countries imbued with Spanish culture, the term duende *carries an aura of the ultimate challenge to every artist. Here in America, the concept is rarely discussed, as such. Upon reading what follows, it will be apparent that we here, all of us—audience, creators and performers—have witnessed and experienced exactly this* Duende *without giving it its name because our language has no word for it. For some its presence is disturbing, even threatening, and for others it is the glow emanating from the art they value most.*

The essay was composed and delivered by Lorca during his stay in Havana en route from the United States; subsequently repeated in Buenos Aires for the Sociedad Amigos del Arts (1934). As translated by Ben Belitt, it is reprinted from Poet in New York *(New York: Grove Press, 1955) by permission of the publisher.*

The Duende[1]: Theory and Divertissement

Whoever inhabits that bull's hide stretched between the Jucar, the Guadalete, the Sil, or the Pisuerga[2]—no need to mention the streams joining those lion-colored waves churned up by the Plata—has heard it said with a certain frequency: "Now that has real *duende!*" It was in this spirit that Manuel Torres, that great artist of the Andalusian people, once remarked to a singer: "You have a voice, you know all the styles, but you will never bring it off because you have no *duende.*"

In all Andalusia, from the rock of Jaen to the shell of Cádiz, people constantly speak of the *duende* and find it in everything that springs out of energetic instinct. That marvelous singer, "El Librijano," originator of the *Debla,* observed, "Whenever I am singing with *duende,* no one can come up to me"; and one day the old gypsy dancer, "La Malena," exclaimed while listening to Brailowsky play a fragment of Bach: "Olé! That has *duende!*"—and remained bored by Gluck and Brahms and Darius Milhaud. And Manuel Tortes, to my mind a man of exemplary blood culture, once uttered this splendid phrase while listening to Falla himself play his "Nocturno dei Generalife": "Whatever has black sounds, has *duende.*" There is no greater truth.

These "black sounds" are the mystery, the roots that probe through the mire that we all know of, and do not understand, but which furnishes us with whatever is sustaining in art. Black sounds: so said the celebrated Spaniard, thereby concurring with Goethe, who, in effect, defined the *duende* when he said, speaking of Paganini: "A mysterious power that all may feel and no philosophy can explain."

The *duende,* then, is a power and not a construct, is a struggle and not a concept. I have heard an old guitarist, a true virtuoso, remark, "The *duende* is not in the throat, the *duende* comes up from inside, up from the very soles of the feet." That is to say, it is not a question of aptitude, but of a true and viable style—of blood, in other words; of what is oldest in culture: of creation made act.

This "mysterious power that all may feel and no philosophy can explain," is, in sum, the earth-force, the same *duende* that fired the heart of Nietzsche, who sought it in its external forms on the Rialto Bridge, or in the music of Bizet, without ever finding it, or understanding that the *duende* he pursued had rebounded from the mystery-minded Greeks to the dancers of Cádiz or the gored, Dionysian cry of Silverio's *siguiriya.*[3]

So much for the *duende;* but I would not have you confuse the *duende* with the theological demon of doubt at whom Luther, on a Bacchic impulse, hurled an inkwell in Nuremberg,[4] or with the Catholic devil, destructive, but short on intelligence, who disguised himself as a bitch in order to enter the convents, or with the talking monkey that Cervantes' mountebank carried in the comedy about jealousy and the forests of Andalusia.[5]

No. The *duende* I speak of, shadowy, palpitating, is a descendant of that benignest daemon of Socrates, he of marble and salt, who scratched the master angrily the day he drank the hemlock; and of that melancholy imp of Descartes, little as an unripe almond, who, glutted with circles and lines, went out on the canals to hear the drunken sailors singing.

Any man—any artist, as Nietzsche would say—climbs the stairway in the tower of his perfection at the cost of a struggle with a *duende*—not with an angel, as some have maintained, or with his muse. This fundamental distinction must be kept in mind if the root of a work of art is to be grasped.

The Angel guides and endows, like Saint Raphael, or prohibits and avoids like Saint Michael, or foretells, like Saint Gabriel.

The Angel dazzles; but he flies over men's heads and remains in mid-air, shedding his grace; and the man, without any effort whatever, realizes his work, or his fellow-feeling, or his dance. The angel on the road to Damascus, and he who entered the crevice of the little balcony of Assisi, or that other angel who followed in the footsteps of Heinrich Suso,[6] commanded—and there was no resisting his radiance, for he waved wings of steel in an atmosphere of predestination.

The Muse dictates and, in certain cases, prompts. There is relatively little she can do, for she keeps aloof and is so full of lassitude (I have seen her twice) that I myself have had to put half a heart of marble in her. The Poets of the Muse hear voices and do not know where they come from; but surely they are from the Muse, who encourages and at times devours them entirely. Such, for example, was the case of Apollinaire, that great poet ravaged by the horrible Muse with whom the divinely angelic Rousseau painted him. The Muse arouses the intellect, bearing landscapes of columns and the false taste of laurel; but intellect is oftentimes the foe of poetry because it imitates too much: it elevates the poet to a throne of acute angles and makes him forget that in time the ants can devour him, too, or that a great, arsenical locust can fall on his head, against which the Muses who live inside monocles or the lukewarm lacquer roses of insignificant salons, are helpless.

Angel and Muse approach from without; the Angel sheds light and the Muse gives form (Hesiod learned of them). Gold leaf or chiton-folds: the poet finds his models in his laurel coppice. But the *Duende,* on the other hand, must come to life in the nethermost recesses of the blood.

And repel the Angel, too—kick out the Muse and conquer his awe of the fragrance of the violets that breathe from the poetry of the eighteenth century, or of the great telescope in whose lenses the Muse dozes off, sick of limits.

The true struggle is with the *Duende.*

The paths leading to God are well known, from the barbaric way of the hermit, to the subtler modes of the mystic. With a tower, then, like Saint Theresa, or with three roads, like St. John of the Cross. And even if we must cry out in Isaiah's voice: "Truly, thou art the hidden God!" at the end and at last, God sends to each seeker his first fiery thorns.

To seek out the *Duende,* however, neither map nor discipline is required. Enough to know that he kindles the blood like an irritant, that he exhausts, that he repulses, all the bland, geometrical assurances, that he smashes the styles; that he makes of a Goya, master of the grays, the silvers, the roses of the great English painters, a man painting with his knees and his fists in bituminous blacks; that he bares a Mosen Cinto Verdaguer[7] to the cold of the Pyrenees or induces a Jorge Manrique[8] to sweat out his death on the crags of Ocaña, or invests the delicate body of Rimbaud in the green domino of the saltimbanque, or fixes dead fish-eyes on the Comte de Lautréamont in the early hours of the boulevard.

The great artists of southern Spain, both gypsies and flamenco, whether singing or dancing or playing on instruments, know that no emotion is possible without the mediation of the *Duende*. They may hoodwink the people, they may give the illusion of *duende* without really having it, just as writers and painters and literary fashion-mongers without *duende* cheat you daily; but it needs only a little care and the will to resist one's own indifference, to discover the imposture and put it and its crude artifice to flight.

Once the Andalusian singer, Pastora Pavon, "The Girl with the Combs," a sombre Hispanic genius whose capacity for fantasy equals Goya's or Raphael el Gallo's, was singing in a little tavern in Cádiz. She sparred with her voice—now shadowy, now like molten tin, now covered over with moss; she tangled her voice in her long hair or drenched it in sherry or lost it in the darkest and furthermost bramble bushes. But nothing happened—useless, all of it! The hearers remained silent.

There stood Ignacio Espeleta, handsome as a Roman turtle, who was asked once why he never worked, and replied with a smile worthy of Argantonio: "How am I to work if I come from Cádiz?"

There, too, stood Héloise, the fiery aristocrat, whore of Seville, direct descendant of Soledad Vargas, who in the thirties refused to marry a Rothschild because he was not of equal blood. There were the Floridas, whom some people call butchers, but who are really millennial priests sacrificing bulls constantly to Geryon; and in a corner stood that imposing breeder of bulls, Don Pablo Murabe, with the air of a Cretan mask. Pastora Pavon finished singing in the midst of total silence. There was only a little man, one of those dancing mannikins who leap suddenly out of brandy bottles, who observed sarcastically in a very low voice: "*Viva* Paris!" As if to say: We are not interested in aptitude or techniques or virtuosity here. We are interested in something else.

Then the "Girl with the Combs" got up like a woman possessed, her face blasted like a medieval weeper, tossed off a great glass of Cazalla at a single draught, like a potion of fire, and settled down to singing without a voice, without breath, without nuance, throat aflame—but with *duende!* She had contrived to annihilate all that was nonessential in song and make way for an angry and incandescent *Duende,* friend of the sand-laden winds, so that everyone listening tore at his clothing almost in the same rhythm with which the West Indian negroes in their rites rend away their clothes, huddled in heaps before the image of Saint Barbara.

The "Girl with the Combs" had to *mangle* her voice because she knew there were discriminating folk about who asked not for form, but for the marrow of form—pure music spare enough to keep itself in air. She had to deny her faculties and her security; that is to say, to turn out her Muse and keep vulnerable, so that her *Duende* might come and vouchsafe the hand-to-hand struggle. And then how she sang! Her voice feinted no longer; it jetted up like blood, ennobled by sorrow and sincerity, it opened up like ten fingers of a hand around the nailed feet of a Christ by Juan de Juni[9]—tempestuous!

The arrival of the *Duende* always presupposes a radical change in all the forms as they existed on the old plane. It gives a sense of refreshment unknown until then, together with that quality of the just-opening rose, of the miraculous, which comes and instils an almost religious transport.

In all Arabian music, in the dances, songs, elegies of Arabia, the coming of the *Duende* is greeted by fervent outcries of *Allah! Allah! God! God!,* so close to the *Ole! Ole!* of our bull rings that who is to say they are not actually the same; and in all the songs of southern Spain the appearance of the *Duende* is followed by heartfelt exclamations of *God alive!*—profound, human, tender, the cry of communion with God through the medium of the five senses and the grace of the *Duende* that stirs the voice and the body of the dancer—a flight from this world, both real and poetic, pure as Pedro Soto de Roja's over the seven gardens (that most curious poet of the seventeenth century), or Juan Calimacho's on the tremulous ladder of tears.

Naturally, when flight is achieved, all feel its effects: the initiate coming to see at last how style triumphs over inferior matter, and the unenlightened, through the I-don't-know-what of an authentic emotion. Some years ago, in a dancing contest at Jerez de la Frontera, an old lady of eighty, competing against beautiful women and young girls with waists supple as water, carried off the prize merely by the act of raising her arms, throwing back her head, and stamping the little platform with a blow of her feet; but in the conclave of muses and angels foregathered there—beauties of form and beauties of smile—the dying *Duende* triumphed as it had to, trailing the rusted knife blades of its wings along the ground.

All the arts are capable of *duende,* but it naturally achieves its widest play in the fields of music, dance, and the spoken poem, since these require a living presence to interpret them, because they are forms which grow and decline perpetually and raise their contours on the precise present.

Often the *Duende* of the musician passes over into the *Duende* of the interpreter, and at other times, when musician and poet are not matched, the *Duende* of the interpreter—this is interesting—creates a new marvel that retains the appearance— and the appearance only—of the originating form. Such was the case with the *duende-*ridden Duse who deliberately sought out failures in order to turn them into triumphs, thanks to her capacity for invention; or with Paganini who, as Goethe explained, could make one hear profoundest melody in out-and-out vulgarity; or with a delectable young lady from the port of Santa Maria whom I saw singing and dancing the horrendous Italian ditty, "O Marie!" with such rhythms, such pauses, and such conviction that she transformed an Italian gewgaw into a hard serpent of raised gold. What happened, in effect, was that each in his own way found something new, something never before encountered, which put lifeblood and art into bodies void of expression. . . .

When the Muse sees death on the way, she closes the door, or raises a plinth, or promenades an urn and inscribes an epitaph with a waxen hand, but in time she tears down her laurels again in a silence that wavers between two breezes. Under the truncated arch of the Ode, she joins with funereal meaning the exact flowers that the Italians of the fifteenth century depicted, with the identical cock of Lucretius, to frighten off an unforeseen darkness.

When the Angel sees death on the way, he flies in slow circles and weaves with tears of narcissus and ice the elegy we see trembling in the hands of Keats and Villasandino[10] and Herrera[11] and Becquer[12] and Juan Ramon Jiménez.[13] But imagine the terror of the Angel, should it feel a spider—even the very tiniest—on its tender and roseate flesh!

The *Duende,* on the other hand, will not approach at all if he does not see the possibility of death, if he is not convinced he will circle death's house, if there is not every assurance he can rustle the branches borne aloft by us all, that neither have, nor may ever have, the power to console.

With idea, with sound, or with gesture, the *Duende* chooses the brim of the well for his open struggle with the creator. Angel and Muse escape in the violin or in musical measure, but the *Duende* draws blood, and in the healing of the wound that never quite closes, all that is unprecedented and invented in a man's work has its origin.

The magical virtue of poetry lies in the fact that it is always empowered with *duende* to baptize in dark water all those who behold it, because with *duende,* loving and understanding are simpler, there is always the *certainty* of being loved and being understood; and this struggle for expression and for the communication of expression acquires at times, in poetry, finite characters.

Recall the case of that paragon of the flamenco and daemonic way, Saint Theresa—*flamenca* not for her prowess in stopping an angry bull with three magnificent passes—though she did so—nor for her presumption in esteeming herself beautiful in the presence of Fray Juan de la Miseria, nor for slapping the face of a papal nuncio; but rather for the simple circumstance that she was one of the rare ones whose *Duende* (not her Angel—the angels never attack) pierced her with an arrow, hoping thereby to destroy her for having deprived him of his ultimate secret: the subtle bridge that links the five senses with the very center, the living flesh, living cloud, living sea, of Love emancipated from Time.

Most redoubtable conqueress of the *Duende*—and how utterly unlike the case of Philip of Austria who, longing to discover the Muse and the Angel in theology, found himself imprisoned by the *Duende* of cold ardors in that masterwork of the Escorial, where geometry abuts with a dream and the *Duende* wears the mask of the Muse for the eternal chastisement of the great king.

We have said that the *Duende* loves ledges and wounds, that he enters only those areas where form dissolves in a passion transcending any of its visible expressions. . . .

The *Duende* works on the body of the dancer like wind works on sand. With magical force, it converts a young girl into a lunar paralytic; or fills with adolescent blushes a ragged old man begging handouts in the wineshops; or suddenly discovers the smell of nocturnal ports in a head of hair, and moment for moment, works on the arms with an expressiveness which is the mother of the dance of all ages.

But it is impossible for him ever to repeat himself—this is interesting and must be underscored. The *Duende* never repeats himself, any more than the forms of the sea repeat themselves in a storm.

In the bullfight, the *Duende* achieves his most impressive advantage, for he must fight then with death who can destroy him, on one hand, and with geometry, with measure, the fundamental basis of the bullfight, on the other.

The bull has his orbit, and the bullfighter has his, and between orbit and orbit is the point of risk where falls the vortex of the terrible byplay.

It is possible to hold a Muse with a *muleta*[14] and an Angel with *banderillas,*[15] and pass for a good bullfighter; but for the *faena de capa,*[16] with the bull still unscarred by a wound, the help of the *Duende* is necessary at the moment of the kill, to drive home the blow of artistic truth.

The bullfighter who moves the public to terror in the plaza by his audacity does not *fight* the bull—that would be ludicrous in such a case—but, within the reach of each man, puts his life at stake; on the contrary, the fighter bitten by the *Duende* gives a lesson in Pythagorean music and induces all to forget how he constantly hurls his heart against the horns.

Lagartijo with his Roman *duende,* Joselito with his Jewish *duende,* Belmonte with his baroque *duende,* and Cagancho with his gypsy *duende,* from the twilight of the ring, teach poets, painters, and musicians four great ways of the Spanish tradition.

Spain is the only country where death is the national spectacle, where death blows long fanfares at the coming of each Spring, and its art is always governed by a shrewd *duende* that has given it its distinctive character and its quality of invention. . . .

Each art has, by nature, its distinctive *Duende* of style and form, but all roots join at the point where the black sounds of Manuel Torres issue forth—the ultimate stuff and the common basis, uncontrollable and tremulous, of wood and sound and canvas and word.

Black sounds: behind which there abide, in tenderest intimacy, the volcanoes, the ants, the zephyrs, and the enormous night straining its waist against the Milky Way.

Ladies and gentlemen: I have raised three arches, and with clumsy hand I have placed in them the Muse, the Angel, and the *Duende.*

The Muse keeps silent; she may wear the tunic of little folds, or great cow-eyes gazing toward Pompeii, or the monstrous, four-featured nose with which her great painter, Picasso, has painted her. The Angel may be stirring the hair of Antonello da Messina,[17] the tunic of Lippi,[18] and the violin of Masolino[19] or Rousseau.[20]

But the *Duende*—where is the *Duende?* Through the empty arch enters a mental air blowing insistently over the heads of the dead, seeking new landscapes and unfamiliar accents; an air bearing the odor of child's spittle, crushed grass, and the veil of a Medusa announcing the unending baptism of all newly-created things.

1930

Notes

1. The *"duende"*: Arturo Barea explains *(Lorca: The Poet and His People):* "Characteristically, Lorca took his Spanish term for daemonic inspiration from the Andalusian idiom. While to the rest of Spain the *duende* is nothing but a hobgoblin, to Andalusia it is an obscure power which can speak through every form of human art, including the art of personality."

2. *Jucar:* river of east central Spain; *Guadalete:* river in southern Spain; *Sil:* river of northwestern Spain; *Pisuerga:* river of northern Spain. *Plata:* river of South America, used by Lorca in the present context to suggest the whole of the Hispanic world outside the borders of his native Spain.

3. *Silverio's siguiriya:* Silverio Franconetti, an Italian "cantaor" who came to Seville and cultivated the "deep song" *(cante jondo)* of the Andalusian gypsy. According to Lorca, the *siguiriya* is a development of the *cante jondo* which combines elements of the primitive musical systems of India, with the indigenous folk tradition of Andalusia. The *flamenco* style, which derives from the *cante jondo* does not take form until the eighteenth century.

4. *Nuremberg:* Lorca is apparently in error here; it was at the electoral Castle of Wartburg in Eisenach that the celebrated encounter occurred.

5. Here again Lorca is either in error, or indulging a playful hoax of his own.

6. *Heinrich Suso:* (1300–1366) German mystic and theologian.

7. *Mosen Cinto Verdaguer:* Jacinto Verdaguer (1845–1902), Catalan poet, author of *La Atlantida.*

8. *Jorge Manrique:* (1440–1479) Spanish poet and soldier, best known for the elegiac *Coplas* on his father's death.

9. *Juan de Juni:* (1507–1577) Spanish painter, pupil of Berruguete.

10. *Alfonso Alvarez de Villasandino:* (1350?–1424?) Writer of lyric and satirical verse, born in the province of Burgos.

11. *Fernando de Herrera:* (1534–1597) Leader of the Andalusian school and innovator in the line of Góngora.

12. *Gustavo Adolfo Becquer:* (1836–1870) Romantic lyric poet born in Madrid, best known for his *Rimas.*

13. *Juan Ramón Jiménez:* (1881–19—) Contemporary lyric poet born at Moguer.

14. *Muleta:* Cloth of scarlet serge or flannel, folded and doubled over tapered wooden stick, used by matadors for defense, the positional manipulation of the bull, "passes" to demonstrate the dexterity and daring of the fighter, and as an aid in the final kill.

15. *Banderilla:* A small dart with a bannerol for baiting bulls, thrust in a series of three pairs into the withers of the bull in the second phase of the bullfight.

16. *Faena de capa:* "cape-task"; the sum of work done by matador in third phase of the fight.

17. *Antonello da Messina:* (1430–1479) Italian painter born at Messina.

18. *Fra Filippo Lippi:* (1406–1469) Italian painter and Carmelite friar born in Florence.

19. *Masolino da Panicole:* (1383–1447) Italian painter born near Florence.

20. *Henri Rousseau:* (1844–1910) The French primitive painter, whose portrait of the poet Apollinaire *(La Muse Inspirant Le Poéte)* is referred to earlier in the essay.

Index

Library of Congress Cataloging-in-Publication Data

Nagrin, Daniel.

The six questions : acting technique for dance performance / Daniel Nagrin.

    p.   cm.

Includes index.

ISBN 0-8229-3974-6 (cloth). — ISBN 0-8229-5624-1 (pbk.:alk. paper).

1. Dancing.   2. Acting.   I. Title.

GV1595.N35   1997

792.7'8—dc21   96-51277